Full Strength Marketing

"Loaded to the brim with valuable information that readers can [use] to boost their profits"

Jay Conrad Levinson, author *Guerilla Marketing*

"Hiring Tom as my media and marketing coach has been the most valuable thing I've done in several years. Learn his secrets in this book!"

Dr. JoAnn Dahlkoetter, author *Your Performing Edge* & coach to Olympians

Praise for Tom Marcoux's other work

"In *Be Heard and Be Trusted*, Tom's advice on how to remain true to yourself and establish authentic rapport with clients is both insightful and reality based. He [shows how] to establish oneself as a credible expert in your own personal endeavor. He provides techniques to resolve conflict ..."

A.P. Ciaramicoli, Ed.D., Ph.D., author *The Curse of the Capable* & *The Power of Empathy*

"In *[Be Heard & Be Trusted]*, Tom teaches potent tools for finding your voice and powerfully expressing yourself, essential for getting what you want in life."

Marcia Wieder, author *Making Your Dreams Come True* and PBS celebrity

"Tom's *10 Seconds to Wealth* contains practical and spiritual ways for you to increase your abundance. Topics include how to increase your confidence, the power of teamwork and the essential element of action. This book is packed with information. Add it to your success library today."

Danek S. Kaus, author *You Can Be Famous! Insider Secrets to Getting Free Publicity*

Full Strength Marketing

*I help people experience enthusiasm, love,
and wisdom to fulfill big dreams.*

TOM MARCOUX

Personal Mission
Caption

Full Strength Marketing

How You Can Use
Your Hidden Strengths,
Break Through Inner Barriers,
and Raise Your Profits

Linda L. Chappo

&

Tom Marcoux

America's Communication Coach
&
The Time-Leverage Detective

A QuickBreakthrough Edition

Book design + indexing by

kunst**+**aventur

see *Collophon* at rear

Dedication

*Tom Marcoux dedicates this
book to the terrific book & film
consultant Johanna Mac Leod.*

Acknowledgements

Linda Chappo: "I would like to acknowledge and thank two people who helped with this project: Tom Marcoux for his creativity, encouragement, patience, and editorial assistance, and Kellie Fennessey-Priest for her support and generous marketing assistance. I would like to dedicate this book to small business entrepreneurs for their dedication and service to their community."

Tom Marcoux: "My heartfelt gratitude to all my other team members. Thanks to the guest authors for their voices of great experience. Thank you to Linda Chappo for her helpful writing that appears in this book! Thanks to Stacy Diane Horn and Joan Harrison for editing. Thanks for comments from my father, Al Marcoux. Thanks to my mother, Sumiyo Marcoux, a kind, generous soul. Thanks to Gregg at Kunst+Aventur for the book's cover, design, fact checking, typesetting, indexing, and production logistics. Thanks to Higher Power, our readers, our clients, and our enthusiastic audiences. "

Contents

Summary Contents

Your Ten Hidden Strengths 3
Envisioning. 9
Transforming 71
Investigating. 121
Identifying 149
Positioning. 185
Defining. 209
Strategizing 235
Energizing 303
Activating 343
Evaluating 395
A Final Note from Linda. 415
A Final Note from Tom. 417

Detailed Contents

LEGEND

📖 *Contribution by guest author*

📄 *Form*

DEDICATION VII

ACKNOWLEDGEMENTS IX

Contents

Chapter **01**

YOUR TEN HIDDEN STRENGTHS

Ten Hidden Strengths 4

Marketing Made Easy 6
Tom Marcoux

Full Strength Marketing 7
Tom Marcoux

Chapter **02**

ENVISIONING

YOUR FIRST HIDDEN STRENGTH 9

How Does the Marketer Gain Clarity? 11
Tom Marcoux

Your Objective for Envisioning 12
Envisioning as a Natural Strength 12

Get More Than Enough 13
Jeanna Gabellini

Envision Your Beacon of Light 16

What's Your Main Purpose? 17
Marc Allen

Marketing and PR as an Act of Faith and Hospitality 22
Pat McHenry Sullivan

Access Your Imagination 26
Identify Your Primary Objective 29
Go for Your Goals 31
Polish the Diamond 32
  The Bonding Facet 33

If You Want to Get Clients, You'll Have to Talk to Them 34
C.J. Hayden, MCC

The Leadership Facet 39
The Gardener Facet 40
The Teamwork Facet 40
The Timekeeper Facet 42
The Creativity Facet 42

The Go-Getter Facet 43
Establish Your Quantitative Objectives. 44
Focus on Quality 46
Meet the Challenge 47
Seven dynamic strategies. 47
Master the Industrial Cycle .49
Create a Master Plan 49
Align with Your Business Plan 52
Build Your Business 53
Communicate with Clarity .54
A Tool for Banks and Venture Capitalists. 54
Business Plan 56
Create a Mission Statement 58

Hidden Power for Your Marketing 61
Dr. Tony Alessandra

Capitalize on the Three C's 66
Campaign 66
Commitment. 67
Consumer 67
Be Visible 68
Envisioning Summary 68
When Do I Take These Steps? 69

Chapter **03**

TRANSFORMING

YOUR SECOND HIDDEN STRENGTH 71
Example from a Highly Successful Person 72
Your Objective for the Transforming Strength. 73
Transforming as a Natural Strength 73
Transform yourself and reach your primary objective 74

Get ready for change 75
Determine Your Needs 76
Change your mental orientation 77

How You Can Set a Marketing Campaign Goal to Expand Your Mind and Your Profits 78
Tom Marcoux

Find the Fear 80

Make Things Happen! 84
Willie Jolley

Overcome Judgment and Self-Doubt 86

How to Market your Way out of Tough Times 88
Patricia Fripp & David Garfinkel

Let Go of the Past 91
Be On Purpose 93
Focus Your Attention 94
Choose Empowering Thoughts 95
Choose Empowering Actions 97
Choose an Empowering Enhancer 98
Determine the Reasons For and Against Change 99
Educate Yourself 101
Turn Lemons into Lemonade 102
Transform Your Marketing Presence 104
Establish Your Marketing Personality 109
Relationship Marketing 109
Create a good track record 111
Take Care of Yourself 112
Develop Your Business's Potential 113
Be a Dynamo 114
Find a Flair for Accuracy 115

Incorporate the Five Factors of Change. 117
Make Powerful Decisions 118
Transforming Summary 118
   When Do I Take These Steps? 119

Chapter 04

INVESTIGATING

YOUR THIRD HIDDEN STRENGTH. 121
   Example from a Top Marketer 122
   Your Objective for Investigating 123
   Investigating as a Natural Strength 123
Be Question-Oriented 125

What Are You Really Marketing? 126
   Tom Marcoux

   Look for Clues 127

📖 ***The Myth of Multicultural Marketing*** 128
   Michael Soon Lee, MBA

   Use Your Resources 135
   Investigate Competitors' Marketing Strategies 138
   Look at Their Benefits 140
   Analyze Your Research. 141
   Find Your Advantage Point. 143
   Win Through Creativity 144
   Recognize the Value of Competition 146
Investigating Summary. 147
   When Do I Take These Steps? 147

Chapter 05

IDENTIFYING

YOUR FOURTH HIDDEN STRENGTH 149
   Example from a Top Marketer 150
   Your Objective for the Identifying Strength 151
   Identifying as a Natural Strength 151
   Identifying Your Target Market. 152

Confident Decision Making 155
   Brian Tracy

   Four advantages of identifying your target market 165
   The four Identifying principles. 165
   Explore Demographics 166
   How to Research Demographic Data 167
   Your local Chamber of Commerce 167
   Surveys 167
   Focus groups 168
   Response marketing 169
   Target market strategy. 169
   How to Make Sense of Your Demographic Research 170
   Produce a Customer Survey 170

Customer Survey 172
Do a "Best" Customer Profile 174
How to Keep Customers 174
   Create Rapport 175
   Cardinal Rules for Building Relationships 176
   How to Improve Customer Service. 176

Marketing Is Trust. 180
   Tom Marcoux

Identifying Summary 182

When Do I Take These Steps? 182

Chapter **06**

POSITIONING

YOUR FIFTH HIDDEN STRENGTH 185

When Marketing Doesn't Feel Good to You 186
Tom Marcoux

Example from a Top Marketer 187
Your Objective for the Positioning Strength 187
Positioning as a Natural Strength 188
Choose Your Position in the Marketplace. 189
Dare to Be Different. 189
The First or Leadership Position 190
The Against Position 191
The New Position. 191
The Niche Position 192
Design Your Own Springboard 193
Write a Position Statement. 194

Why Presenting Public Seminars is a Great PR and Marketing Tool to Promote and Prosper 195
Raleigh R. Pinskey

Case Study 1. 196
Case Study 2. 197
Case Study 3. 197
Find Your Niche. 198
Be a specialist. 199

Personal Branding Makes Marketing Easier 200
Mark Sanborn, CSP, CPAE

Dependability 200

Novelty 201

Attitude 201

Look at the Big Picture 203

Become an Infopreneur 204

Initiate the Four Principal States of Presence 205

Positioning Summary 207

When Do I Take These Steps? 207

Chapter **07**

DEFINING

YOUR SIXTH HIDDEN STRENGTH 209

Your Objective for the Defining Strength 210

Defining as a Natural Strength .210

Win with Clarity 212

Position first, then define. 212

Define Your Business Image 214

Create a Synthesis 217

Establish Your Image Package .218

Your personal image 218

Your public image. 218

Marketing materials 219

Media package 220

Becoming the Conversation on Twitter and Facebook 220
Karmen Reed

How to become a conversation on Twitter. 221

How is Facebook relevant to your business? 224

Integrating the two images 227

Adopt the 'Mirror' Concept 228

Employees Who Make a Difference 230

Define Your Spirit 230

Where Do You Get Your Inspiration? 231
Tom Marcoux

Make a Lasting Impression .232
Defining Summary 233
When Do I Take These Steps? 233

Chapter **08**

STRATEGIZING

YOUR SEVENTH HIDDEN STRENGTH 235
Example from a Top Marketer. 236
Your Objective for the Strategizing Strength 236
Strategizing as a Natural Strength. 236
Market Strategies. 237

The Real Secret of Success 238
Noah St. John

Create the Energy to Manifest What You Want. 240
Tom Marcoux

Basic human motivators 242

What Do People Really Want? And How Can You Get 'Em to Buy?
. 242
Tom Marcoux

Gain Energy so You Do the Rough Parts of Marketing 244
Tom Marcoux

Call a friend. 244
Draw "balloons". 245
Ask, "Where is the joy?" .245

Determine Your Approach 245

 Do Your Homework 246

 Pull It Together 247

 Set the Direction 248

 Make a Balanced Decision 248

Create a Sense of Expectancy. 249

Slice the Pie 250

Get Ahead of Your Competition 251

 Review 251

 Campaign. 251

 Communicate 252

Choose from Sixteen Strategies for Better Marketing. 252

 Network Your Way to Success 252

 Make a BIG Deal out of Seasons, Holidays, & Events 253

 Diversify. 254

 Choose Your Opportunities. .256

 Solidify Team Spirit 257

 Use Creativity to Your Advantage 258

 Make a Splash, and Follow with Ripples 259

 Build a Professional Reputation 259

 Choose your Target Market Carefully 261

 Be Focused 261

 Emphasize the Benefits. 261

 Meet Needs and Desires 262

 Provide Value 263

 Make Changes When Necessary 264

 Overcome Resistance 265

  Cost. 265

  Needs 266

  Habits 266

  Belief. 267

 Start a Sideline Business. 267

Calendar Strategy 268

    Marketing tools 268

Plan a Calendar of Events 268

The Five Advantages of Advance Planning 269

Events Calendar Process 270

Maintain Balance 270

Choose Social Promotional Events 271

    Remember your primary objective 272

    Six success secrets to event planning 272

Develop Your Media Plan 274

    Public relations 275

📖 *You Gotta Pitch It to Promote it so You Can Tell it to Sell it!* . . .275
Gayl Murphy

    Questions to self for creating "The Power Pitch" 278

    Print media 280

    Advertising 280

    Direct mail advertising 280

    Magazine and newspaper advertising 282

    Yellow pages advertising 282

    Broadcast media—radio and television 283

    Digital media 285

📖 *Get Started with Online Marketing* 286
Danek S. Kaus

    What to put on your website 286

    Blogs 288

    Podcasts 289

    Article Directories 290

    Forums 291

The Power of Your Blog 292
Paul Gillin

Promotion Reminders 298
    Make Final Decisions 298
    List Exact Media Details for Each Promotion 299
    Do a Product and Equipment Analysis .299
Strategizing Summary 300
    When Do I Take These Steps? 301

Chapter **09**

ENERGIZING

YOUR EIGHTH HIDDEN STRENGTH .303
    Your Objective for the Energizing Strength 304
    Energizing as a Natural Strength 304

How You Can Be a Marketer Who Goes to Sleep Happy 306
Tom Marcoux

    Energizing Your Marketing Campaign .307
Energizing With a Financial Investment .307
    Empower Your Dreams 307
        Five principles to Energize your marketing campaign 308
    Make a Financial Commitment 308
    Define Your Budget 310
    Plan a Financial Strategy 311
Your Communication System 313
    Energize Your Messages 313
        Define benefits to customers 313

Would You Like Fries with That? 314
Craig Harrison

    Up with selling 315

Sales crossing ahead 315
Suggestive selling salient in our lives 316
Service through sales. 316
Let's play Bridge 317
Define your message 319
Educate the public 321
Add impact to your messages. 322
Energize with a Graphic Identity System 323
Analyze your competitors' graphic identity system 323
Logo design 324
Design an eye-catching logo 324
Buy a professionally designed logo 325
Contact an Art School and Engage a Student 327
Choose Coordinating Colors and Typefaces 327
Choose Paper Stock 328
Business Card Guidelines 329
Design Your Brochure 331
Write to persuade. 331
Illustrations and photos 332
Find a good printer. 332
Five Secrets to Better Brochures. 333
Small and home-based business menu 334
How to Develop a Timeline 335
The week-by-week schedule 335
Example Schedule 336
Example Backward Schedule 337
Hire Outside Professionals 338
Five Methods to Attract New Customers 339
Energizing Summary 341
When Do I Take These Steps? 342

Chapter **10**

ACTIVATING

YOUR NINTH HIDDEN STRENGTH 343

Your Self-Esteem Can Boost Your Marketing 344
  Dr. JoAnn Dahlkoetter

  The 3 P's for Your Performing Edge 345
  Your Objective for the Activating Strength 346
  Activating as a Natural Strength 346

A Celebration of Your Life Transformed—Really? 347
  Tom Marcoux

Develop Ethics in Advertising 349

Being Good Means "Good for Your Business" 349
  Tom Marcoux

Can Marketing Be Spiritual? 352
  Tom Marcoux

Choose Your Distribution Methods 353
Launch Your "Rocket Ship" 355
  Actualize 355
  Plan 355
  Repetition 355
    Activate your marketing campaign 356
    Activate public relations 356
      Press Releases 357
      Press Kit 359
      Strategic publicity power .359
    Activate direct mail marketing 360
      Nine secrets for planning a direct mail campaign 360

Contents   Detailed • xxix

Introductory letters 362

Direct mail coupons. 363

Direct mail catalogue. 365

E-newsletters 365

Helpful hints for e-newsletters. 366

Don't "Throw Away" Your Prospects 368

Ed Gandia

Activate Advertising 371

Advertising approaches. 371

Advertising decisions 372

Closing an advertisement 372

Free Advertising 373

Advertising media. 374

Newspapers. 374

Ethnic newspapers. 375

College/university newspapers 375

High school newspapers 376

Local newspapers 376

Yellow pages advertisement 378

Activate Outdoor Advertising 378

Balloons 378

Billboard advertising 378

Activate Broadcast Media 382

Activate Digital Media. 382

Converting Web Traffic Into Sales .383

Allison Bliss

Want a Huge Twitter Following? 386

Here's how to get more twitter followers

Danek S. Kaus

📖 ***Promotions on $0 Budget: Use Twitter for a Purpose*** 389
Beth Barany

    Before we begin—Twitter basics. 389
    Grow your fan base. 390
    Build your book buzz 391
    Book sales 391
  Activate Transportation Advertising 393
Activating Summary 394
  When Do I Take These Steps? 394

Chapter **11**

EVALUATING

YOUR TENTH HIDDEN STRENGTH

YOUR TENTH HIDDEN STRENGTH 395
  Your Objective for the Evaluating Strength. 396

How Can You Evaluate a Marketing Campaign—and Keep Up Your Morale? 397
Tom Marcoux

  Evaluating as a Natural Strength 398

📖 ***Get Out Of Your Own Way—Overcoming Ambivalence and the Fears That Hold You Back*** 399
Elayne Savage, Ph.D.

    Where does ambivalence come from? 401
    Uncertainty, confusion, anxiety. 401
    Tips for taming ambivalence 402
Evaluate Critical Areas 404
Measure Short & Long Term Results. 406
Review Your Vision 407
Keep a Marketing Ledger. 408
Include Your Team Members 408

Learn Strength Enhancement 409
Data Sheet 410

📖 ***Networking Encouragement*** 411
    Jill Lublin

Evaluating Summary 412
    When Do I Take These Steps? 413

Appendices

A Final Note

FROM LINDA 415

FROM TOM 417

   Coach to Action 418

   Set Effort Goals and Result Goals 418

   Make It a Game You Can Win 419

   Keep Score and Achieve More 419

   Use Your "For the Team" Tendency 419

SPECIAL OFFER FOR OUR READERS 423

Glossary

SPECIAL TERMS III

Bibliography

FURTHER READING XVII

Index

TOPICAL INDEX XXI

About the Authors

Linda L. Chappo XXXI

Tom Marcoux XXXIII

COLLOPHON XXXVII

OFFER XXXVIII

1

Your Ten Hidden Strengths

Imagine that you and I sit on the deck of a luxurious ocean liner. Sun reflects off the glorious waves of the Caribbean. Then, a warning siren blasts; crew people run to and fro. Henry, a friendly waiter, pauses just a moment in response to our question, "What's going on?" He says, "The Captain fell overboard, the first officer is ill, and we're off course!"

Is your small or home-based business off course? Feel like you have somehow left the rudder of your business? With this book, *Full Strength Marketing*, you can stop worrying. How? In these pages, I* share something revolutionary: *ten hidden strengths* you already possess. You can use these strengths to create your marketing plan. Upon implementing that marketing plan, you'll have your business on course for improved profits.

. . . .

* This book is written in Linda Chappo's voice. Tom's contributions are contained in the interspersed articles signed by him and in his roles as general editor/writer and catalyst bringing together the guest authors.

You'll learn how to keep your ship on course, and allow all your passengers (your employees and clients) to have fun, stay safe, and feel secure. They'll know they're in good hands, that all through their journey, their captain (you) is capable, conscientious, and confident.

What are these *ten best marketing strengths* and how will they impact your marketing campaign? They function like navigational tools to build your business and take you from where you are today to where you want to be in one year and beyond.

Ten Hidden Strengths

Envisioning. Remember that you have always used envisioning to create an image or idea of something you wanted. Then use this process to creating a primary objective for your marketing campaign. You focus on creating a catalyst to ignite your desires.

Transforming. Recall times you transformed situations in your life and gained valuable experience, knowledge, and fulfillment. Now, take those memories to inspire you to transform fear into confidence so you act in favor of your vision or primary objective.

Investigating. Remember how you investigated situations before you took action. Apply this process to investigating similar businesses that appear to control the marketplace.

Identifying. Recall how you gained clarity. Then, apply this process to identifying your target market.

Positioning. Remember times when you "positioned" yourself to improve your personal situation. Then, use positioning as a competitive strategy.

Defining. Recall defining something and having a better understanding of its components. Then, use current information effectively and share it with others. Now, you'll apply the definition process and your understanding to your business image. The process of building a business plan is helpful here, too. A business plan includes knowledge of your competition.

Strategizing. Remember how you used strategy to get something you desperately wanted. Then, take this information and passion, and use it to realize a winning strategy for your business.

Energizing. Recall times when expending energy has brought you joy and satisfaction. Energize your campaign with confidence, money, and printed support materials.

Activating. Remember times when you acted with determination and strength to attain something you really wanted. As a result you gained a sense of power. You will now apply that enthusiasm to strengthen your business's presence in the marketplace.

Evaluating. Recall when you've measured end results. Then, measure your current effectiveness—what techniques worked and which ones didn't. Evaluate the results of your marketing campaign.

These ten natural strengths are the essence of making marketing easy, as my co-author Tom Marcoux elaborates.

Marketing Made Easy

Tom Marcoux

How can you experience marketing as an easy process? It's all about making an easy system. Here's an example. Someone calls a speaker-author, Mai. She doesn't have to think about her process; she just opens her Marketing Plan (in a binder) and goes through these steps:

1. Receive inquiry from a new prospective client.

2. Answer questions during the call and inquire about what the person needs and wants.

3. During the call, offer a choice of three free articles.

4. Email the chosen article to the prospective client.

5. Make a follow-up call and …

You see that Mai doesn't have to start from scratch with each incoming phone call. She has a plan.

And this is how you can make your marketing easy. As you read this book, jot down ideas that impress you as: "That sounds good. I can try that." Place your notes on methods and the ten marketing strengths in a binder, using tabs to organize the elements. Soon you will have your own marketing plan. I call this the "Easy Part Start."

As Tom mentioned, it helps when you use a binder and jot down ideas to create your own marketing plan.

These ten strengths are the core of *Full Strength Marketing*.

Full Strength Marketing

Tom Marcoux

When I saw Linda's ideas about the qualities that we all naturally possess, I was impressed.

At first, many of us find that marketing seems to be foreign and unknown territory. Some of us actually look upon marketing as distasteful.

Then I had the idea that expressing your hidden strengths is really just a little shift. That's when the phrase "full strength marketing" blossomed in my thoughts.

Let's face it. Many of us (before now) have only devoted half-hearted efforts towards marketing. But that is *not* for you.

Now, through this book, we'll release your full strength. You will find that Full Strength Marketing feels easier and even more fulfilling than standard marketing efforts. Why? Because you're engaging your natural inner resources. Inevitably, you must be more effective.

Now, that's a relief … and it's your path to truly attracting and serving new customers.

Let's more forward.

2

Envisioning

Your First Hidden Strength

A marketing plan truly begins with our first strength –envisioning. The first step is to envision where you want to go with your business.

Success is the progressive realization
of a worthy ideal.

EARL NIGHTINGALE

Imagine a time when someone gave you a gift: a big, colorful, beautifully wrapped package with a delightful bow. Envision how you held that mysterious package in your hands, shook it, studied it, and fantasized about its contents. You eagerly wondered what kind of happy surprise was inside. Would this be one of the many things you've always wanted? Could it be a dream come true? Your overwhelming curiosity was almost too much to bear.

Envision now that you receive a similar gift, one that could take your business to the next level of success. You were born with natural strengths; gifts that were meant to be expressed as you grow in experience and performance. You'll apply the gift of insight throughout this book and bring a new level of success into your life.

> *This first strength—Envisioning—focuses on your ability to create a vision and primary objective for your business. It answers the most important question about your business, "Who are you now, and who do you want to become?"*

When you've completed the envisioning *Action Steps*, you'll have a vision for your business, a beacon of light to guide you towards the success of your dreams.

About envisioning: Walt Disney began with discomfort he felt on "Daddy's Day." On Saturdays, he took his daughters on trips. He grew tired of merely sitting and watching them flow past on the Merry-Go-Round and was dismayed that amusement parks were not truly family-friendly. Walt envisioned a place where parents and children could have fun together. This vision became Disneyland, where parents and children sit on rides together.

But envisioning an appropriate marketing strategy is not always easy, as Tom Marcoux discusses.

How Does the Marketer Gain Clarity?

Tom Marcoux

How do you boil down your marketing message to a simple, clear, impactful statement? A mile of ink, a hill of printed pages and twenty earfuls of talk. That is, you try a lot of things; you talk with a number of people … and you explore.

For example, one of my interns was working on a revision of one of my websites. He proposed the catchphrase: "Leverage yourself above everyone." Did that fit as a description of what I do? Well, it was a bold statement.

But I hesitated. It did not feel like me. On one hand, I certainly like "leverage" and I have spoken on "Time Leverage" for years. But the "above everyone" had my colleagues and me hesitating. For instance, I'm the "Be Heard and Be Trusted" guy. (*Be Heard and Be Trusted* is the title of one of my books.) I am not into ruthless competition.

Here's the solution (for now): we use "leverage your best life." In marketing, I like the words "you" and "your" for getting attention.

Am I done with "leverage your best life"? Probably not. But this catchphrase is currently on the website and doing its job—until a better idea comes along.

So get out there and try some details and pay close attention to the feedback you get.

Your Objective for Envisioning

Your objective is to remember how you have always used envisioning to create an image or idea of something you wanted with all your heart and soul, and apply that remembrance to creating a vision and primary objective for your marketing campaign. A point of reference from which to act is our objective for the envisioning strength.

Envisioning as a Natural Strength

We practiced envisioning as children and teenagers when we fantasized about who we'd like to grow up to be. Maybe you wanted to be a fireman, nurse, doctor, pilot or actor. At 11, I envisioned myself as a teacher. I felt great joy and appreciation for the teaching profession. As I grew in age and experience, my visions changed periodically, and so did my vocational desires.

Before I opened my hair salons, I envisioned them to be full-service salons with plush contemporary equipment and decor, creating a trendy atmosphere. I'd have a full menu of services by licensed and trained cosmetologists plus numerous retail products. My team would serve the community through extended hours of operation and by participating in social, seasonal, and holiday events. This vision helped me to set goals and boundaries, and I became more focused.

Envisioning is a creative ability that is natural to us. Whenever you start to express a hidden strength, always begin by envisioning the finished product or service. On day one of my first college printing class our teacher provided us with correctly printed samples, so we could see what an ideal finished piece actually looked like. We quickly identified some goals. He pointed out that the printed piece had good ink coverage and was in "registration." After we learned to recognize accurate printing, then we learned how to run the printing presses. After the teacher revealed the 'whole picture' to us, we followed a step-by-step procedure. The same process applies to marketing strengths; envision your finished product first, then implement the necessary steps to its achievement.

Sometimes, we don't envision something in a big or invigorating way. No one became excited about doing something to just get by. Jeanna Gabellini invites us to reach higher.

Get More Than Enough

Jeanna Gabellini

It's common to just make do with what you have. You may be suffering slightly but other people are worse off than you, right? Why should you complain? But you do. It feels annoying to not have the amount of income or investments you want. You may even feel strapped financially. It may even be affecting your health.

Now, your health itself may be fine, in general, but you lug around extra weight or have bad allergies during Spring. Maybe you have a bum back, knee or shoulder. What about your relationship with your family or clients? Are you tolerating something less than desirable there?

It's easy to accept situations that are less than ideal but not yet really painful. You may put up with them without realizing they are even there. It's like a broken drawer. You may not use the drawer much but when you do it is so irritating. How about not only fixing it but having one of those self closing devices put on there for smooth gliding? You don't need that luxury but when it's there it is awesome!

Check out your own life for a minute. Do you absolutely expect the best case scenario every time? Are you preparing to have each of your goals delivered in an easy and relaxed manner … just the way you like it? Is your health amazing? Do you have enough money to pay your expenses, have an extreme amount of fun, invest in whatever you like and have some left over? Do all of your relationships fill you up? How peaceful do you feel on a scale of 1-10?

What if on a scale of 1-10 (10 being over the top good) you rated all areas of your life a 20? What about 100? Here's the deal. Life can continue to get better no matter what your score. You'll always find ways to create more joy and fulfillment but you have to expect to receive more than enough!

Yes, I know some of you can't imagine living from that perspective. The perspective of always having more than enough. Getting what you need and want and more. You'd be happy just to have enough dough to pay the bills and go out to dinner once in awhile. You'd be happy to just have a day all to yourself with nobody expecting anything of you. You'd be happy to just have a pain free day. It will be easier to get to those places I just mentioned if you start expecting things to go better than you can imagine.

In order to have more than enough, you have to start thinking and planning for more than enough. The abundance of well being may only trickle in at first. Then momentum will eventually take over and you will have more than enough. It may take you a year of practicing this new way of thinking. I still catch myself planning for something not ideal. But then I work my way up the ladder of more than enough thinking.

Here's an example: Taxes are due next month. I look at the money in my checking account and wonder how I will pay for the quarterly taxes. I just got through shelling out a lot of money for my new products and marketing for my new classes. I want to pay everything in full next month. I can take out of my savings and investments. Nah, that's not ideal but it's a good backup plan. I will generate new income. I will do this. I can have it my way. In fact, I'll generate more new income in this coming month than I ever have before. Okay, that feels really good! And so it is!

Look at your intentions on a daily basis. Decide that you will have more than enough. Take action from this powerful place. You won't be able to stop the abundance you will receive. Enjoy every morsel.

Jeanna Gabellini is the Extreme Abundance Coach, author, speaker, trainer, and radio show host who blends strategies and fun with the Law of Attraction. She coaches individuals and teams to go BIG ... effortlessly!

Check out her book co-authored with Jack Canfield, Mark Victor Hansen and Eva Gregory, *Life Lessons on Mastering the Law of Attraction*.

Jeanna@MasterPeaceCoaching.com
MasterPeaceCoaching.com
(707) 747-0447

Jeanna's comments can inspire us to devote time and efforts to envision better and bigger outcomes for our marketing and our business. Aim for something that you can get excited about.

Action Step

List three examples from your past when you naturally used your envisioning strength.

Envision Your Beacon of Light

You walk into a darkened room and try to find your way around. You may stumble, run into things, hunting for the light switch. If you don't run into anything at all, you'd feel that you're cast adrift in a space with no boundaries or in a sudden unknown abyss. It's an uncomfortable situation, and elicits fear because you have no vision, and therefore no reference points for finding what you're looking for. Owning a business without a vision is like walking around in a darkened room. You don't know where you're going and have no point of reference for measuring your success.

When we envision, we turn on the light. Now, you can see the contents of the room and feel comfort and safety.

In the mind, this process is called 'enlightened,' which relates to the inner light. It generates an expanded awareness and it's where brilliant ideas come from.

Here, we're referring to your small business—how it will evolve, take shape and become everything you desire.

Begin with a vision, a beacon of light to guide you in the direction of your most vivid dreams. Vision helps you make an improvement, an innovation, or do something to benefit humanity. This guiding light directs you and gives you a sense of purpose. Think of your vision as an idea or a product of your imagination that has the potential to become a reality. Your entire business should be based on your vision, which is essentially the perfect business situation for you. For example, your business might be animal grooming; your vision might be rescuing animals.

Now, Marc Allen shares the value of identifying your main purpose.

What's Your Main Purpose?

Marc Allen

"What's your main purpose in all this?" Bernie [an old gentleman and potential investor in my fledgling business] asked me.

"My main purpose?" That question surprised me. I certainly hadn't given it much thought. In fact I hadn't given it any thought at all. Fortunately Bernie gave me some time to reflect a bit.

"In doing this plan," he said, "in raising this money—hopefully—you have some kind of purpose. What is it? Do you want to make a ton of money? Do you want to retire in a mansion? Be honest, now."

I had no other choice. I couldn't face his gaze and lie to him. But he was asking a very difficult question.

"When I try to put my main purpose into words," I said, "it comes out sounding pretty hackneyed, or something. But I'd like to help people. I'd like to do something significant, something meaningful … something that makes a valuable contribution to people and maybe even helps the world in some way be a better place to live in …"

I paused, searching for words. Bernie was in no hurry. There was a silence.

"That's as close as I can come at the moment, I guess." It wasn't a very good statement of purpose. I'd forgotten what we had put in our mission statement at the beginning of the plan. But Bernie didn't seem too disappointed.

"Good," he said, "you're on the right track. You have to have a higher purpose than making money in a business. If you have a higher purpose, you marshal all kinds of forces behind you and within you that support you in reaching your goals. You get support from all kinds of places—some you plan on, some that you can't possibly plan on. It's almost mystical—I think it is mystical—I've seen it happen over and over. If your purpose is just making money, you wither and die. You might even be successful, to some degree, but you're still unfulfilled, and you wither and die. I've seen that happen over and over, too.

"Money is essential in business, but it's secondary. Money is the lifeblood of the business, but the business has to have a higher purpose to survive and thrive.

"There are a lot of people who believe that the purpose of business is to make money. I feel sorry for them. They have such a tough row to hoe. You sense it all the time, from the little guys who'll do anything to make a buck to all the big corporations whose leaders are always using phrases like 'maximizing shareholder value.' It leads to stupid business decisions that can have disastrous results for the company and the environment.

"That kind of thinking is just stupid—well, I should call it *ignorant* instead, because some very bright people believe this way. But they're ignorant, they don't understand the results of their actions.

"It's as ignorant as believing that the purpose of our lives here on earth is to keep blood pumping through our bodies. Sure, we need to have blood pumping through our bodies in order to be alive, but our purpose in life is something far greater, far more significant."

He looked back at [my business] plan and flipped through it casually, glancing at random at different pages. It was nerve-racking. I knew he was giving me valuable advice, but it was hard to focus on it.

"Each of us is different," he said, looking back at me again, and stressing his words so that I had no choice but to listen, "and each of us has a unique purpose for living. Each of us has been given some unique talents and abilities to accomplish that purpose. There is something you can do, and something I can do, that no one else can do in quite the same way.

"We all have these natural gifts. Sometimes it's difficult for us to discover what they are—and sometimes it's because they're so obvious; it's so easy for us to perform in a certain way that we take it for granted and we don't value it, we don't realize what a gift it is.

"Each and every one of us should spend some time—however much time is necessary, and whenever necessary—to reflect on our purpose, and discover our purpose. Our purpose involves service of some kind, and love, always; it is something that contributes to humanity and to the planet."

Excerpted from *Visionary Business*, revised edition, by Marc Allen.

Marc Allen is an internationally renowned author and president and publisher of New World Library, which he co-founded (with Shakti Gawain) in 1977. Marc is a well-known musician and composer as well, having produced five albums of music for his label Watercourse Media. His latest book is *The Greatest Secret of All*. He is the author of *The Type-Z Guide to Success*; *The Millionaire Course: A Visionary Plan for Creating the Life of Your Dreams*; and *Visionary Business: An Entrepreneur's Guide to Success*. He has also produced an audio CD, *Stress Reduction and Creative Meditations*. His books, audios, and workshops have been highly rewarding experiences for thousands of people, and he has produced a 12-CD audio *The Success with Ease In-Depth Course*. Marc and his wife Aurilene have founded the Brazil Hope Foundation to help street kids in Brazil. www.marcallen.com

---

Marc reminds us to begin at the beginning—our main purpose.

Many small business people have a lofty vision of what their business could be, yet they seldom start at that level. They grow into their vision. It's like children who play 'dress up' with their parents' dresses, hats and shoes that are too large for their little bodies. Children accept this and realize that someday they'll grow up like their parents. The same process applies to your vision. Your current business may seem small and insignificant by comparison. With time, patience, and persistence, you grow and fit into that vision. For example, you could offer incentives for your customers to adopt another pet. Endless possibilities exist for you during your creation of a vision for your business.

Action Step

> Name at least two businesses whose owner or founder began with a vision (perhaps, do a Google search).

Envisioning is a part of each of the ten hidden strengths, so you'll be practicing your envisioning strength throughout the book.

Tip: Know yourself.

Marketing excellence and effectiveness depend upon one critical factor: knowing who you are as a business entity. Keep focused on why you are in business (your mission) and what you plan to accomplish. It's important to know your strengths, weaknesses, and how you differ from similar businesses. The brief *Action Steps* throughout the book help you become clear on exactly what you are marketing, to whom, and for what reasons. It is a mirror image of you.

The *Action Steps* stimulate the creative part of your mind and help you answer questions regarding the crucial details of your business.

Now, Pat McHenry Sullivan shares ideas that can help many of us develop more comfort with the marketing process.

Marketing and PR as an Act of Faith and Hospitality

Pat McHenry Sullivan

What if your marketing could be done as easily, as graciously and as ego-free as offering someone a tissue when they need one? How can marketing express your deepest values, even be an act of compassion or hospitality? Here are some tips I have learned from many sources: Start with a vision of your marketing as an act of hospitality. When you invite honored guests to your home for dinner, you naturally do all you can to make them comfortable. You spend way more time putting them at ease and listening to them than you do focusing on your own comfort or putting your message across.

Carol Costello, author of *The Soul of Selling*, offers information and inspiration about how selling can be done "with ease, in the spirit of service, and in a way that feeds your soul." (soulofselling.com) I suggest taking that idea into your meditation, with an affirmation like: "I choose to see clearly how my marketing can be done easily, in the spirit of service, in a way that feeds my soul." Then, when your heart speaks, take good notes. Keep playing with the guidance from your heart and soul until you have a clear vision for your marketing plan.

Consider all marketing an act of faith. You've got to have some kind of faith in yourself, your offerings and the market to stay in business. Problem is, fear can drown out the quiet wisdom of faith with self-talk like "Who do you think you are?" or "It's a jungle outside, so you've got to be tougher, more vicious, more trendy, especially in this down economy!"

HR consultant Roseanne Roberts (robertsresources.com) taught me a simple affirmation: "My need for income perfectly matches another's prayer for my product or service." Rev. Sarah Hargrave, a staff minister at the Golden Gate Center for Spiritual Living in Corte Madera, ggcsl.org/ministry/rev_hargrave.htm, inspired a great continuation to Roseanne's affirmation: "With the help of the Universal Marketing Committee, I now see clearly how I am called to connect with those who most need my offerings."

Still faithless? Consider Hebrews, chapter 11, verse 1 in the *New Testament*: "Now faith is the substance of things hoped for, the evidence of things not seen." Do your marketing homework. Blend spiritual guidance with practical marketing guidance.

Offer your services or products as simply and graciously as you offer a tissue. This tip came from Carol Costello recently. Hold your product or service away from you, at an angle where you and your potential customer can see it objectively. Engage fully with the other person(s) while also detaching yourself from the outcome. Know that when you do this authentically, at the least you will have a fascinating interchange with a fellow human being. Whether or not that person does business with you, he or she will be blessed with at least a little of what's most authentic and good about you.

Seek not to be understood and appreciated but to understand and appreciate. Trader Joe's stores are famous not just for their amazing variety of inexpensive, tasty and often organic foods from around the world but also for their quirky and fun branding. Thus, some of Trader Joe's boxes of tissues feature a different message in old-fashioned type saying "I'm here when you're sad" or "I'm here when you have to pick up icky things," or run out of toilet paper or you're sick. Accompanying each "I'm here when you ________" is an old-fashioned photo and script saying things like "love, Tissue," or "kindly, Tissue," as if the tissues actually speak to us. What can you learn from this model?

Treat marketing as a respectful way to share good news. Without marketing and PR, people just can't discover what we offer. How selfish we are when we're too shy or nervous or whatever to help them find us!

In Christianity, "gospel" literally means "good news," but not pushing your will on people. Jesus' parables invite us to stop hiding our light, to stop refusing to exercise (spend or invest) our talents. Do your work as if you were doing it for your beloved, our Hindu friends say. Make no split between what you do in your prayer time and your work, say Muslims. Buddhists promote right livelihood, which means to do all work—including marketing—with compassion and consciousness. The book of Proverbs in the Hebrew Bible (aka *Old Testament*) is for many a soulful marketing and business manual.

Pray, meditate or reflect about your marketing plan and activities. One of my affirmative prayers has been simply my commitment to notice more opportunities to let my light shine. When Susan Harrow invited newsletter readers to submit guest blogging ideas, I wrote "Marketing as Spiritual Practice" (examiner.com/x-977-SF-Marketing--PR-Examiner~y2009m10d1-Marketing-as-a-Spiritual-Practice). Then I took the concept to meditation and wrote this for a post on my own blog at spiritworkandmoney.com

Marketing requires faith in our true selves, which are connected to all creation, not to our egos, which have a more limited, selfish viewpoint. Our real selves are as comfortable with potential rejection as babies are comfortable picking themselves up each time they fall; our egos would rather avoid anything potentially painful.

Marketing requires faith in our products or services. If we can't have faith in them, it's either time to reshape the product or service so we deeply respect it and can stand on its value—or it's time to offer other products and services that are more ethical, meaningful and useful.

Marketing requires faith that there is room in the market for quality and integrity. Whatever bandwagon of hype or fear is popular today, marketing with faith calls us to stay true to what we know to be true. If that means a smaller market share, so be it, and bless it. By being true to ourselves, we will always have enough.

Pat McHenry Sullivan, owner of Visionary Resources in Oakland, CA, helps people create business visions and bankable plans that are built around their truest values. Her blog often features creative marketing tips and inspiration. Pat is the author of *Work with Meaning, Work with Joy: Bringing Your Spirit to Any Job.*

visionary-resources.com
Blog: spiritworkandmoney.com
(510) 530-0284

Pat's ideas can help many of us who have had a knee-jerk reaction of "I don't like marketing." Instead, we can focus on service. When you perform the *Action Steps* in this book, you'll think through your ideas about the birth and growth of your business and create an intimate relationship with your business. The result is that you'll know and understand your current or future business from the inside out, so a marketing plan can be successfully implemented. You'll also gain an awareness of where your business stands in the marketplace. Having that knowledge puts you in the driver's seat, where you belong.

Access Your Imagination

Imagine a time when you got something you really wanted. You knew that your life or situation would improve, and that thought brought you feelings of peace. Attach that memory to your next step: imagine one year from now and how you will feel when you create these benefits: an expanded business, more money, more clients, more recognition, and more peace of mind.

> *The imagination is a creative tool for gaining new insights. There is a causal level of intelligence where all ideas are born. Jose Silva, whose methods have helped thousands of people attain mental clarity and focus, called this mental level the Causal Domain. I refer to it as the Quiet Imagination. By allowing your mind and thoughts to become still, quiet, and focused, you are able to access this causal imaginative level and achieve the clarity that you need.*

> *Using this creative part of your mind helps you access specific images or ideas. It's a useful tool for creating what is possible in reality. Use the four tools of imagination: daydreams, intuition, meditation, and visualization.*

Meditation is the most interesting process, because you derive so much from doing virtually nothing. No physical activity is involved; it's all mental discipline. The goal is essentially to have no mental activity, and that appears to be the challenge for many people. Quieting the flow of busy thoughts requires persistence and patience. After two weeks of daily practice, I began taming those intruding thoughts. Closing your eyes during meditation allows you to relax and avoid distractions.

The answers or solutions are available to you within your mind. Once you are able to totally relax your mind and become open to possibilities, your mental processes and imagination work together to help you find a solution. This process helps direct your efforts. Your solutions may come in the form of images, ideas, or impressions. Constant practice will help to speed up this process. Write your solutions in a place where you can conveniently see them. Then you can work through any details.

Napoleon Hill, author of *Think and Grow Rich*, wrote "If you can imagine it, you can become it." He referred to the incredible power of your imagination and its link with your destiny. We'll apply this power to the first step and envision your primary objective.

Action Step

> **Visualization.** Plan to invest at least twenty minutes of time alone. Find a place to relax your body and peacefully access your imagination. Close your eyes, take a few deep breaths, relax your mind, and draw upon your inner resources to give you a direction in which to go for the year. I like to form a clear question in my mind before I begin, so that I am using my relaxation/ problem-solving time to the greatest advantage. I focus

on the question for a while, then let it go, and let my mind become an empty vessel, waiting to be filled.

It helps to alternate visualization exercises. Ask a question one time, then the next time visualize many new customers calling for appointments, products or services. Notice how happy they look as they receive value from your business. Build a clear image of consumers writing checks or giving cash as payment. Then visualize your own joy as you deposit the payments into your business checking account. Make it realistic and believable. Prepare for it to happen and it will.

You may also want to prepare an affirmation, a simple positive statement in the present tense that affirms your vision: "I am now receiving prosperity and happiness." "I am now enjoying my newly renovated business." "I easily attract many new customers."

Action Step

> Note briefly "what is your small or home-based business vision?" (Daydream a bit and describe your business's potential: location, image, customer profile, price structure or any other aspect which you find intriguing.)

For times when you lose your focus, be sure to establish a beacon or a guiding light. It's important to annually establish an objective for your business, and you will have a lighthouse to guide you. Your primary objective is usually based upon the idea of creating something easier, faster, or better than what already exists, without sacrificing quality. It is essentially a yearly mini-vision that guides you towards the achievement of your grand vision.

Identify Your Primary Objective

The next integral step is to envision your primary objective: the one important thing you want to accomplish this year. You must be crystal clear as to exactly what you want to happen. It must be something to which you are emotionally attached. You can't be ho-hum about it. Your primary objective must be something you really desire or that is incredibly important.

Objectives are features and characteristics that can be measured realistically. Some examples of this year's primary objectives are:

- Increase the sale of products

- Introduce a new line of products

- Increase services

- Create business for a new employee

- Remodel your business

- Improve your business's image

The first questions to ask yourself are "What do I want to come of this? Is this just a fantasy or is this something concrete that will give value to consumers? Will it help my company to grow? Is it an objective that I am capable of achieving?"

Once you formulate your critical questions, then you need to brainstorm ways to meet your objective. Later in this book, you will choose promotions that accomplish it.

Your ability to envision and decide on a primary objective puts you at a distinct advantage. Having an objective gives you a precise direction in which to go. The risk of meandering or becoming stagnant is greatly diminished, because you are motivated by its benefits.

Tip: Remember to shift gears.

Recently, I heard a story of a man who went out to his car early one morning, turned on the ignition and revved up the engine, but the car didn't move. He gunned it again and still nothing happened. The reason the car didn't move was simple: in his half awake state, he didn't shift gears from neutral to first. Sometimes it's that way with a business. The owner wants it to improve and take off, but it doesn't. The business remains in neutral because the owner is stuck and unmotivated. The owner hasn't shifted the gears in his or her head. A shift in your business doesn't happen until you shift from neutral to first. Then you can get going.

If you have trouble deciding on a primary objective, use the visualization *Action Step* to help achieve clarity. Making profit is one of your major benefits and is generally a by-product of your primary objective.

Action Steps

1. What is your primary objective for the year? (And set a Target Date.)

2. What will you give in return for the attainment of your objective?

Plan for the Future: You may have secondary areas of your business that you eventually want to develop. You may not invest as much money or time promoting them, but planting the seeds this year could allow secondary objectives to bloom next year or sometime soon.

Action Step

List secondary objectives, if appropriate.

Go for Your Goals

As a strong marketer, look ahead to where you want to be and how you will achieve your vision and primary objective. Setting and aligning short- and long-term business goals are important parts of any business. Your yearly marketing campaign and primary objective are associated with your short-term goals, because you achieve them in one year. They need to promote your long-term vision. For example, your primary objective might be to create a website. Your vision will likely be promoted on the website.

Action Step

What are your small or home-based business goals? Where do you want to be? At this point, write down a preliminary guess as to how you will get there—in one year, in five years, and in ten years

Polish the Diamond

Envision the strengths you now have as a diamond with extremely rough edges. When you polish each of these facets within yourself, the resulting brilliance will contribute more value to your objective. Self-mastery depends upon your commitment to excellence. It begins with personal development and ends with personal accomplishment.

Have you ever stayed awake at night thinking about how you could do more, be more or have more? Having it all takes giving your all. Years ago I heard the dynamic speaker, author and motivator Zig Ziglar. He said one thing that stills stands out in my mind, "You can get everything you want in life by helping enough other people to get what they want." If your visionary business includes abundant success, then improving your own personal strengths is the first step to making your dreams come true.

Take a few moments to reflect upon your marketing strengths thus far. You may be new to marketing or you may have some experience. The knowledge you are beginning with can always be refined and improved upon for further success. Integrate these seven critical facets, and become a polished diamond.

The Bonding Facet

Form an exceptional emotional attachment to your primary objective in order to go the distance and accomplish it. These three bonding agents are critical to the achievement of your objective: desire, belief and acceptance.

Desire. Your objective will be achieved when you truly desire it. You can't feel lukewarm about something as important as the attainment of your objective. You must desire its achievement in your mind, heart, and gut. When these three areas are in alignment, you are ready for achievement.

Belief. Do you really believe you will achieve your objective? If you have an unwavering belief in your ability to succeed, and in the campaign that will take you there, then you're way ahead of everyone else. Belief is a powerful factor to add into a marketing campaign. Your honest belief in yourself will support you through the times when you feel challenged by unforeseen circumstances.

The movie *Field of Dreams* is an inspiring motion picture about a young man who hears an inner voice that often whispers to him ,"If you build it, they will come." Eventually, baseball stars who have passed away magically arrive from the corn fields of Iowa to play ball in his baseball field. At first, he is the only one who can hear and see this mysterious event, but eventually it is revealed to all.

Field of Dreams is a story that warms the heart and spirit, and inspires us to follow our inner direction towards our dreams. What the young man in Iowa built was not a baseball field, but the belief that dreams come true. Build your belief in yourself, your strengths, and your business, and "they will come": increased cash flow and more new customers.

Acceptance. Some people make half-hearted decisions and then are surprised by roadblocks in their path to success. You can remove roadblocks by bringing true acceptance to your business decision-making process. Will you accept full responsibility and willingly make the necessary efforts? The success you achieve in this one year will be the springboard for many more successful and profitable years.

Now, C.J. Hayden reminds us that the marketing process involves the acceptance of a crucial activity.

If You Want to Get Clients, You'll Have to Talk to Them

C.J. Hayden, MCC

"I've done everything I can think of to get clients," a desperate self-employed professional wrote to me. "I launched a website, I had a brochure designed, I've been sending out mailings, and I've placed all sorts of ads in print and on the web. But no one is hiring me. What am I doing wrong?"

This unhappy professional has made a common mistake. He has fallen into the trap of believing that spending money on marketing materials, mailings, and ads will somehow produce clients without the direct involvement of the business owner. And he truly believes that this is "everything" he can do.

Perhaps professionals who make this mistake are trying to follow the model of big business. They hide behind a company name, expensive marketing literature, and a website. They spend hundreds or thousands of dollars on ads, directory listings, and trade show booths. Far too many self-employed professionals don't even disclose their own name in their marketing, even when they are operating a one-person company!

But people don't buy professional services from an anonymous company whose name they don't even recognize; they buy them from either: 1) nationally recognized firms who have spent millions to gain name recognition, or 2) individual people they have learned to know, like, and trust. The more personal—or the more expensive—the service you offer is, the more likely this is to be true.

If you are a financial advisor, career counselor, or life coach, you are asking people to trust you with the most intimate areas of their lives. If you are a web designer, IT consultant, or corporate trainer, you are asking your clients to trust you enough to spend thousands of dollars with you. You don't earn people's trust by placing an ad or sending them a brochure.

Independent professionals and small professional service firms simply don't have the resources to build name recognition and trust by way of high-priced, anonymous approaches like advertising and mass mailings. In fact, the approaches that work best for most professionals to get clients are less expensive—and more personal.

Here are the five best ways for professionals to get clients:

1. Meeting prospects or referral sources in person, at events or by appointment

2. Talking to prospects or referral sources on the phone

3. Sending personal letters and emails to prospects who already know them

4. Following up personally with prospects over time

5. Speaking to groups likely to contain prospects at meetings and conferences

And here are the five things self-employed professionals most often try that don't result in clients:

1. Placing ads in the Yellow Pages, trade publications, or pay-per-click ads on the web

2. Distributing or posting brochures or flyers around their community

3. Mailing mass-produced letters or brochures to strangers

4. Sending their newsletter or ezine to people who haven't asked for it

5. Building a website consisting of nothing but promotional copy for people to read

The main difference between these two lists is that the first group of approaches require you to talk to people. The second list consists of anonymous activities that allow you to hide out and never meet the people you are in business to serve.

If you want people to become your clients, they need to get to know you, learn to like you, and believe they can trust you. And for that, they really do need to meet you.

It is understandable why so many business owners gravitate to the least effective marketing tactics—they are so much easier to accomplish! To buy an ad, all you have to do is put up the money. To send a mailing, all you need is a mailing list and postage. It's much more challenging to go out and meet strangers, or to call people on the phone, or to speak in public.

But the reality is that this is what it takes to get clients. Even if you have the world's most compelling copy on your website, it's a rare client who finds their way to your site, reads it, and decides then and there to work with you. The same is true for an ad or a brochure. All these marketing tools are simply that—tools. Just like a pair of pliers, they need a person holding them in order for them to work.

What clients want is to get a sense of who you are as a person. They want to see your face or hear your voice, to get to know you over time. If you don't have enough confidence in your business to speak to people in person about it, how will they ever have enough confidence in you to hire you?

What you'll discover if you begin to meet prospects in person, talk to them on the phone, and speak with them directly about how you can help them, is that it gets easier the more you do it. It will build your confidence in yourself—and the confidence your prospective clients have in you—at the same time.

If you're in the business of serving people, your best marketing tool can be your own voice. So put it to work and start talking to them.

C.J. Hayden is the author of *Get Clients Now!*™ Thousands of business owners and independent professionals have used her simple sales and marketing system to double or triple their income.

Get a free copy of "Five Secrets to Finding All the Clients You'll Ever Need" at getclientsnow.com.

C.J. reminds us that marketing involves making a personal connection. Along these lines, we realize that some people are afraid of success and are not comfortable with the changes it brings or how it will impact their lives and the lives of their loved ones. If this is an issue for you, focus on the hidden strength *Transforming*, discussed later in Chapter Three. This strength addresses any blockages in your mind that may hold you back from the success and prosperity you deserve and includes numerous ways to create a healthy space for a prosperity consciousness. You'll begin to expand your life with wealth, power, and success.

The three critical elements that enable your objective are your desires or passion, your unwavering belief, and your wholehearted acceptance of responsibility for success.

Action Steps

1. What actions will you take to keep yourself motivated?

2. Measure your desire for your objective by rating it on a scale of one to ten. How do you feel about it?

3. Measure your belief in yourself and your plan on a scale of one to ten. How do you feel about it?

4. Measure your objective acceptance level on a scale of one to ten. How do you feel about it?

5. Write about your personal beliefs and attitudes toward your profession.

The Leadership Facet

"Leaders are made, and not born" is a thought that has inspired many people to devote time to learn to express their strengths. Placing yourself in a leadership position by starting a business is a primary responsibility. Your ability to act directly affects the economic future of your business, the financial well-being of your employees, and your contribution to the community where your business is located. Strong marketers wear many hats, and wearing the leadership hat requires that you lead your business forward by envisioning an objective, an ideal business situation that is both realistic and attainable. It may pertain to size, structure, quantity, a look or style.

Professional motivators encourage entrepreneurs to 'think big,' and to focus on realistic and attainable goals. I encourage business people to evaluate their ability to take appropriate risks.

Action Step

What steps can you take to create and maintain a positive attitude toward your small or home-based business marketing campaign?

The Gardener Facet

Envision your business as fertile soil for cultivating everything you desire. Seek to harvest the benefits of your business and reap the rewards by getting in alignment with what the *ten hidden strengths* are all about: that you have within you everything you need to grow your business and become successful. Nurture it with the love and compassion of a gardener, and you'll see growth and expansion.

Our American culture highly respects the growth process. It's a major aspect of a capitalist society. The growth of your small business will contribute to and support various businesses, as well as our governing agencies. It's like a vine that spreads across many walls. People who are successful at gardening are said to have a green thumb. On some level they feel a oneness with nature. Sincere expression of that oneness leads to a bountiful harvest. And you too will harvest your goals and dreams.

Action Step

What will you do today to cultivate your dreams?

The Teamwork Facet

It's easy to spot winners: they're the group that works together for the benefit of everyone. Sharing your objective with others is a positive and powerful way to multiply your results. If your small business has more than one employee, share your objective with the entire team. Bring it to their awareness so they understand what you want to achieve and how they can cooperate with you.

Find out what their goals are when you hire them; then you'll know if their goals will align with yours and support a common purpose. Then, your whole team will be motivated by the same enthusiasm and dedication.

Be sure to explain the benefits of aligned goals; growth, opportunities, prosperity, security, flexible schedules, profit sharing, pride or others. Employees will rise to the occasion when they clearly understand the benefits they, personally, will enjoy. The team objective becomes a powerful team project. Employees welcome goals and objectives, as long as the situation doesn't become too stressful or in some way affects their health and well-being. People feel better when things are clear: they know the target and what is expected in terms of performance.

Without goals to attain, employees either create their own goals or become bored and unmotivated to act at all. Be an effective leader and engage employees in a unified objective, so the powerful force of the team will work together toward its accomplishment.

Strong marketers share their objectives and dreams with everyone to make them partners in a team effort. I know a man who shares his dream of an island venture with everyone he meets. It's a way of attracting people who may have similar visions. My co-author Tom Marcoux says: "To get people on board with your dream, learn to tell your vision in the form of stories. When you express a story, you avoid stimulating anyone's natural resistance."

Action Steps

1. When will you meet with your employees to share your marketing plan?

2. How will you encourage your team to brainstorm new marketing ideas?

The Timekeeper Facet

Set your intentions in a clear and strong way with a timeline. When you become comfortable with setting timelines, your projects will flow in a more congruent manner. A timeline is one guiding tool to help set boundaries for completing tasks. You realistically have twelve months to accomplish that one important milestone, the primary objective.

Action Step

Write down three possible one-year goals. Now, search your feelings. Which of these goals feels most appropriate to you?

The Creativity Facet

Polish your creative spirit, and this facet of your life will make all others shine with superb brilliance. Your creativity is a facet that you can influence with some regularity. According to *Webster's New World Dictionary*, creativity is defined as having or showing imagination; artistic or intellectual inventiveness. Let each strength (as you practice and experience it) be enhanced by your unique creative spirit and inventiveness. Try new ideas, stretch your imagination, and everyone will take notice.

Action Steps

1. Make a list of your past creative endeavors (painting, drawing, jewelry and candle making, music, writing and others).

2. How can these past experiences contribute to your current creative spirit—and how can you apply this to your marketing goals?

The Go-Getter Facet

If you've been waiting for the right set of circumstances or the perfect situation, you are only holding yourself back. Set your intentions and go after what you want. Are you serious about increasing your cash flow and attracting a consistent flow of new customers into your business? Does reaching your primary objective mean something to you? Polish your go-getter side and don't let the rough edges hold you back.

Remove the rough edges by focusing your attention to discover what it is you want. Nobody really wants marketing, they want the things that marketing will bring them. Take a few minutes to realize the things that marketing will bring you. Is it more new customers? Is it more cash flow? Is it prestige from having a successful business? Is it worldwide travel, a college education for your children, a new car or boat, investment capital, more money for expansion or a secure retirement? As I mentioned earlier, Zig Ziglar says, "You can have everything you want in life by helping enough other people get what they want." Become a go-getter by helping other people, which in turn helps you to get everything you want.

Action Step

What are the things you want that marketing will bring you?

Establish Your Quantitative Objectives

Add a quantity factor to your objective and you have a measurable result by which to gauge your marketing success. This is called a quantitative objective. Increasing sales by 5% or 10% gives you a solid number to work towards. You might want to attract 5-10 new customers a week, or 20 per month. Be very specific about what objectives you want to achieve. They must be attainable, yet still be challenging. Another important point is this: you may not reach your objective of 100 new clients this year, but if you get 60, and those 60 people return to your small or home-based business and become repeat customers, then you have certainly multiplied your profits for the year. You must keep that fact in perspective.

Realistically estimate what your sales objective would be for the year. For example, let's assume your objective is to sell $10,000 worth of products this year. Begin by breaking down this amount and establishing a monthly sales goal, which would be only $833 per month. Four employees would each need to sell $208 worth of products in one month, which is a very small amount of products.

Sales goals are more easily attained when you break them down to a realistic amount. What once appeared impossible is now almost effortless.

It's easier to be enthusiastic about campaigning for something that is meaningful to you. All of your marketing efforts should reflect your annual objective. Below are some examples of objectives:

- Increase the sale of products by 50%.

- Increase services by 10%.

- Increase profits by 20%.

- Create business for a new employee (5 new clients a week).

- Create value for consumers (receive 20 coupons per month).

- Increase awareness of your business (do one promotion each month).

- Create a compelling image for your business (remodel interior, give exterior a fresh new look or add new signage).

- Enhance your current image through printed materials (develop a splashy new identity system).

- Rise above your competition by getting more media exposure (3 publicity events per year).

- Create fun and entertaining promotions for employees and clients (use each holiday as a springboard for your success).

Action Steps

1. What are your business's quantitative objectives this year? Formulate in terms of sales, new clients, new employees or whatever is important to your business.

   (*Example:* increase sales by 50% this quarter, or sell to 10 new clients per week.)

2. List three actions you want the consumer to take

   (*Examples:* come in and purchase retail items or products, call to make an appointment with a new employee, or others).

3. What kind of sales goals are your business/employees capable of achieving?

Focus on Quality

Customers will define you and your business by the quality of products and services you offer. This is true whether you own a restaurant, hair salon, furniture store, shoe or clothing store, or sell computer software and hardware. Whether you offer less quality at a low price or high quality at a high price, you must define that to yourself first, then to your customers. Different types of people are attracted to low- or high-quality services and products for different reasons. For you to attract the right repeat customer and establish customer satisfaction, you'll need creative ways to attract the people who align themselves with your brand of quality.

Action Steps

1. What standard of quality is your product or service?

2. What buzzwords will attract the right customer for you?

Meet the Challenge

Strong marketers must meet the challenge of increasing income and volume in order to maintain profitability. The cost of doing business increases yearly as rents increase, product prices accelerate, utilities skyrocket and advertising costs escalate. In order to cut costs, many small business owners reduce the money they spend toward a marketing presence in the community. This detrimental practice only decreases the flow of new consumers into your business. Instead of reducing marketing costs, owners must find practical, cost-efficient strategies. It begins with a sensible marketing plan and attainable goals.

Seven dynamic strategies

1. Set an objective that benefits you and gives value to your customers. Make it a win-win situation.

2. Set a quantitative objective to increase the number of customers per week or per month.

3. Set a quantitative objective to increase product sales.

4. Establish quality control to keep valued customers.

5. Create a timeline for your objectives.

6. Create magnetic promotions that attract the right customer.

7. Raise your prices when it's feasible.

One way to increase your cash flow is to raise your prices. Whether you have a service business, or a products and service business, raising prices should always be done with thought and reason. You may lose customers by raising your prices too often. Project how many customers you'll lose, or how much more money you'll gain by raising your prices. It's always smart to review your bookkeeping and overhead to determine if you must raise prices.

Action Step

> What actions will you take to attract customers and increase your cash flow?

The marketing campaign is the vehicle that can reach your objectives and goals—by driving your business to a profitable state.

A precise plan will act as a road map to success and the future you desire. You do not want to leave your marketing to chance, so create some type of marketing plan that focuses primarily on promotion.

Master the Industrial Cycle

Typically, businesses go through an industrial cycle, which is essentially a life cycle. By actively nurturing your business with a marketing plan, you have some control over the duration of each phase.

1. The Start-up Phase consists of the first year or two of business operation. These are generally 'building' years with very little growth. You'll invest the most money marketing your business: creating effective signage, an identity system, promotional materials and more.

2. The Growth Phase happens when consumer awareness coincides with consumer needs. This phase will last as long as innovation is prevalent.

3. The Maturity Phase begins when your company has a consistent market share and ends when you either enter the growth phase again or the decline phase.

4. The Decline Phase happens when you fail to innovate and market share diminishes. Business starts to drop off. (The solution is to pre-plan your next marketing campaign *and* take action.)

Create a Master Plan

To keep pace with today's competitive marketplace, create a Master Plan that keeps your company in the growth phase. Here are two suggestions that will assist you.

Constant improvement: Constant improvement means constant growth and profits. I've seen small business owners who didn't reinvest in their businesses, and allowed their businesses to deteriorate and so they entered the decline phase. It's too easy to take your profits and put them elsewhere. You will find these solutions helpful:

1. Train employees more thoroughly.

2. Constantly refresh your image. Be current.

3. Make great customer service a priority.

4. Review and update your marketing materials.

High visibility: Remind customers that your business exists. Keep your marketing materials and promotions consistently in front of the public eye. Be relentless.

Tip: Be consistent.

Inconsistency is the number one reason small businesses fail to make an impact on the marketplace. Instead of implementing a campaign, many small businesses will occasionally advertise in the local newspaper or with a flyer. The results are minimal because two or three advertisements go virtually unnoticed. The real key to a steady flow of new customers is a consistent media presence in the marketplace.

Perhaps you've made this mistake. You advertised one or two promotions in the newspaper or handed out flyers and coupons, and nothing happened. You didn't gain even one new customer. So out of the fear of wasting money on advertising (and we've all done it) you do absolutely nothing more. It becomes frustrating because your business doesn't grow or grows at a snail's pace.

> *Marketing is the single most important business activity that affects your bottom line. You can't afford not to spend money promoting your business, if you want to stay in business. Through consistent marketing, your business becomes more profitable for you.*

Establish long-term loyalty with existing clients by offering consistent quality, value, and service. The number one reason that people don't return to a business is a lack of consistent quality and service.

Nurture your business through educating yourself. Also, your strengths in marketing, leadership, communication, and management—plus a bit of good luck—will determine how long your business remains in either the growth or maturity phase.

Action Step

What will you do to create a Master Plan, and keep your business in the growth phase?

- Remember that it may take anywhere from three months to a year before you see any results from your marketing efforts.

- It's always productive to spend some time visualizing your success. Productive daydreaming can lead to interesting results, and perhaps some innovative ideas.

Align with Your Business Plan

Imagine that you want to build a new home, and you've won the lottery so money is no object. You envision your home's size, style, bedrooms, kitchen, bathrooms, yard, and so on. You know exactly what you want and communicate that to your contractors. This information is translated into a blueprint or an exact plan to accomplish your dream.

> *Likewise, an entrepreneur with a business plan and a marketing plan has the advantage of a blueprint for every phase in the evolution of his or her business.*

First, align your marketing objectives with your business plan, which provides the overall direction of your business. Your business plan takes your vision (before you opened for business) and makes adjustments to it so it becomes realistic and attainable. In this way, producing your business plan is a vital part of the envisioning process. Look at your original business plan and note if a strong marketing plan is included. If not, then now is the time to align the two plans. Your plan converts your vision into a better possibility of becoming a reality.

A business plan is a practical tool that serves six dominant functions:

1. To support your objective.

2. To synchronize all your marketing efforts for the year.

3. To bring you closer each year to your original vision.

4. To attract investors or bankers. (It's an investment tool.)

5. To develop ideas about how the business needs to be conducted.

6. To assess the business person's actual performance over time.

If you don't have a business plan or know how to write one for your business, it's never too late to develop one and plan for your renewed success.

Build Your Business

When a new building is designed, the architects provide for a strong and durable foundation. You set up a foundation during the development phase of your business, and like all foundations, it must be durable enough to support the weight or stress that will be placed on it later.

You'll find value in writing your business ideas and plans on paper. It's similar to a blueprint, which will cause you to be organized and know how your business will operate. The process of creating a business plan forces you to take a realistic, objective and critical look at your business in its entirety. It doesn't matter if you are just beginning or have been in business for several years. It's never too late to develop clarity. You don't have to be an expert to develop an effective plan. To be efficient, the plan is necessary.

Communicate with Clarity

The business plan is the chief instrument for communicating your ideas to associates, bankers and employees. It allows you to give clarity to any vague thoughts you may have.

A business plan is a written summary of what you plan to accomplish and how you intend to organize your resources to attain those goals.

It's important to become aware of what your finances really are, and how far they can be stretched. It's great to dream of big things, and your next step is to make a realistic plan. One advantage of a business plan is how it assists you in discovering something previously overlooked. Its best use is to help you identify both your weak areas and your strengths.

A Tool for Banks and Venture Capitalists

Venture capitalists or financial institutions will need to see several elements in your business plan, such as:

1. The number of employees you currently have or intend to hire.

2. Last year's sales figures.

3. Your profit and loss statement.

4. Your legal form.

5. If you are a corporation, include the date and state where the corporation is located. List the founders' names.

6. Describe the nature of your business.

7. Describe any trademarks you may own.

8. Describe your geographical area.

9. Furnish a physical description of the business.

10. Describe your major suppliers.

11. Describe a list of major customers.

12. Describe any employee benefits that you intend to provide.

13. State the type of business loan you are seeking.

14. Describe what types of insurance coverage you will purchase.

15. Identify whether your real estate is leased or owned.

16. Explain your bank relationships and your credit lines.

17. It's a good idea to furnish copies of brochures, mailers, publicity releases, newspaper and magazine articles (in appendices).

18. Determine the qualities that set you apart from others who are in the same business. (This process does require you to systematically observe your competition.)

19. Include a projection of growth from your market research.

20. Provide a forecasted budget detailing how loan funds would be used.

Remember in developing a business plan that nothing is written in stone, and your plans may need to be revised as necessary. A financier will assess your plans and base the decision to give you a loan upon this information.

You show precisely how the money is going to be used. Backers will know what you are all about, and how you are physically, mentally, and emotionally capable of starting and operating a business.

Business Plan

Here are elements of an effective business plan:

1. Table of Contents—include a history of the company, a business summary, a plan for personnel, the products and services you plan to use, your marketing and sales program, a report on the competition, your management potential, and all financial reports.

2. Executive Summary—list of major topics and a one- or two-sentence description of vital points.

3. Management Team—list personnel, expected turnover rate, any benefits program or incentives. Add resumes of key personnel, business and personal references, reputation, capabilities, and attitude. List salaries or commissions, and enclose proposed contracts with employees. Include information about the owner here.

4. Long-range and short-term goals.

5. Financial forecast.

6. Your market for the product or service—a history including product brand names, price ranges of products and services, size of market, trend of product or service, suppliers and references.

7. A marketing plan, analysis, and strategy—advertising and promotion, location, sales earnings, percentage of market share, new competition, competitors' prices.

8. Describe any potential changes that could contribute to your success. List any properties that you own. Explain the state of your equipment: its condition, value estimate, owned or leased.

9. Operational plan, timetables and strategy—profit and loss statements.

10. Ownership and Equity—anything substantial that you own.

11. Potential Pitfalls—any concerns you foresee.

12. Appendices.

Writing a business plan is similar to writing a resume. You must shape and tailor the inside information to suit the needs of the lender. (loan officer, venture capitalist, friend). Don't bore the reader by making it long and complex. Make it comprehensive; numerous lenders prefer about fourteen pages.

A business plan can help you avoid a business venture that is doomed to failure. Also, notice that no matter how well written and documented, the plan must be followed in order to succeed.

Business owners who feel less confident about writing their business plan can supplement their efforts with the advice of a professional.

As business owners, we can get caught up in daily activities and forget to take care of the business. This can cause us to miss out on opportunities.

Action Steps

1. What is the purpose of your business?

2. State your philosophy with regard to your profession.

3. State your philosophy with regard to your business.

4. What are you doing now according to your business plan?

5. Is your business plan sound?

6. Is your service or product marketable?

7. Can you make money with your product or service?

   (This last question may seem obvious, but remember the dot-com bust when many Internet companies had no viable plan to earn profits.)

Create a Mission Statement

Complete your business plan with a mission statement or a mission caption. They are creative tools whose purpose is to share the essence of your business's purpose. You are the messenger and your mission statement is your message to the world. According to Raleigh Pinskey, author of *101 Ways to Promote Yourself,* "A vision statement can be based on a vision, goal, or ethics. It can be a slate of objectives, an environmental policy, an operating policy, or a basic business philosophy." Your mission statement (as one sentence) can be used on your business card, in your brochure or newsletter, on your letterhead, in your advertising and public relations messages or on a banner within your place of business.

According to Laurie Beth Jones, author of *The Path, Creating Your Mission Statement for Work and for Life*, a good mission statement has three simple elements:

1. A mission statement should be no more than a single sentence long.

2. It should be easily understood by a twelve-year-old.

3. It should be able to be recited at gunpoint.

In creating a good mission statement, it is important to look at the big picture. A mission statement will help you to accomplish the goals you set. Mission statements are for individuals or companies who are on a mission to do something inspiring, helpful or enriching for a targeted group of people. Think about your vision, your purpose and who you want to reach with your message. At the very core, what do you want them to know about you? Your mission statement will say who you are and what you intend to do for your customers. It will express what you and your business stand for.

Mission statements require action, which requires that you use verbs. Choose three action verbs that describe what action you will take.

It may be to brighten, delight and entertain. Or educate, encourage, and enhance. You could prepare, inspire, and promote. How about serve, protect, and respect? Your three choices should be meaningful and purposeful. Ultimately your mission statement will apply to a group, presumably your target market.

My co-author Tom Marcoux emphasizes the "mission caption" in his book, *Be Heard and Be Trusted*. He emphasizes that, "A traditional mission statement can be pages long, and many people look at it infrequently. A mission caption is like the line below a photograph in a newspaper. It's best to memorize your mission caption. Or you can look at your mission caption every day. It takes only two seconds for you to ensure that you're on a fulfilling and successful path."

Individuals may also create a mission statement or caption for themselves. A caption must be brief, flexible, and distinctive. Here are examples:

1. Mark Victor Hansen, well-known speaker and coauthor of the *Chicken Soup for the Soul* series uses this mission caption: "Motivation for the Betterment of Humanity."

2. Tom Marcoux has the mission caption: "I help people experience enthusiasm, love and wisdom to fulfill big dreams. "

3. Toastmasters uses a mission statement: "The mission of a Toastmasters Club is to provide a mutually supportive and positive learning environment in which every member has the opportunity to develop communication and leadership strengths, which in turn foster self-confidence and personal growth."

Action Step

What is the mission statement in your business plan? If you don't have one, create it now. For yourself, create a "mission caption."

Now Dr. Tony Alessandra brings additional insight to the mission statement process.

Hidden Power for Your Marketing

Dr. Tony Alessandra

You need a clearly defined mission to be successful!

To get anything significant accomplished, you must work hard, possess energy, and demonstrate drive. But to truly influence others, you also need a mission.

It isn't enough just to come up with a "mission statement" that merely sounds good or looks sharp on paper, though that's a start. Instead, to be effective, your mission has got to come from your heart. It's got to grow out of a sense of what's important in your life and in your world.

The most effective missions involve helping others. Often, it's acquiring that mission that catapults people into a leadership role, which puts them in a position to exercise personal power.

Steve Jobs and Steve Wozniak didn't start up Apple Computer just to make money or to make people more efficient; their mission was to develop a "user-friendly" machine that would revolutionize people's lives. Their sense of purpose propelled them to perform brilliantly. And, characteristically, when they later sought to attract John Sculley, widely respected as a marvelous marketer, they didn't emphasize money or prestige, both of which he already had in abundance as Pepsi's president and CEO.

Instead, according to Sculley's autobiography, Jobs and Sculley were walking near Sculley's home when Jobs asked, "So, what do you want to do, John? Do you want to sell sugared water for the rest of your life—or do you want a chance to change the world?" Sculley, faced with that kind of challenge and that kind of vision, knew what he had to do. He acquired a new mission and joined Apple.

Candy Lightner's defining moment came in 1980 when her daughter Cari was killed by a drunk driver. Her anger soon turned into her mission: a burning desire to do something about such wasteful tragedies. Within a few days, she held a meeting with a few friends—and that was the beginning of Mothers Against Drunk Driving, better known as MADD. Candy Lightner had no position of power when she began. Yet she is living proof of Andrew Jackson's famous epigram: "One man with courage makes a majority." Or, in this case, one woman. "If you care enough," Lightner says, "you can accomplish anything."

As usual, your attitude can affect how you choose to frame your mission. Perhaps you look around and say, "Here I am, stuck in a dead-end job. How can I possibly develop a mission?"

But where we are, or what happens to us, is not as important as what we think about where we are or what happens to us. My point is, maybe we can't all have missions echoing the grand but simple nobility espoused by Salvation Army founder William Booth: "Others." But we can all look outside ourselves as we try to figure out our life's purpose. And looking outside ourselves will not only help us fashion a mission, it will also help draw people to us and our mission.

Spell out your own success with SMART goal-setting: Striving for and attaining goals makes life meaningful. Goals create drive—but only if you set yourself to achieving them in the proper way. I have found that the letters in the word SMART are very useful in articulating goals.

SMART reminds me that my goals must be Specific, Measurable, Action-Oriented, Realistic & Relevant, and Time-Bound.

Specific and Measurable relate to how you phrase your goal. Vagueness goes hand in hand with lack of genuine commitment. You do not think a world-class pole-vaulter, for instance, just says, "I want to jump higher next year." No, he has a certain height in mind.

Therefore, instead of "I will be more fit in six months so I can hike into mountains and help with a reforestation project," you might say, "In six months my resting blood pressure will be ten points lower."

Alternatively, "In six months I'll be twenty pounds lighter." "I'll be running three miles in four to six months" is more effective than "I'll be running more in four to six months."

Or if your goal is to become a standout salesperson so you eventually can rise in the firm and change its focus, you'd be better off proclaiming, "I will increase my sales next year by twenty percent" rather than "I will sell more next year."

In order to ensure your goal is Measurable, you need to know if you are making progress. You need to set up interim goals or checkpoints along the way. Depending on what your goal is, you might be checking your progress every day, once a week, or once every two months.

Action-Oriented means that your goal will involve taking action. We cannot move toward our goals by standing still, and stating your goals in such a way that denotes action releases the power that you inherently have available internally.

The statements above include the action that will be taken. Words like "hike" and "running" make the goal real, powerful, and motivating.

Realistic has to do with the goal, which should be just beyond your reach, making you stretch. It should be attainable, yet challenging. The goal must also be Relevant to your overall plan and direction or it will be a distraction or have a detrimental impact on your overall goals and aspirations.

If it is almost impossible to achieve, a goal can be de-motivating. On the other hand, a goal with 100 percent chance of achievement is not really a goal; it is a given. That defeats the purpose of goals, which is to move you forward by making you work harder, or by gathering more resources than you had in the past.

The last rule of smart goal setting is Time-Bound. Until you set a specific time frame in which your goal will be accomplished, it is merely a wish, not a goal. Set the exact time that the goal will be accomplished, and if it is a longer-term goal (over three months), you should also set up short-term checkpoints when you will measure progress, and take corrective action in order to get back on track if necessary.

You may discover that your goal is not attainable or realistic within the time frame you have set. However, be flexible about your game plan before you reconsider your goal. Nothing ever goes exactly according to plan, so you may have to make adjustments in order to stay on track and keep up your motivation.

Some other suggestions about goals:—Write them down. It's one thing to think about your goals, but it's quite another to dignify them by putting them on paper. Trust me on this! Writing them down makes them more tangible, more meaningful, and more imperative. Instead of being nothing more than a vague musing, your list of goals becomes a call to arms, a goad to action, and a pact with yourself.— Make them personal. They must be sincere and something you want to do rather than something you think you should do. Whatever your objective, the reasons must be strong enough to fuel your desire to work to attain your goal.—Make them positive. The mind cannot refuse to think of something when instructed to do so. So if you say, "I will not smoke today," your mind automatically ends up thinking more about smoking than if you had said, "I will breathe only clean air today." Same purpose—more effective.

Dr. Tony Alessandra has a street-wise, college-smart perspective on business, having been raised in the housing projects of NYC and eventually realizing success as a graduate professor of marketing, an entrepreneur, business author, and hall-of-fame keynote speaker. Dr. Alessandra was inducted into the Speakers Hall of Fame in 1985 and is a member of the Speakers Roundtable, a group of 20 of the world's top professional speakers. Tony's polished style, powerful message, and proven ability as a consummate business strategist consistently earn rave reviews and loyal clients.

Dr. Alessandra is a founding partner in The Cyrano Group and Platinum Rule Group—companies which have successfully combined cutting-edge technology and proven psychology to give salespeople the ability to build and maintain positive relationships with hundreds of clients and prospects.

Dr. Alessandra is a prolific author with 18 books translated into 49 foreign language editions, including the newly revised, best-selling *The New Art of Managing People*. He is featured in over 50 audio/video programs and films, including *Relationship Strategies*.

Products: PlatinumRule.com
Speeches: Holli Catchpole, (760) 603-8110, Holli@SpeakersOffice.com

---

Capitalize on the Three C's

The three C's of marketing are Campaign, Commitment, and Consumer.

Campaign

In presidential elections, each candidate travels nationwide to communicate how he or she plans to benefit voters. Each campaign manager will have a winning strategy. Certain media is chosen to reach voters to place the candidate into office. The same is true of a business marketing campaign. You are essentially campaigning for local support—for potential consumers to become clients and invest their money in your products and services.

According to *Webster's New World Dictionary*, a campaign is a series of organized, planned actions for a particular purpose. The whole purpose of your marketing campaign is to organize and plan the actions that will best reach your primary objective for the year. A marketing campaign is a commitment and an investment in the future life and prosperity of your business.

Commitment

It's just like a successful marriage, which calls for a commitment to the relationship. Proof of your commitment to marketing must be shown by efforts beyond only three or four times a year. Every day you make a conscious choice for the relationship. Continued commitment and effort are needed to make the relationship a rich one.

You have a similar relationship with your business. Single advertisements and promotions are ineffective. The best way to increase the flow of new customers into your business is to consistently stay in the public eye, and you accomplish that with a marketing campaign. For example, Microsoft invests in a big media blitz every time they release a new product. Although you may not afford an expensive advertising campaign, you can use your creativity to make an impact on a much smaller scale within your community or industry. As a sidenote: Pepsi recently dropped having a Super Bowl commercial in favor of devoting money and effort to a social media campaign.

Consumer

Remember the consumer's part in helping you to reach your objective. Your market campaigning has a circular movement; it is directed from you, through the media, to a specific customer, and back to you again.

Consumers are bombarded with thousands of advertising messages a day from radio, television, newspapers, magazines, books, billboards, t-shirts and the Internet. To be recognized in your community you must make a real impact, which is achieved by making the consumer a partner in your business venture.

Be Visible

Strong marketers maintain high visibility. In step one, we created a beacon of light. That beacon will help the world to focus on your vision and primary objective. All of the steps thus far lead you to move on to the next strength, transforming this vision into reality.

Envisioning Summary

Take the following steps to access your hidden strength to envision.

1. Envision your beacon of light.

2. Access your imagination.

3. Identify your primary objective—the one main thing you want to accomplish this year.

4. Go for your goals.

5. Polish the diamond.

6. Establish your quantitative objectives.

7. Master the industrial cycle.

8. Align with your business plan.

9. Capitalize on the 3 C's.

10.Be Visible.

When Do I Take These Steps?

Identifying your objectives is generally done, along with your business plan, before you open for business. You'll identify a new primary objective at the beginning of each year. It is your yearly mini-vision that leads to the accomplishment of a larger overall vision of your business.

3

Transforming

Your Second Hidden Strength

You are seated in a large auditorium, waiting for the first speaker to address an enthusiastic audience. You've finally made it to the popular self development seminar that you've always wanted to attend. Friends and colleagues rave about these personal growth seminars and the profound difference they've made in their lives. They quickly learned how to move past procrastination, self-doubt, and fear. You noticed how confidently your friends moved towards their goals, and are now significantly happier and more at peace. They finally discovered the inner gifts they possess. As you look about, you wonder if the other participants are business owners, factory workers, counselors, sales people, ministers, or stay-at-home parents? People from all walks of life have a desire to transform their lives into one of quality and fulfillment. You have come, as they have, to a place where you'll gather the resources you need to achieve your dreams. The house lights dim, you settle back into your chair, and the first speaker begins, "Change is a natural part of our lives, and transformation is the process that enhances it."

Whenever we are about to embark on a new journey, one that involves stepping into unknown territory, many of us have a certain amount of anxiety that may temporarily confuse us and cause us to hold back in our endeavors. Anxious thoughts can be laid to rest when we've gone through a transformative process. Once we get important information, we gain in self-confidence and the courage to move toward our dream.

Strength 2—*Transforming* focuses on your ability to transform your business into one that meets your expectations. You'll learn to move past barriers that stand in the way of your success.

Complete the transformation *Action Steps*, and you'll benefit through personal growth and self confidence. You'll be empowered to charge forward and create the successful business you deserve.

Example from a Highly Successful Person

Movie producer Lynda Obst has learned how to transform tough situations into success. In 1994, her world came to a heart-wrenching crash when she lost the race against a rival producer at a competing studio. Her rival had placed his movie *Outbreak* into production first. In essence, Lynda was beaten because her studio cancelled her similar movie based on the book *The Hot Zone*. It had been a tough struggle to gain name stars including Jodie Foster. But Lynda's efforts had ended in ashes.

Lynda now advises women to say "next" and move on, and have multiple projects. She has a number of productions in various stages at any given moment. And she has enjoyed producing a number of successful films including *Contact* (with Jodie Foster) and *Sleepless in Seattle*.

Humor helps. Lynda's friend Nora Ephron (director of *Sleepless in Seattle*) had a unique response when someone rejected her script and said, "Don't take this personally." Nora responded, "How should I take it? As a group?"

Your Objective for the Transforming Strength

Your objective for the transforming strength is to remember how, in the past, you transformed things and situations in your life and as a result gained valuable experience, knowledge, and fulfillment. You will easily apply that remembrance by acting with confidence in favor of your vision or primary objective.

Transforming as a Natural Strength

Children demonstrate this strength by transforming or changing things in their young lives. When my brothers were small children, they played with a toy called a Transformer. With moveable parts and a quick shift or two, the toy could be transformed from a vehicle to a combat warrior and then back again. Little girls play with dolls that can be easily transformed by changing the hair, costumes, and props. Many children are now computer literate, and computer software offers a vast array of transformation tools. Everyone at some time in their life has changed their residence, career, relationships, body shape, and home furnishings. We've changed many other small and large situations. In some ways, we can define transformation as a significant change(s) that start us on a new path. Welcome transformation as a part of the evolutionary process.

Action Step

> Write about two examples from your past when you used your natural transformation strengths.

Transform yourself and reach your primary objective

A strong marketer knows that the road to success or profits is smooth when you know what you're doing, where you're going, and how to get there. So the most important question becomes, "How do I accomplish this objective, which may now be applied to a profitable and service-oriented business, in the most direct and expedient way?" The answer to this question can be found by transforming your vision into reality.

At this point you have an overall vision for your business. You believe that your primary objective will bring attention, growth and profits to your business. You'll use your transformation strength to transform your primary objective from something illusory or abstract into something visible. You'll make it all happen by taking firm steps throughout the year towards that objective.

The previous *Action Steps* in Chapter 2– *Envisioning* hold your creative ideas, so you're off to a good start.

Get ready for change

Transforming is just as much about getting ready for change as it is about the change itself. Let's first look at the word transform. According to *Webster's New World Dictionary,* "trans-" means on the other side of, across, or through. "Form" means appearance. Your objective will take a form or appearance, which is an idea in your mind. You will then change it into physical form. Ask yourself several important questions regarding your readiness for change. Do you welcome it? Will you accept change into your life, into your business adventure, into your consciousness? If your answer is no, or you're not sure, then perhaps you need to rethink your objective, and put it into alignment with what you are willing to change.

Let's assume that you are ready to make a change, or transform your objective into a real thing or situation. Since you want something new and specific to happen, you must do something different from what you are now doing; otherwise, there is no change. You must be the one to determine what to do that is different. You are the visionary.

Action Steps

1. On a scale of one to ten, with one as the least excited, and ten as the most excited, how would you rate your enthusiasm towards your primary objective?

2. What components would you have to add to raise that rate to a ten, if it isn't already a ten?

When you think of a butterfly, you know that it evolves naturally through various stages before it becomes a fluttering, elegant butterfly. Those stages are not comfortable for the caterpillar and temporarily leave it in a vulnerable and weakened state. Yet it instinctively knows that its destiny is to become something ultimately greater than a caterpillar. The promise of beauty and freedom compel the caterpillar to naturally transform itself into something greater than before.

Determine Your Needs

Take this step in the transforming process to determine what actions are needed to accomplish your primary objective. This may take a great deal of investigation on your part or it may take a few simple phone calls; it really depends upon the complexity of your objective. Consider this step a brainstorming session. It isn't necessary to come up with concrete solutions. It's more important to find creative ideas and new directions in which to proceed.

For example, if a new business image is your primary objective, then at the end of the year you can expect to have a new identity system, new signage, improved brochures and advertising. You'll begin by assessing what is necessary to make the new identity system a reality. You may need to take desktop publishing classes, or call a graphic design firm for estimates.

Maybe your primary objective is an improved reputation, more strengthed employees, or a large or expanded retail area. You'll take concrete steps to make that happen. For example, if you want a new employee, you'll first decide what strengths are necessary. Then you'll write an advertisement defining your requirements, use Internet resources or an employment bureau, and then interview candidates.

If your primary objective is to improve your business's interior, then you'll change the image in your mind into the physical manifestation of newly painted walls, new equipment, and anything else that is meaningful to you. You might look at interior design or trade magazines to get innovative ideas. Talk over new trends with a professional interior designer and get estimates. Or ask a friend for a referral. Your benefit from achieving your primary objective will result in a higher retention of customers and referrals, which leads to larger amounts in cash, checks, or credit card sales.

Determine your needs so you have a starting point from which to begin your actions.

Action Steps

1. What do you believe is needed in order to reach your primary objective?

2. What does the customer need?

Change your mental orientation

You begin moving from vision to reality by changing your mental orientation from stagnation to motivation. Some people find it easy to make that phone call or get that estimate. Other people procrastinate, worry, or bury their goals and dreams under a pile of other things to do. If that's the case, then you need to dig deep. For example, I met a woman who studied hypnotherapy but was deeply afraid that her home town in the "Bible-belt" would not welcome her new hypnotherapy business. She felt they would reject her and perhaps run her out of town. She moved through her fears by talking to people in her industry, who pointed out the advantages of her new business. Her new mental orientation provided her with a better attitude. She marketed herself through television advertising that included testimonials of people who overcame cigarette smoking and weight problems. Her business skyrocketed. As the only hypnotherapist in the area, she found her niche. She changed her mental orientation and reaped large rewards.

Action Step

> What is your mental orientation (fears) toward your business? What three things can you do to change your mental orientation?

How You Can Set a Marketing Campaign Goal to Expand Your Mind and Your Profits

Tom Marcoux

Have you ever set a marketing goal and felt overwhelmed? Some of us set goals that are too small; and others set goals that are too tough. Either way, you might drain your energy.

Now, learn an empowering way to set goals that can get you to think in new ways and to achieve extraordinary results. This process was innovated by author Raymond Aaron, and he calls it "MTO" (Minimum, Target and Outrageous).

Here's an example—my client Kerrie sets these goals:

Monthly Goals:

- **Minimum:** Sell 11 books on Amazon.com—per month

- **Target:** Sell 33 books

- **Outrageous:** Sell 3,000 books

If she sells 11 books, she is still happy. The magic happens when she considers how to sell 3,000 books. Her mind starts flowing with new possibilities to try. To sell 3,000 books she might want to contact other authors who have e-subscriber lists. To sell 2% (3,000 copies) she would need to make an arrangement with 8 authors, each with a list of approximately 20,000 e-subscribers.

You can see how this goal-setting process is empowering. Now try the "MTO" process on one of your first-guess goals.

Tom has shown that we can use Raymond Aaron's "MTO" process so that we improve our goal-setting steps.

Look at all the angles. When you look at a box, you see that it has many angles. Unless you turn it in different ways, you won't see the opposite sides, where something else may be hidden. Look at your goals and visions from a totally different angle. It's like using the magnifying glass to focus on what is there. Notice areas for improvement like social etiquette, image, finances, or contacts.

It begins when you consciously focus on what you want. Start with your first thoughts of how you can create a better place to live, work and play. You are in a powerful position because you are a business owner, interact with many people in your community, and influence the quality of other people's lives. You are essentially a model for what is possible.

Secondly, take stock of who you know and how they can help you forge ahead with confidence. Your friends, family, colleagues, and networking companions can give valuable suggestions and expand your opportunities. Look for hidden potential.

I've known many successful business people who walked their talk and became pillars in their community. They had many wonderful traits: vision, determination, and compassion. They learned how to look at all the angles.

Action Step

> Brainstorm for a few minutes and write down some abstract ideas about how to manifest your primary objective. It can be anything wild or zany. Don't limit yourself.

Find the Fear

Imagine that several people who grew up in your community went away to college and eventually became powerful corporate business owners. They believed in their personal strengths and abilities, and became fabulously successful. They know how to transform their fear into power. The second step in transforming is to find the fear that is blocking you from taking those necessary steps to growing your business.

Fear is the major emotion that holds most people back from living a truly fulfilled life. If we allow it, fear can paralyze the quality of our journeys. Fear can turn a wonderful heavenly adventure into a hellish one. Think about your concerns: things that keep you from transforming your business into something bigger and better than it is now.

Fear is the most destructive and limiting mental state. Without your intervention, fear can …

1. Limit your potential to have a successful business.

2. Prohibit you from having an improved quality of life for you and your employees.

3. Stop you from giving back to your community.

4. Prevent you from realizing profits.

5. Prevent you from realizing your dreams and objectives, and it is the number one block to success and prosperity.

Many of us hold our visions in our minds for a long, long time without ever acting on them. Our minds become a holding chamber where our visions or objectives are held prisoner. They are stuck there mostly because we fear change. As a hypnotherapist I found that these feelings are usually associated with incidents from the past: childhood or early adulthood.

Most people know what is holding them back from achieving their business goals. Many times it is fear of success or failure, or feelings of low self-esteem and unworthiness. Perhaps it is an unsupportive mate, a lack of motivation, or burnout.

We can choose to free ourselves from that which keeps us from accomplishing our dreams. Since fears are just thoughts about things, and not things themselves, that means they can be transformed or changed.

Action Steps

1. Determine what it is you're afraid of—make a list of everything that comes to mind. When written down, they lose some of the power that vague, fearful thoughts have in your mind.

2. Find a quiet place to close your eyes, and relax your mind and body. Record this *Action Step* on a recording device and play it back to yourself, giving yourself enough time to apply the points, or ask a friend to read you the points. Use this five-part *Action Step* process to quickly move through your fear:

   a. Identify the incident that caused the fear. It may be a recent incident or one that happened at an earlier time in your life.

   (Was someone else involved, and how did they contribute to your fear? You can't change this incident, but you can change how you perceive it. How could you perceive it in a way that is non-threatening?)

b. Identify another time when you were successful in overcoming that fear. Pay particular attention to your happy feelings. Escalate those happy feelings.

c. When you experience happy feelings, anchor that response by doing something unique, such as snapping your fingers, touching your temple, or a similar activity ("anchor" means connecting your happy emotions to your body).

d. Replay incident No. 1 using the new positive response and snap your fingers, or other activity, to anchor a happy feeling.

e. Any time the fear returns, snap your fingers to trigger happy feelings and successfully overcome any traces of fearfulness (you may also use one of your recently created affirmations).

(*Note:* some fears may require that one gets some form of therapy.)

3. How has your understanding of fear changed?

I firmly believe that there are enough customers to go around, and that a strong marketer can be as prosperous as he/she gives themselves permission to be. Giving yourself permission means to "go beyond any fears" of failure or success, and embrace a "can do" attitude. An enthusiastic attitude means everything and is a required component for success. You can do it.

Now, Willie Jolley encourages us to make things happen.

Make Things Happen!

Willie Jolley

What's more important than a business plan? I believe you need a hustle plan.

For example, when I was just starting my speaking business, I took audacious action. I knew that members of the National Association of College Activities Convention were choosing speakers for the year. But I didn't have money to pay the registration fee so I couldn't enter the convention hall. I didn't let that stop me. I gave out my little flyers about my speaking business outside the convention hall.

Soon, my friend twice admonished me to stop handing out flyers: "Man, this is not how we do it. You are embarrassing yourself!" After he left that second time, I started back up and continued until I had given out all of my flyers.

Later, a man hollered at me when I walked past the convention hall. I thought he was security and was going to yell at me about breaking rules. Instead, he asked if I had been the guy giving out the flyers in the morning.

"Yes. I confess … it was me!"

"Good!" he replied, "I have been looking for you all day! I am the owner of the biggest college booking agency, and I think that if you have enough guts to hustle and work like you did today, then I think you will be a help to our agency."

From this moment when my hustling paid off, he became my biggest booking agent for colleges!

When asked what keeps them from being successful, most people will blame the government, the economy, their families, or the "isms" of life (you know … sexism, racism, ageism, etc.). But the one thing most people avoid in their list is that which is most important! It is the person we see every day in the mirror … it is us! We are the main obstacles to our success in life! Instead, we must make things happen.

It has been stated, and I believe it is true, that success follows the 80/20 rule: 80 percent of the work usually comes from 20 percent of the people. In personal achievement, this means we are responsible for 80 percent of our failure to hit our goals, and outside obstacles are only 20 percent of the problem.

The old African proverb states, "If you can overcome the enemy on the inside, the enemy on the outside can do you no harm!" We must be brutally honest with ourselves and come to the realization that we are the biggest challenge to our own success!

If you want to win, you must stop letting things happen and start making things happen. Remember, when all is said and done, much more is said than done … so let's go get it done!

Today … make a commitment to overcome yourself, so you can reach your goals!

During tough economic times, some people sit and wait for the economy to change. They talk about how bad things are, and they just want to survive the storms. Yet there are others who do not wait for things to happen, they make things happen.

This article includes Willie's story of handing out flyers that is one highlight from his book *Turn Setbacks into Greenbacks*.

Willie Jolley is America' s premier celebrity speaker-singer-author … inspiring millions with music and motivation! *Success Magazine* hailed Willie Jolley as the "Comeback King"—when he successfully helped Ford Motors avert the need to accept bail out dollars. Ford took Willie on a speaking tour to present to all their employees. Willie was named

"One of the Outstanding Five Speakers in the World" by Toastmasters International. Willie earned the CPAE/Speaker Hall of Fame Award from the National Speakers Association. Willie authored the best-selling book *A Setback Is A Setup For A Comeback*. Willie's new wealth-building book *Turn Setbacks Into Greenbacks* is on its way to becoming another bestseller. Willie hosts "The Willie Jolley Weekend Show" on XM Satellite radio. He holds a B.A. in Psychology and Sociology from The American University and a Masters Degree from Wesley Theological Seminary. His mission in life is to help people maximize their God-given talents and abilities so they can "Do More, Be More and Achieve More!"

Visit WillieJolley.com

Overcome Judgment and Self-Doubt

Judgment and self-doubt form a barrier to success. Transform your opinion of yourself by developing your confidence. Participate in events that help you to stretch beyond your self-imposed boundaries. Here's an example of how I once had a breakthrough and overcame judgment and self-doubt.

In 1992, I was the first one to arrive for a class at the World School of Advanced Healing Arts in San Francisco. I was in training to become a Holistic Health Counselor. I sat down and noticed several rows of 1"-thick boards lined up against the wall. I picked one up and impulsively gave it a good karate chop, thereby hurting my hand!

When class started the instructors told us that we were going to literally 'break wood' and have a breakthrough in some area of our personal life. My hand was still throbbing, and I thought, "I'm not doing this, no way." We were being trained to 'stay in the present moment and just listen intently.' By the end of the session, I was psyched up to have a breakthrough—I knew I could break that board. My classmates lined up and each one broke the board like it was a cookie. But I hit the wood with my hand, and it didn't break. I tried it again and again and it still didn't break.

I was then asked to practice some more while other students took their turn. I practiced in the background, all the while hearing my classmates being cheered on. At this point I decided that wild horses couldn't stop me from achieving my breakthrough. I tried several more times and finally broke the wood. My classmates cheered, and I was pleased with my achievement.

The importance of this story is not about breaking the wood. My breakthrough was overcoming my negative personal judgment and self-doubt. When I got enough information, I knew I could do it. It led to reclaiming my confidence and personal power. Judgment and self-doubt are the roadblocks that keep us from having breakthroughs in our life's journey.

Action Steps

1. What action could you take to overcome judgment and self-doubt?

2. List at least 2 incidents from your life when you achieved something that you initially thought you couldn't.

Sometimes, we allow self-doubt to arise from listening and believing the bad news stories emphasized by the media. People will say, "It's hard to get a job in today's economy," or "Sales are down in today's economy." What we need to remember is that statistics do not indicate the truth for every individual.

Now, Patricia Fripp and David Garfinkel show the marketing strategies that work even in a so-called slow economy.

How to Market your Way out of Tough Times

Patricia Fripp & David Garfinkel

There's gloom and uncertainty in the air, and most businesses are making a terrible mistake right now in their efforts to ride out the tough times. They're cutting back on marketing and waiting until the economy improves.

In an economy like this, cutting back on marketing is flirting with business suicide. What you should do instead is increase your marketing without increasing the amount of money you spend. This will not only protect you from sales declines, but will also strengthen your business against the threat of deep-pocketed competitors, who may see tough times as a great opportunity to outmaneuver you and grab some of your customers.

How do you get more marketing bang for fewer marketing bucks? By using proven lower-cost, higher-yield methods. Here are five sure cures for marketing woes in tough times:

1. Get back in touch with old customers. It's all too easy to ignore your old customers, but they are often your best source for new business. Sometimes sending a personal note, making a phone call or inviting an old customer to lunch is all it takes to rekindle a business relationship.

If you want to do this through direct mail or email, you can give old customers a special "Welcome Back" offer—a freebie, a discount, or a bonus when they resume doing business with you.

2. Offer prospective customers a free sample. This is an obvious but often overlooked strategy that certainly can work for your business. Everyone from grocery stores (who offer tidbits of food) to high priced consultants (I spoke to one last week who snared a $10,000 personal coaching client by offering a free first hour) can use this strategy effectively. Don't think it will work in the corporate world? Hmmm ... ever hear of a company called AOL?

3. Focus your advertising. Many businesses think "keeping your name in front of the public" is a valid advertising strategy. It's questionable at best, but it's way too risky and low-yield in tough times. Instead, make sure your advertising is only in publications that reach your best prospects, and—this is the most important part—make a specific offer and call to action to get readers of the ad to call you.

One of my clients used this strategy and progressed from 10 lukewarm leads that wouldn't turn into customers, into signed contracts with 35 customers representing millions of dollars worth of business.

4. Let your customers help you out. Business is always a two-way street. Some of your customers who you've helped in the past will be glad to return the favor. Often, all you have to do is ask. Two things you can ask for: testimonials and case studies you can use in your sales presentations and advertising.

Another way they can help you: by giving you referrals. And if you have an influential customer who's appreciative of what you've done, ask that customer to write and send an endorsed letter to others recommending your business. Offer to pay for the printing and postage, and help with the writing if necessary.

5. Give extra attention to high-integrity behavior. If you think you're the only one who's a little nervous about a lot of things right now, you're not alone. Recent tragic events have increased feelings of distrust across the board. To set yourself apart in the marketplace, go out of your way to conduct business in an especially trustworthy manner. Bend over backwards to be fair about refunds and exchanges.

Do all you can to act in your customers' best interest, even if it means referring them to a competitor (if you don't think you're the best choice for what they want). High-integrity actions can hurt a little in the short-term, but payback is remarkably quick and well worth any sacrifice you may have had to make. If you get (or strengthen) a reputation for being trustworthy, that can be the most precious marketing asset of all in the times ahead.

This is also a great time to invest in sales training. If you would like to know more about how Patricia Fripp can help, email pfripp@fripp. com or see everything you need to make an educated decision fripp. com. Hundreds of companies can't be wrong!!!

David Garfinkel has been described as "the world's greatest copywriting coach." He's a successful results oriented copywriter and the author of *Advertising Headlines That Make You Rich*, which shows you exactly how to adapt proven moneymaking headlines to your business. Find out more about David Garfinkel at davidgarfinkel.com

Patricia Fripp, CSP, CPAE is a San Francisco-based executive speech coach, sales trainer and award-winning professional speaker on change, customer service, promoting business, and communication strengths. Fripp offers fresh, usable ideas on getting, keeping and deserving customers. She is Past-President of the National Speakers Association, author of *Get What You Want!*, *Make it So You Don't Have to Fake It*, and numerous video and audio programs on presentation strengths, marketing, sales, customer service, leadership, team building and more! Meetings and Conventions magazine calls Patricia "one of the country's 10 most electrifying speakers." Her clients include IBM, Sears, Merrill Lynch, Pfizer, American Payroll Association.

Patricia Fripp,
Sales Presentation Trainer,
Executive Speech Coach,
Keynote Speaker.

fripp.com
PFripp@ix.netcom.com
(415) 753-6556

Patricia and David remind us that there is a lot we can do to make our marketing efforts go well even in a slow economy. Another thing we need to do is move beyond our past efforts and fears.

Let Go of the Past

Let go of any negative experience from your past that may apply to a marketing situation. Learn to let go and begin again in a fresh new way. Anthony Robbins, author of *Awaken the Giant Within* says, "The past does not equal the future." Holding onto past failures keeps us in a stagnant position and away from trying new methods of success. Maybe your promotions or advertising in the past didn't work, and you felt that they were a waste of money, time, and effort. It's necessary to review what you did in the past that did or did not contribute to your success. Look through your records for clues.

Ask yourself essential questions. What technical aspects of your previous marketing plan were weak? Did you follow your business plan? Was the copy effectively written to attract your target market? Were your mailings targeted? Was your budget adequate? Answer these questions, then evaluate how your previous campaign stopped short of evolving your business in positive ways.

What about you personally? Did you inadvertently do something to sabotage your success? Did you believe and accept your plan or vision? Did you create the mental or emotional space for success?

Identify what you are saying to yourself that is negative or harmful to the accomplishment of your objective. You may have feelings of self-doubt, that you are undeserving of success and prosperity.

There is also the issue of someone who says "been there, done that."

Tip: Don't be arrogant.

An American reporter went to Japan to learn about Zen from a monk. The monk immediately asked him if he would like some tea. "Sure," replied the reporter. The monk poured tea into the cup until it overflowed onto the table, then the floor. "Wait, stop!" cried the reporter. "The interview is over," said the monk. The reporter replied that he came three thousand miles to learn about Zen. The monk softly explained, "You are like the cup; you are so full of tea that there is room for no more." The moral of this story is that before you can learn anything new, you must first empty your own cup. Business people who insist "I've heard that before … .Been there, done that" are admitting to being "full of tea." It helps when we approach a situation by being "present and in the moment." It is in the present moment when we can have a new perception and discover something different—that can make a big difference in our life.

Arrogance can be one of the largest blocks to a business person's success. I've known business people who were so consumed with their own self-importance that they failed to create a bond between their business and the community. They lacked compassion. Other owners were afraid of giving back to the community, fearing that they might not receive their just return. We need to turn our thoughts from fear to a compassionate mode of interacting with people.

Action Step

> Make a list of your concerns: things that are keeping you from moving forward with your objectives (money, effort, time, other).

Be On Purpose

Transform your business by being on purpose. You have goals and an objective that are important to you. They are worth your effort. People who act with purpose devise a plan and act on it in a way that gives them a sense of strength, authority, and control. To get on purpose, you'll take deliberate actions to get specific results. You'll expand your positive results as you apply the rest of the Ten Hidden Strengths throughout this book. Sometimes it means letting go of things or situations that don't work.

Action Step

What actions could you take to be more on purpose?

Focus Your Attention

Whatever you focus your attention on grows and expands. Focusing your attention on your purpose or objective allows it to appreciate. It's an investment in whatever is valuable or important to you. Focus on learning self-mastery. Here is an example of how the power of attention leads to self-mastery.

When I was a child my father became interested in archery. He learned many steps including how to hold the bow properly, line up the arrow, place his face near the string so he could get an accurate aim, and finally pull the string back with necessary force. He bought bales of hay for attaching his many paper targets. I watched him practice daily in our yard, over and over for what seemed like years. Sometime later he took our family with him to an archery exhibition for the Boy Scouts of America. Far across the room his target was an apple, tied to a string, swinging rapidly back and forth. I watched with anxiety. My father raised his bow. The arrow zipped through the air and went through the swinging apple. The crowd cheered, and I learned about the power of attention through my father's determined practice.

Action Step

> What areas in your business or career need your attention? When there are more than one, list them in the order of priority.

Choose Empowering Thoughts

Self-mastery comes from placing our thoughts and our energy on a physical action that leads to accomplishment. My father began with the intention to become an accurate and successful archer. He accomplished his intention through determination and practice. Our intentions are our mental plans, and our determination to achieve a desired result. Having an intention gives you a purpose or goal toward which to direct your thoughts.

In Chapter 2, *Envisioning*, you envisioned a purpose for your business in the form of a primary objective. The purpose of the transforming strength is to ensure that you actually transform your vision or objective into an accomplishment. You'll do that by consciously choosing thoughts that are positive and empowering.

We can become more disciplined in our thinking or cognitive processes. Your disciplinary strengths are those that you develop from birth which allow you to control and correct what doesn't actually serve you. You have more control over this area than you might expect. Choosing where to place your attention is an important step forward in your goal of choosing powerful thoughts.

> *Whenever you find yourself thinking of or saying something negative about yourself or your vision, exercise your disciplinary strength and immediately choose to stop. Use the empowering action of immediately replacing negative thoughts with powerful ones.*

First, identify and focus on those specific negative thoughts. Replace the sentence with something success affirming. I remember how I turned my thoughts around as I expanded my salon business. I developed a positive affirmation that brought me to a positive state of mind. I wrote it in the first person, present tense, as if it already exists now: "I am the successful owner of a salon with seven hair stylists." Repeating it helped me to keep my momentum going. As a result, I evaluated what I needed to do, and, almost automatically, took extra measures to improve my marketing and business.

My experience with affirmations and thought control have been miraculous. I find that in about two or three weeks of mentally exercising control over my thoughts, I become aware of subtle differences in my relationships and also in my life circumstances. I encourage you to practice raising your thoughts to a higher level of certainty.

Now it's your turn to affirm that you are an accomplished, successful person. Think of two or three short positive statements, in the first person, that express how you see yourself in an ideal situation. For example, "I am now enjoying my new cafe.—I find pleasure in keeping it clean and neat.—I enjoy promoting my successful new cafe.—I am happy to see many new customers.—I am a successful and prosperous business person.—I enjoy making large bank deposits." Make sure they are simple and easy to remember. Write your affirmations on paper and place them in areas of your home where you can see them often. Practice saying them throughout the day. Before long, your thoughts will be positive, supportive and successful ones. Once you have reached success here, it is time to learn an empowering way to choose your actions.

Action Steps

1. What is your intention for this year's marketing campaign?

2. List three positive affirmations that will empower you.

Choose Empowering Actions

It is our actions that ultimately bring about a fulfilling career and life. In this second level of focusing your attention, you'll begin to choose your actions based on the information you learned above. You know that accomplishment depends upon where you place your attention. You also answered the question about your intention: your objective this year. Now, you choose actions that are in line with your intentions.

Funnel all of these actions into your decision-making process: Actions that ...

1. Support your objective.

2. Are effective.

3. Influence other people in positive ways.

4. Help you to amplify your inner strength.

5. Help you become accurate at what you do.

Change your actions from self-defeating to self-empowering by making a daily commitment to accomplish the most important tasks.

If your affirmation was, "I am happy and peaceful—I smile and give compliments," then support your affirmation by smiling at everyone and freely giving compliments. Don't worry about the responses you receive. Some people will accept and enjoy them, and other people will act as if they're in a coma. The outcome doesn't matter. As long as you follow through, you'll gain from the commitment and the interaction.

If your intention is to have a more friendly business, then share your intention with your teammates. You'll work together to spread goodwill.

Action Steps

1. Choose three actions that will empower you.

2. Choose three actions that will empower your business (primary objective).

Choose an Empowering Enhancer

We've talked about choosing empowering thoughts and empowering actions. It's all very deliberate, yet there is something more that is needed, something powerful that enables you to move in the direction of your desires. In order for you to act with passion you must determine what your actions will bring you: recognition, inner peace, prosperity, love, happiness, respect, prestige, fulfillment or any number of things. In other words you need an Enhancer, an element that instantly touches your heart. For example, my co-author Tom finds that the soundtrack music of *Indiana Jones* or *Superman* immediately energizes him and raises his mood—helping him improve his productivity.

Action Step

> What element can function as an Enhancer for you? What touches your heart and raises your energy level?

Determine the Reasons For and Against Change

Many people are unable to make changes due to internal conflicts. Generally, two situations pull us in different directions: one related to comfort and the other focused on fear. If you're unable to let go of a negative situation and make a change, it's because you are somewhat comfortable with it. Or there is something in that situation that you think you need. You may be under the impression that you can't get your needs met anywhere else. You may also fear the new direction, which you may think of as the dark unknown. You stay with what you know; therefore, you don't evolve to the next level. The transforming strength is about taking you to the next level.

Dissatisfaction with your current situation can motivate you to move forward. It must be either more important for you to change, or less painful to change than it is to stay in the same rut. At the end of this strength we'll discuss in detail the Five Factors of Change, beginning with dissatisfaction.

There is a mental *Action Step* that I always like to do when faced with a situation or decision that I am unsure about. You'll find this *Action Step* helpful.

Action Step

Take out a fresh sheet of paper and write your particular situation at the top of the page, usually in the form of a question. Underneath, write the words "for" and "against." Then draw a line down the middle of the page between both words. Begin listing all the reasons for making a change and then all the reasons why a change would not be in your best interest.

Once you take the time to write all of the pros and cons, then you must evaluate the list. Which side has more items? Prioritize the items in order of importance to you. Determine the critical issues, the necessary issues, the trivial ones, and your impressions of the results.

Action Step

Suppose you decided to go for the change. There is another *Action Step* that might contribute to your peace of mind. Turn the sheet of paper over and divide it in half. On the left side write: What would be the best thing that could happen when I choose to make this decision? Write on other side of the paper: What would be the worst-case scenario if I choose to make this change. Then list everything that might apply. What are your impressions of the results?

To get different results, do something in a different and better way.

Educate Yourself

Transform your strengths and your business by educating yourself. Before you can take any solid steps toward marketing your business, you need to ask yourself one critical question: "What do I need to know in order to do this?" You'll need a certain amount of knowledge and experience to become adept at a particular task. The purpose of this book is to help you quickly implement a marketing campaign by transferring your hidden strengths to learn marketing principles.

Learn marketing skills and you win in four critical areas:

1. Your business benefits from the increased flow of customers.

2.. Your customers become aware of your business's benefits.

3. Your business and your entire industry will gain a better reputation and be perceived as professional. Along with professionalism comes respect and, consequently, a better quality of life.

4. You enjoy increased cash flow.

Locations for additional education. Community colleges are a good place to go for classes. The Chamber of Commerce and the Small Business Administration has a supply of either free or inexpensive literature. Learning centers offer short-term classes on various subjects. There are also trade seminars that may offer the knowledge you seek.

Bookstores, libraries and newsstands carry an incredible amount of information. Well-known entrepreneurs share the powerful secrets of their success, so you have an opportunity to learn from the pros. Many of their ideas can be tailored to the small business with a more narrow budget. Tele-seminars and online courses can be helpful (Visit FullStrengthMarketing. com). I have my own library of success and motivational books, and I refer to them often. Sometimes all we need is a little positive reinforcement.

Action Step

> List three ways you will expand your marketing education.

Turn Lemons into Lemonade

Perhaps you can relate to my personal story of how I turned my lemons into lemonade. I started my business on a shoestring, like so many people do. My entry into small business was a quick one, so I had no time to take a college course. The trade school I attended didn't teach marketing skills. Unfortunately the small business owners I worked for had no idea of how to put a promotion package together. The result of this inexperience was that I began my small business with two major handicaps.

My first handicap was the awareness that I wasn't properly prepared to market my business. The second handicap I faced was that my business's location was less than admirable, so I started my business with two lemons. The absence of marketing knowledge and a poor location often lead to failure for many businesses, but these initial disadvantages—lemons—were blessings in disguise and gave me the opportunity to transform my marketing weakness into a marketing strength—lemonade— thereby growing into a knowledgeable entrepreneur.

I incorporated the ideas I learned from marketing experts into twenty-one years of experience, and developed shortcuts that can save you years of trial and error. The constant flow of traffic into my small business was a reflection of that effort. You only need to invest hours to invoke the power of this system.

I realized that great word-of-mouth advertising is helpful, but it's slow and limited. I also knew that my business was never going to take off until I learned how to organize and execute a marketing campaign. So I read every marketing book available and attended management and marketing classes. I learned through trial and error and eventually developed my strong marketer program and this book *Full Strength Marketing*.

Action Steps

1. In what three ways is your experience, or lack of it, an advantage to you?

2. In what three ways is your experience, or lack of it, a disadvantage to you?

3. What lemons are you now holding?

4. What actions will you take to turn them into lemonade?

It's critical to your business's profitability and success to "do it right" the first time, then build on that success.

Transform Your Marketing Presence

People won't know your business exists until you have a presence in the marketplace. Your marketing campaign is the vehicle that educates consumers as to what you do and the problems that you solve. I mention this material here because the idea of educating yourself is for specific purposes: to improve how your create your marketing presence and your marketing campaign. Your marketing presence is determined by four important factors:

The quality of your campaign. This refers to the degree of excellence that you maintain in your printed materials, your radio or television broadcasts, your website, or your public relations efforts. It has more to do with image than with money. People notice innovative ideas.

The frequency of your marketing efforts. The only way to get a marketing presence is to advertise, promote or use public relations frequently. Networking and positive word of mouth from current clients is helpful too. In other areas of this book we discuss Twitter, Facebook, and LinkedIn, and social media can be a free process to help you get the word out. How much is enough for a small or home-based business? I believe that your target market should see your name through various media (print, broadcast media, or social media) at least once a month, and more often if possible.

Action Step

What will you do to ensure a quality campaign and frequent marketing efforts?

The value you give to consumers. Typically, marketing is everything you do to attract consumers to your business — mainly public relations, advertising and promotions. Customers are conditioned to expect value, and value marketing is simply the act or process of helping people to solve problems. In order for you to reach your objective, you must help your clients to reach their objectives. Discover what they need or what problems need to be solved and solve them in the most creative way. Explain how you solve the problem ("benefits" you provide) in your marketing materials.

Secure your position in the marketplace by becoming more competitive. Accomplish this by creating the right mixture of value and service for your target market. When I take my nephews to a fast food restaurant, we purchase food at a low price, however, we must stand in line to order our food, pay for it, wait until it is ready, take it to our table, and then bus our table when we are finished. We are expected to serve ourselves and pay less for the inconvenience to do so.

When my friends and I go to a full-service restaurant, we expect to pay a bit more to be seated at a table where someone takes our order, fills our water glass, brings our meal or anything else we might need, and cleans up after us. Included in the price is the cost of ambiance, a convenient location, and possible entertainment.

Successful marketing results happen over time with patience and persistence. Results are not always immediate—realizing results may take anywhere from three months to a year. We market for the short term and the long term. It's like investing in the stock market or real estate. You don't expect to get in and make a quick buck, although that does sometimes occur. Growth is generally slow and constant. That's why it's important to make a commitment in the beginning and stick with it.

Market your small or home-based business consistently, and your promotions gain momentum in the community. A marketing presence and high visibility is the benefit to you. As more people see your advertisements more often, they have more opportunities to respond. When people remember a name, they'll remember you.

Action Step

> List at least three ways you plan to give value to consumers.

The value you create for your business. A strong marketer must find the delicate balance between creating value for customers and also earning a profit for themselves. Creating value is not meant to take away from your profit margin. Be creative in finding ways to keep a steadily rising profit:

1. Talk to a business consultant to help you solve problems. SCORE is a volunteer program put on by the

Small Business Administration. Retired executives act as business consultants. My co-author Tom Marcoux also coaches business owners (reach him through TomSuperCoach.com).

2. Learn to do a few tasks yourself to save money, if you can use an efficient bookkeeping program (for example). Ask for help from your spouse, children or teenagers.

3. Delegate certain tasks to employees, so your time can be spent making sales or thinking of profit-making opportunities.

4. Lower your overhead costs.

5. Print your marketing materials in one or two colors rather than four. Use less expensive paper. Ask your printer for economical ways to print your materials.

Your future prosperity is dependent upon your ability to make an investment toward proactive marketing.

In order to be profitable, you must ask yourself, "What can I do today that will generate more profits tomorrow?"

Tip: Honor your marketing principles.

The Four P's are well-known primary marketing principles also named as the marketing mix—the 'right' mixture of product, price, place and promotion. Your chances of selling your product or service and making a profit increase dramatically when you have the right products/services at the right price, in the right place, and with the right promotion. Honor these marketing principles to get better results from your marketing efforts.

1. Product or service must be one that the consumer wants or needs.

2. Price of your services or products must be appealing to the consumer. Charge a price they are willing to pay.

3. Place (or location) must be convenient and easily accessible to the consumer. Consider your competition and think about having good physical distribution for your products.

4. Promotion is essential. It won't matter how good you are, or what great prices you have, if no one knows your business exists. To attract a constant flow of new customers you must consistently promote your business name, location, products, services, and prices.

Remember that the Four P's are important, but they aren't everything. Outstanding quality service is equally important. Add your superb service, and it's like putting the icing on the cake. It adds a taste of brilliance to what is already dynamic.

Kelly Fennessey, a marketing specialist for Safeway, Inc. in Pleasanton, California, says that you can overcome a poor mixture of The Four P's if your business is strong in other areas such as employee talent, connections in the community, a large customer base, a larger cash flow or other strengths.

Some marketing strategists add four more P's to the marketing mix: package, premiums, personal selling, and publicity/advertising.

Value marketing is the process of reaching the people you want to reach and helping them get the services and products they need. In return, you get results by accomplishing the objectives set forth in your business plan.

Establish Your Marketing Personality

Many years of business ownership and working in a service industry have led me to believe that the owner or manager needs to develop a marketing personality. The following aspects are key to successfully marketing a small service business:

Relationship Marketing

Relationship marketing is about establishing a rapport with customers and finding common ground. Building a relationship takes the edge off selling and emphasizes your humanity. You aren't just another salesperson, you're a compassionate human being who cares about people, not just the sale. My co-author Tom Marcoux says, "In tough economic times, we need to realize that trust overcomes fear. People buy from people they trust. That's why I emphasize 'be heard and be trusted.'"

Be sure to know the customers' birthday, husband or wife's name, their vocation, how many children they have, where they vacation, and their state of health. People like to do business with people they know. We all find comfort with familiarity.

It's always to your advantage if your customers personally like you. Your honest and sincere interactions with customers and your personal integrity will indirectly impact your campaign. As a small business owner or manager, there is more importance placed on your own public image than you might like to believe. You can spend as little as $500 or as much as $20,000 on a fancy marketing campaign.

You can also have the most talented employees in the area, but if your negative behavior turns customers off, you'll lose in the long run. People are quick to make judgments about you.

> *Even if their service was satisfactory, they may resist returning if the owner or manager was apathetic, unfriendly or short with them. I've seen it in many businesses I've worked for where the owner constantly gossiped, belittled customers who weren't politically connected, argued incessantly to make a point, failed to apologize when an apology was in order, or harassed employees in front of customers. This is bad public relations, which falls under the marketing umbrella.*

In large businesses and corporations, owners are somewhat shielded from the public eye, except in special cases where a CEO becomes a celebrity. On the other hand, small business owners are accountable for their good or poor social strengths.

As the small business owner or manager you'll act as the main marketing representative. Because most small business owners seldom have the cash flow to implement a full-fledged marketing campaign through an advertising agency, the business's overall success lies mainly on the marketing personality of the owner or manager. You interact with customers, the general public and business associates on a daily basis. The quality of those interactions and relationships will, in large part, contribute to or detract from the popularity of the business.

The owner of a very small business, Arthur, didn't market his business through the media, but used social networking instead. This kind of campaign is inexpensive to implement but requires some unique social strengths and the freedom to always be in a social environment. Networking was extremely successful for Arthur, until he got tired and slowed down his efforts. This caused his business to abruptly decline. Successful network marketing requires you to be consistently visible, making contacts and building a favorable image for your business.

Action Step

> Imagine that you are a friend of yours. How would you rate yourself, on a scale of 1-10, as to your likeability factors: 1) attentively listens, 2) keeps commitments, 3) is polite, and 4) develops pleasant rapport?

Create a good track record

There's much to be said for having years of marketing experience behind you. After several years of planning your marketing campaign, you'll find that it's easier to put a promotion package together. It's less work when you're aware of the shortcuts. You know which ideas worked in the past, which ones didn't, and how they can be improved.

There are three advantages to creating a good track record:

1. You'll have established relationships with printers, graphic designers, and media representatives. Comparative shopping gives you the competitive edge.

2. Experience leads you to the best prices for supplies, props, and decorations.

3. You'll understand your target market better and easily create promotions that appeal to them.

Action Step

How will you increase your track record?

Take Care of Yourself

There's no doubt about it, it takes a lot of energy to stay on top of the business scene. I was 27 years old when I opened my first business. My enthusiasm and youthful energy carried me through those early years, riding the waves of business ownership. As small business owners, we wear all the hats, which means we have plenty of jobs to do. As a salon owner I stood on my feet from early morning to late evening, with my appointment book keeping me racing to stay on time, and business duties demanding too many hours of my precious time off. Year after year of this hectic routine can wear down even the heartiest soul.

If you are past fifty and are opening your first business, I suggest:

1. Make certain you are super passionate about your new career.

2. Learn how to delegate or expect to get a slow start if you are doing it alone.

3. Use your past experience and contacts to their fullest advantage.

4. Set boundaries on your work hours. Take time to rest during the day.

5. Take care of yourself with plenty of sleep, good nutrition and exercise.

6. Take additional night classes if necessary. Fill in the gaps in your education.

A number of older individuals run their own business, work full or part-time and still do a good job. Their prior experience and ability to delegate carries them through quite well. If you're older, you might consider a business without manual labor.

Develop Your Business's Potential

Your business has the potential for greatness particularly when you are filling an un-met need. Now, this is a wonderful element of your marketing personality. How do you want a current customer to talk about your business? Wouldn't you like your current customer to respond to a friend by saying, "Oh, yes! That business is great in doing … "

First become aware of how your business can improve and grow through change. Review the vision and the objective you established in your business plan. Become aware of what that means to you, and how you will prosper by having attained it. Then review your primary objective for the year and affirm that it is something you are willing to work towards.

Also be open to the possibility that the vision and/or the objective must change in order for you to reach your potential.

Be a Dynamo

If you desire success, then you must be open to the concept of dynamics. The dynamics must change in order to move an entrepreneur's business from one state to another state: from the profit potential state to the profitable state.

The dynamics are where the power is, the force that moves a business forward. Apply these three dynamics to transform and make your objectives happen: willingness, discipline, and simplicity.

Willingness expresses your intention and determination to control your actions. No one else can force you to move ahead on your objective. You must have a strong and fixed sense of purpose, knowing that your vision will provide benefits and value to others and to you. Your deliberate actions or intentions express your willingness to follow through on your objectives.

Discipline is a critical dynamic which, when incorporated into behavior patterns, will result in finished projects and personal satisfaction. Self-control, orderliness, and efficiency are favorable aspects of a disciplined leader or entrepreneur. See and feel the advantage of adding discipline to your schedule.

Simplicity in your projects or objectives makes them less complex and easier to achieve. Too many details can become overwhelming and prevent you from taking action. Brainstorming ideas with your team is one creative way to establish simplicity in your marketing campaign.

A conscientious business sense and a good attitude lead to loyal employees, business growth and better profits.

Action Step

> Regarding your objective, what two things could you do that would help you to become more disciplined?

Find a Flair for Accuracy

Years ago, my friends and I participated in slalom auto races with the Sports Car Club of America. Solo drivers are given a map of a complicated driving course. The winner is the driver who stays on course, knocks over the least amount of pylons, and finishes in the least amount of time. We notice that the race car driver utilizes specific strengths similar to organizational strengths.

Experienced drivers have a much better command of the road due to four primary abilities: confidence, perception, judgment and balance. The best race car drivers are not afraid of speed nor the vehicle they drive. They push it to the max. Confidence is a big factor; it's a certainty or belief in your own abilities. Excellent drivers know how the course is best articulated and how to shorten the length of the track. At the subconscious level, the best race car drivers are able to use good judgment and balance in order to adapt their speed to the curves, corners and longer stretches of the course. The best auto racing strengths can be transferred to other areas of life, like business and marketing. As you continue with *Full Strength Marketing,* use confidence, perception, judgment and balance—especially for making an important decision.

Many business people think that marketing is a race, and its primary importance is to get those profits as quickly as possible, without thought of how the race is driven.

In my experience, accuracy is just as important as speed. An accurately driven auto race, utilizing the *ten hidden strengths* discussed in this book, got me to the finish line as quickly as other drivers who pushed harder and drove faster but were sloppy when it came to the strategic elements.

> *You'll get more satisfaction, and ultimately more profits, from your marketing by using the ten hidden strengths with accuracy.*

Your passion is another area of prime importance. Someone with a burning passion for driving race cars is ultimately in a better position to win than someone who is not. Only you can determine how passionate you are about succeeding in business. Your passion is the fuel that will accelerate your marketing vehicle and put you in first position.

More than ever, the owner must make a commitment to listen carefully to customers' needs, preferences, and complaints— and act to serve them better each day.

Incorporate the Five Factors of Change

Expand your horizons and learn problem-solving strengths by using five factors of change. Change and transformation is a continuing process, so be prepared to exercise patience and free yourself from restrictions.

There are five basic factors that elicit a simple change: dissatisfaction, inquiry, visualization, realization and action. Let's use these factors in an example we can all relate to—a Bad Hair Day:

1. Experience dissatisfaction with the status quo. You look into the mirror and UGH, you dislike what you see. You're unhappy with your current situation and recognize that you need to look more professional.

2. Inquire into how your hair can look better. Your hairdresser's recommendation and styling books are a good place to get ideas. You look through magazines for something suitable to your lifestyle.

3. Visualize something new, and how that particular style would look on you.

4. Realize the pleasure that you'll gain from making the change. This realization motivates you toward taking the fifth step. If there is no realization of pleasure, improvement, growth or a benefit, then the fifth step is not taken.

5. Take action by making an appointment, going to the salon and changing your hair. Taking action depends

upon your success with steps two, three, and four. You have gone through five steps just to change your hair.

Action Step

Think of one thing you want to change in your business or your life, and apply these five factors to bring about a new, happier situation.

Make Powerful Decisions

Have you ever wondered how some people accomplish so much, and other people do not, even though they make their best effort? I've discovered that what differentiates the accomplished people from the wannabe's is their ability to make powerful decisions. They get all the information they need, evaluate it, and decide on the most powerful decision. It's the one that will support their goals and objectives.

Action Step

Name one powerful decision you could make today.

Transforming Summary

Take the following steps to access your hidden strength to transform.

1. Determine your needs.

2. Find the fear.

3. Overcome judgment and self-doubt.

4. Let go of the past.

5. Be on purpose.

6. Focus your attention.

7. Determine the reasons for and against change.

8. Educate yourself.

9. Establish your marketing personality.

10. Incorporate the five factors of change.

11. Make powerful decisions.

When Do I Take These Steps?

Take these transforming steps after you envision your primary objective, and when you are ready to make a commitment to change.

4

Investigating

Your Third Hidden Strength

Imagine that you are a famous private investigator like Sherlock Holmes or one of Charlie's Angels—or detective Kate Beckett (TV series *Castle*), except that it's really you as a private eye in your own hometown. You heard on the streets that a mysterious company has stolen an extremely valuable, highly treasured ball. Now undercover, you investigate who has this highly valued ball, where they're located, and the methods they use to keep control of it. Good news! This mysterious company happens to be a visible, high-profile business. If you somehow captured the ball, you'd gain more customers, wealth, prestige, and more of everything that a great business would bring you. Are you interested in this assignment? You'd discover that this mysterious company is really a small business who controls the ball, which is an analogy for controlling the marketplace. Now are you interested in becoming a private investigator? Are you interested in that valuable, extraordinary ball? Mastering this strength helps you to answer some important questions: "Who are my competitors, what are they doing to get customers, and how can I compete?"

The advantage of detective work is that you will realize the differences and likenesses, strengths and weaknesses.

The hidden strength of Investigating, focuses on researching and outsmarting your competition in order to control the ball. Answer the *Action Step* questions to determine who has control of the ball (marketplace).

You'll benefit by creating a distinctive marketing plan. Get control of the ball to attract the most customers, increase your cash flow, increase your name recognition, and make a better contribution to your community or industry.

Example from a Top Marketer

Ruth Handler, co-founder of Mattel and the creator of the Barbie doll, investigated what dolls would appeal to girls. She noticed that her daughter and friends did not want dolls like themselves, but preferred paper dolls of grown-up women. Ruth proposed the Barbie doll, but her colleagues were unconvinced for five years. Ruth investigated a "Lilli" doll in Germany that finally made Barbie a reality. "Lilli" came in six versions each with a different costume. Back at Mattel, Ruth showed "Lilli" and insisted that girls would enjoy an adult doll. Barbie now sells over the billion-dollar level.

Your Objective for Investigating

Your objective with the investigating strength is to remember the many times in your life when you received value from investigating a situation first, before you took any action. You'll apply that remembrance to the task of investigating similar businesses that appear to control the marketplace.

Investigating as a Natural Strength

Babies investigate everything within their grasp. We are born with a natural curiosity mode, and grow up wanting to know how things work. When my three younger brothers were children, I would watch in horror as they pulled apart many of their toys, investigating what made them work. As human creatures with a natural urge to explore, we carry the investigative tradition throughout our lives.

Envision the last time you went into a bookstore and an interesting title or book cover attracted your curiosity. You probably read the information on the inside jackets, the back cover, and the table of contents. You scanned a couple of chapters for clues to the book's content value. Once you completed your investigation, you were able to make a buying decision. The same process applies when you buy a car, a home, a diamond, or a fishing pole.

Remember when you wrote your first business plan? That's one recent example of how and when you used your investigative abilities. You'll use them again this year to initiate your marketing campaign.

One of my favorite cartoons begins with a man who stands on the deck of a luxury ocean liner. He's dressed in a bathing suit, diving into a beautiful, refreshing pool. He emerges to find himself in the middle of the ocean with the cruise ship off in the distance. We can all laugh at the surprised look on his face, but it's not so funny when something similar happens to you. Always investigate the waters before you leap.

The hidden strength of Investigating is crucial. What you learn can prevent embarrassing situations and expensive mistakes. Investigate first, so you aren't surprised and find yourself lost at sea.

Your investigation will determine what needs your competition is meeting. Then you can determine different or similar needs you want your business to meet.

Transfer your natural investigative strengths to one of the most critical marketing principles: make a thorough inquiry regarding your competitors. Use this strength to investigate competitive businesses and find out who has control of the ball.

Action Step

> List two examples from your past when you used your investigative strength.

The advantages of your investigative strength are that you'll learn who has the competitive edge and why. This information will save you from making unnecessary mistakes. It's always better to do it sooner rather than later. Your most thorough search is helpful for your very first campaign, and whenever you are creating a new identity system or new marketing materials.

Always keep a watchful eye on the marketplace in case the competitive situation changes.

To be a great investigator, you need:

1. A strong sense of curiosity.

2. A willingness to go beyond the obvious.

3. An insatiable hunger for clarity.

Be Question-Oriented

To further develop your investigative strength, a strong marketer must be question-oriented. You must ask specific questions and be prepared to find the answers, no matter what. An effective investigator focuses on who, what, when, where, why and how of what's going on in the marketplace. You need to know who's got control of the ball, and what they are doing to keep it. Where are they succeeding, failing? Why do people buy their products or services? How are they solving the customers' problems? How are they solving problems that are typical to your industry? How are they adjusting to changing technologies?

Here's an example of small business owners who didn't investigate their own industry. Jane and Millie owned a small clothing boutique between 1965-1980. Their initial endeavor as a 'dress shop' was a booming business for them; however, the clothing market changed in the middle 1970's. Many of their women clients switched from dresses to denim. These boutique owners didn't change inventory fast enough and were forced out of business. These business owners weren't driven under by competitors. They just didn't foresee what was coming.

Jane and Millie could have kept in touch with the marketplace in a number of ways: a) a survey given to regular clients pinpointing their needs, b) a comprehensive study of trade magazines and newspapers for current trends, and c) visiting competitors' stores.

At the same time, a nearby store's dress business boomed through this era and continues to do well. The difference is that they knew their very selective customers, and the items they wanted to buy.

The general economic situation could also have an impact on your business, in a positive or a negative way. This fact makes your investigative strength extremely valuable.

What Are You Really Marketing?

Tom Marcoux

If you were selling soap, what are you really marketing? Feeling clean. I recall TV commercials in which beaming people enjoyed feeling "Zestfully clean" (Zest is a brand of soap).

I was working with an intern and the question arose: "What are we really marketing?" With three of my books, we notice:

- *Be Heard and Be Trusted*—"a relationship that brings good feelings or what you want [trust will get you a closed sale]"

- *Truth No One Will Tell You*—"hope"

- *Nothing Can Stop You This Year*—"comfort and encouragement"

So now with your product or service ... what are you really marketing?

Tom has started you off with a valuable question ... and here are others.

Action Steps

1. What questions will you ask about your competitors and the marketplace?

2. Name your five major competitors.

3. Which competitive businesses are also competing for the same target market?

4. Regarding their location, what does it cost them to operate?

5. Who are their employees, and how do they help that company to become a top performer?

Look for Clues

Drive around your neighborhood to get a bird's eye view of competitive businesses. Write down your impressions. Note the appearance of their storefront and any outstanding signage. Are they appealing? Do they attract your attention? Are they neat and professional looking, or an embarrassment? What messages do they send to the consumer about that business? Is there easy access to their business? Are they busy during various times of the day and/or days of the week? Do they have a convenient first-floor location, or are they hidden? Get the scoop on your competition's location, image, and clientele, so you can make critical decisions regarding your own business.

My first business was located on the second floor of an office building. A sign on top of the building and another in the downstairs window attracted passersby. Anyone wanting to investigate my business would have to come upstairs and look around, and sometimes they did.

Look in the phone book or in local newspapers for information about competing businesses.

Action Step

List at least 3 clues about your competition.

Now, Michael Soon Lee will guide us with details about marketing to people with various cultural backgrounds.

The Myth of Multicultural Marketing

Michael Soon Lee, MBA

Hispanics, African Americans, Asians, and Middle Easterners buy over $2 trillion worth of goods and services annually. As a result, U.S. firms are scrambling to implement multicultural marketing campaigns. In fact, reaching minority customers is the fastest-growing area in consumer marketing today. They are spending fortunes to target their advertising to reach culturally diverse consumers.

To effectively market to minorities advertisers must first determine exactly who they want to reach. For instance, Hispanics are not one monolithic culture but are actually six major distinct groups which include: Mexicans, Puerto Ricans, Central Americans, South Americans, Cubans, and Dominicans. Blacks include: African Americans, Jamaicans, Haitians, Africans and many other groups. Asians include: Chinese, Filipino, Japanese, Koreans, Vietnamese, Asian Indians, and others.

Multicultural ads must be in-culture and possibly in-language. To be in-culture ads must use images and words that connect to their target audience. For instance, Asians can tell the subtle differences between pictures of Chinese, Japanese and Korean subjects. In addition, appropriate images would reflect the culture of the group you are trying to reach. Take, for example, the word "family" in which Hispanics might imagine a large group including grandparents and children while Asians might picture a large group which could include children and their families. At the same time African Americans might envision a traditional family or a female head-of-household with children.

In addition, words used in multicultural marketing must connect with the audience. Words that are important to Hispanics might include: "family", "faith" and "children"; some of the words that connect to African Americans are: "respect", "faith" and "individuality"; and a few of the words that especially get the attention of Asians are: "family", "tradition" and "value". Do some research and find out what words grab the attention of the group you are trying to target. Be sure to run the ad past a focus group that can help you catch any mistakes or problems.

Whether your ad has to be in the native language of your intended audience depends on how long they have been in the United States. The longer they have been here, the more likely you can reach them in English. The shorter the time they have resided here, the more likely you will have to reach them in their native language. If this is the case you will obviously need people who can respond to calls, emails and other inquiries in that language. Again, just a little research will quickly tell you which language will be most effective in reaching your potential customers.

However, many companies have bought into the myth that all you have to do is do a little bit of multicultural marketing to earn the business of ethnic consumers. The reality is that all of this money is wasted if minority customers are not treated with sensitivity when they come into your store or office. Just as marketing must be adjusted to meet the unique needs of diverse customers, so must your sales presentation, store layout, staff, products, services and much more be adjusted.

Multicultural customers do not buy products and services in the same way as European American consumers, nor do they want to be treated the same. They may prefer goods that are customized for them. For instance, homebuilders may need to change the types of models they offer, the amenities available and even orientation of the property on the site. Grocery stores must carry the foods that are familiar to ethnic customers.

Just a few of the other differences that affect retailers and service providers include: building rapport, negotiations and contracts. For instance, it's a little-known fact that not all people throughout the world are comfortable being greeted in the same way. As Americans, we assume that everyone wants to be met with a firm handshake, which is not necessarily true. In fact, the most common greeting in the world is the bow, not the handshake, which can actually be offensive to many people such as traditional Japanese, Asian Indian or Middle Eastern women.

The first step in building rapport with any person, regardless of culture, is never to assume how they want to be greeted. In other words, let them determine the most comfortable greeting by hesitating before extending your hand and see what they do first. Most men in the United States, regardless of culture, will offer a handshake and may even nod as they do so. Simply do likewise.

Recognize that some cultures are used to hugging and even kissing people on the cheek. If this happens to you please take it as a sign that they are comfortable with you and do likewise. American men are not used to having strangers, especially other men, kiss them on the cheek. Gentlemen, be forewarned, if you turn away as someone is about to kiss your cheek you will get the next one squarely on the lips!

Immigrant men from the Middle East often shake hands with a slight nod or bow and then exchange kisses on both cheeks. Traditional Muslim men may shake hands and then touch the right palm of their hand to their heart as a sign of friendship. Men from this country generally do not shake hands with women. They often do not introduce women who accompany them nor is it expected that you shake hands with her.

The global rule of greeting is: never assume anything! Greet the customer verbally and then hesitate for a moment giving him or her the opportunity to offer the kind of greeting that is most comfortable to them. Then, of course, simply return the gesture.

Next, training must be provided so salespeople understand that many new immigrant women do not want to be touched by strangers. This is especially true for traditional Japanese, older Indian and Saudi women. My studies show that 60% of these women do not want to have their hand shaken, meaning that if salespeople are not trained to be culturally competent they are likely offending a majority of multicultural buyers.

Therefore, it is crucial after shaking a male's hand to be sure to drop your hand to your side before turning to a woman companion. If she does not offer her hand, simply nod in her direction to acknowledge her presence and begin your sales presentation.

There are other cultural differences of which store owners and service providers should be aware. Personal space varies among cultures. In the United States we are used to shaking hands and then standing about two-and-a-half feet apart. This is not always comfortable for some people from more formal countries like Japan, where they bow or shake hands and then take a step back. When this happens to an American we feel difficulty in communicating across a distance that seems like the Grand Canyon so we step forward. If you've ever had your personal space violated you know how uncomfortable this can be, so a Japanese person will naturally step back to reestablish a more comfortable distance for them. You can easily see how this could result in you "chasing" the customer all over the store or office!

Other cultures may prefer to stand closer than Americans when communicating. Among these are the Middle Easterners and many Hispanics who will often hug you and simply stand at that distance. This is much too close for Americans so we naturally step back to a safer distance. Of course, this is probably too far away for the other party so they naturally step forward, violating our own personal space. If this continues they will steadily chase you all over your establishment. Obviously, this makes communications difficult and uneasy. It also does not start your relationship on a very positive note.

Another difference Americans should be aware of is the amount of eye contact to expect from people from diverse cultures. In the United States we equate strong, direct eye contact with honesty and respect. On the other hand, many Asians and Native Americans avoid direct eye contact as a sign of respect for you. They feel that looking someone in the eye is intrusive and rude so they look down to honor you. Unfortunately, this is extremely uncomfortable for people from this country so we do everything possible to catch their eye.

The solution to lack of eye contact is simple—look down. You can also use this as an opportunity to show them brochures, pictures, price charts or other material since they are already looking down at your desk.

As usual, not all cultures behave the same way and there is a tendency for Middle Eastern people and some Hispanics to give very direct and strong eye contact. In fact, there is a saying in the Middle East that the "eyes are the windows to the soul". People from these groups may make Americans somewhat uncomfortable with their intensity. Just get used to it is the best advice you can get.

Many new immigrants come from countries where negotiating is a way of life. Unfortunately, here in America we have gotten into the habit of paying full price for nearly everything except cars and houses. This puts us at an extreme disadvantage when dealing with people who are used to haggling over everything from clothes to food. If you have many customers who hail from negotiating countries it would obviously be a good idea to enroll in a negotiating class as soon as possible!

Contracts are also not the same around the world. In the United States we put everything we agree upon in very detailed writings. When we sign a contract here it ends all further negotiations. In many other countries signing a contract begins the bargaining process, so again, a negotiating class would probably be a good investment.

Minorities in America are growing at an astounding rate because our families are younger and larger. According to the U.S. Census Bureau, the Hispanic population in America swelled 58% from 1990 to 2000, during the same period Asians increased in numbers by 48% and the African American population jumped by 16%. At that time, it was estimated that from 2000 to 2010 these groups will expand their numbers by 31%, 13%, and 20%, respectively.

These consumers can be an increased source of income for companies who are willing to adjust, just a little, to make people from diverse cultures more comfortable in doing business with them.

Another way to make people from other countries comfortable is to have someone who can speak their language on staff. Hiring and retaining bilingual salespeople, cashiers, receptionists, and others requires special talent, knowledge and contacts.

Packaging must be done in accordance with cultural principles. For instance, it is bad luck in the Asian culture to package any product in groups of four. For the same reason, pricing should avoid the number four while the number eight is considered lucky. This is because the number four, when pronounced in Chinese or Japanese, sounds like their respective words for "death". Similarly, the number eight sounds like the words for "rich" or "fortune".

You can see that multicultural marketing must be done in conjunction with cultural competency training; otherwise, multicultural customers will still not buy from you.

Michael Soon Lee, MBA, is a cultural expert and author of several books on selling to multicultural customers. He also was a producer for the ABC Television Network and a Marketing Director for the State of California. Mr. Lee is the first Asian American to earn the Certified Speaking Professional (CSP) designation in the history of the National Speakers Association and is the former dean of a university business school. His company, EthnoConnect™, provides keynote speeches, training and consulting on diversity and selling to the ethnic markets in America.

EthnoConnect.com
(800) 417-7325.

Michael reminds us to keep on the lookout for the various preferences and cultural differences among people we'd like to market to. Now it's time to focus on the resources available to you.

Use Your Resources

Never underestimate the value of investigation, whether you are using it to research the competition, your target market, or a new business. Use your resources to keep informed and to avoid expensive mistakes. Network with your contacts and their referrals. Ask for what you need, and put that information to work for you.

Who you know can be helpful. I made it a habit to ask salespeople who called on me about competitive businesses.

They always knew the scoop on new and seasoned businesses and were willing to share that information.

> *Ask, Ask, Ask! Also, just walk into a competitive business and ask for a brochure, a business card, or any other pertinent information. You can ask the receptionist questions about the business or look around for a price list. You'll benefit by going there and seeing it first hand.*

> *If your competitors know who you are, you may not be comfortable with this procedure; your second option is to call on the telephone, or have a friend call and ask pertinent questions. You won't be able to ask every question over the telephone, so you'll need to find additional sources of information. You also won't be able to ask how they are doing financially, but by frequently driving or walking by, you might get a good idea of their business volume. (This only works for businesses with window exposure.)*

Keep a notebook handy so you can organize and log important facts about each competitor as you receive the information. Confusing notes quickly scribbled on scratch paper won't make sense to you later when you need to analyze your information.

Ask your co-workers, family, and friends about competitive businesses. They may have worked in a competing business at one time and will have first-hand knowledge. They may have friends who are now working in a competitive business or who own one. Ask your customers if they ever frequented a competing business.

Look up your competition in the phone book and notice the size of their yellow pages advertisement. They pay a lot for a large ad. In your opinion, is their advertisement innovative and effective enough to warrant the price they pay? You could learn something from this. Their website will also reveal detailed information about their image, products, services, and prices. My co-author Tom Marcoux says, "Find out how customers feel about a business: type up something like 'Acme Hair Brush, Inc. problem' in Google search and discover if the particular business is failing their customers in some way." Research the competition in trade publications and requests for proposals.

Identify who the experts are in your field and learn from them. Trade shows and Chamber of Commerce events are a good place to go to meet the experts. Learn about your business, and all business in general. Attend marketing, sales, leadership and motivational seminars that target people in your line of business. Make time to read self-improvement books and listen to audio programs. You can usually apply that knowledge to your own circumstances.

Become successful by studying your competition. You absolutely need to know what they're doing so you can either do something different, do something better, or just do something.

Action Steps

1. Who can you ask about your competitors?

2. What do people say about your competition?

3. What do people say about your business?

Investigate Competitors' Marketing Strategies

Let's investigate the strategies of competitors who control the ball with strength and passion. A savvy strong marketer has a campaign that accurately defines where they're going and how to get there. They have well-designed campaign materials and use them consistently.

You must take the initiative and find out what other businesses are doing to gain customers. Are they advertising in local newspapers, using direct mail, upgrading their premises, lowering or raising their prices, handing out coupons on the street or through the Internet or something else? Pay attention to the frequency of your competitors' newspaper advertisements (or Google Ads). Be aware that a frequently placed ad is working for them.

An important part of your marketing plan is determining which businesses compete for the same target market. Learn about their image, atmosphere, size, number of employees, services, fee structure, educational requirements and any unique characteristics. Do some research to find businesses with a comparable image and price point that are located near your business.

Notice that some businesses use billboard advertising, especially those that are located in a rural area where rental prices are less costly than in the city. Is it effective? If you know another small business owner or any similar service business owner who has done it, be courageous and call them. Ask if billboard advertising was effective for them.

I once owned a home-based hypnotherapy business. My marketing campaign included an advertisement on the back page of the local TV Guide. Other than the front page, this is the most visible and valuable spot for your advertisement. Although this advertising spot was a substantial expense, it did bring me more calls than any other advertising effort. Someone actually did call me to find out if it was worth the cost. He obviously noticed the frequency with which I advertised in the TV Guide.

Take some time to notice how the large corporations develop their competitive marketing strategies. They're always looking over their shoulder to see what the other guy is doing.

Tip: Be a copycat.

Everyone has the potential to become an innovator, but not all people try to exceed their perceived limitations. If creative problem solving is not your forte at the moment, then you may achieve success by following in the footsteps of others.

One of the first strengths we express is imitation. Psychologists report that babies only a few days old begin to imitate their parents when they make funny faces at the newborn child.

Rich Little, the well-known impersonator, has become as famous as the celebrities he imitates. He's one example of someone who studies a celebrity's personal characteristics and uses that information as entertainment.

Study the habits of successful leaders and learn how they develop their ideas. Integrate useful strategies into your own ways of doing business. Trade magazines regularly write feature articles about small and home-based business innovators. Top performers reveal the secrets they use to attract new customers and make larger profits. You don't have to reinvent the wheel. Learn great ideas from knowledgeable business owners.

If you can't come up with a new gimmick first, you can play copycat like large corporations do. Imitate the tactics of successful corporate marketing campaigns by following their lead and incorporating winning strategies.

Keep a file folder full of sample marketing pieces from competitors and noncompetitors alike. You'll gain a fresh perspective and stay current with what marketing strategies other businesses are using. (Also, add a new twist of your own.)

Unfortunately, many small business owners run their business as if they were wearing blinders. You must become a self-starter and motivate yourself to continue to control the ball in the most innovative and entertaining way.

Action Step

> What is your competition's advertising like? Show and analyze three to five examples (subtle, bold, colorful, humorous, interesting, attractive, professional, bland, informative, non-existent, elegant, other).

Look at Their Benefits

You must know what benefits your competitors offer to their customers. What do their customers find appealing about them? What are they doing to control the ball? What is unique about them? What do they do that you don't? Some benefits that attract customers are convenience, low cost, prestigious image, great customer service, overnight delivery, location, consistent quality, entertaining, fast service, relaxing, and good reputation. They may not do anything better or different—because they are established, they have credibility.

Action Steps

1. List the names of competitive businesses in your town, city or online.

2. List the benefits and weaknesses of each competitor.

Analyze Your Research

Finally, analyze your research to become aware of how you do or don't measure up to your competition. Are you not meeting some standard? Is there something more you can do, but are afraid to take a risk? Look at all the facts to understand which competitive business rules the marketplace and why. You might even find that no one is doing anything special. If that is so, then you'll have a better chance of standing out. Your advantage would be less marketing effort and a smaller investment.

Perhaps you'll find that you are the most popular, innovative, efficiently run small business in your area. Take a bow—that's something to be proud of.

Action Steps

1. List weaknesses your business has in comparison to your competition.

2. Identify steps you'll take to overcome those weaknesses.

3. How do you distinguish yourself from the competition?

4. Which products or services does your competition sell?

5. Of your five main competitors, which one has the most appealing image and what makes it so?

6. Of your five main competitors, which one would you most like to surpass with regard to image, reputation, service and sales?

7. Which benefits or features does your competition offer that you don't?

8. What do you offer that they don't?

9. What are they doing that is right or wrong?

10. What more can you do to retain current customers or gain new ones?

11. Who is your competitor's client? (List gender, age, social class and more.) Identify details for six competitors:

12. What is the quality of their service or product?

13. What percent of the market do they have?

14. What kind of reputation do they have?

15. What valuable ideas or insights did you gain from this investigative process?

Find Your Advantage Point

Find your advantage point by learning strategies from competitive sports. In baseball or football, each coach has a strategy—he uses a series of specific plays or techniques to place his team at an advantage. He'll play investigator and review on video past performances, assessing the strengths and weaknesses of both teams. By organizing this information, the coach has a crucial understanding of how his team can gain the advantage over the other team and win the game.

By studying the other team's weaknesses, the coach will find a loophole or the weakest link for scoring points. A business owner who understands how this strategy works has a greater advantage in the marketplace than one who does not.

What can you do to put your business at an advantage and the competition at a disadvantage? When you know or do something first, regarding a new service or product, you place other competing businesses at a disadvantage. Let's say a service or product is successful; customers are overjoyed and tell everyone they know. You're the only business who knows how to perform the service or sell the product. You are unique, and you have control of the ball. You've cornered the market and gained a reputation, all in one swift swoop. This happens often. Make certain that you publicize your advantage by sending out a media release (previously known as a press release).

Tip

When you're the first to do something new and attach a new name to it, customers leave the competition and come to you who have the special knowledge. It makes everyone else look inept, and you look on the ball.

Action Steps

1. How are you better than your competition?

2. How is your competition better than you?

3. How are they not as effective as you?

4. How will you compete with your competition?

5. What more can you offer to customers?

For your advantage point, two areas contribute to your good reputation: integrity and ethics. Integrity concerns your moral principles, the rules of conduct by which you operate your business and interact with the public. It encompasses your honesty and sincerity. Many industries have a code of ethics, a list of ethical business procedures and laws by which they abide. The public is not blind and deaf; they know when you are meeting ethical standards and when you are not.

Win Through Creativity

Earl Nightingale, author of *The Strangest Secret*, wrote that "instead of competing, all you need to do is create." By tapping into the creative part of your mind, you'll develop a flow of new ideas, insights, concepts, and techniques that will take you far and above the competition. You'll create within yourself a point of reference, a resource that will serve you much better than any underhanded scheme for one-upping the competition. When winning through creativity is of interest to you, please review the Envisioning strength for techniques to enter your quiet imagination.

Here are two good examples of large businesses that used creativity to the maximum level: Walt Disney and hotel owners in Las Vegas.

Walt Disney envisioned a place where people could take their children and everyone could have a happy experience. He created a world in itself of adventure, excitement, fun, and amazement. There are other amusement parks, but Disneyland and Walt Disney World are places created to help you forget your problems for a while and bask in a fantasy world of cartoon characters and family entertainment.

Las Vegas is sometimes called 'the adult Disneyland.' More than just a gambling Mecca, Las Vegas is a popular vacation spot for the whole family. Casino owners currently compete with each other by creating bigger and more complete themed hotels, casinos, restaurants, shopping areas, entertainment and amusements. Bigger and better services and products are king in Las Vegas. In this one city you can enjoy recreations of Egypt, Monte Carlo, Italy, New York, New Orleans, Rio de Janeiro, a tropical paradise, and other major attractions. Las Vegas is a prime example of competitive creativity at its most extreme.

In the world of small business, I recall how Wally Amos promoted his cookies by giving two cookies with every business card he gave out—and in this way the brand Famous Amos rose to great heights.

Action Step

> What unique idea can you implement to gain a creative edge over the competition?

Recognize the Value of Competition

I believe that every person has, at their core, an essence or spirit that is connected to everything else in the universe. We are here to help each other learn and grow in our personal development. I like to think of each individual as our helper. We know some helpers through close associations: such as friends, family members, co-workers and neighbors. Other people help us indirectly. They may be police officers, welfare workers, doctors, or museum curators. They may be environmentalists who oversee the well-being of endangered species, rainforests, and other environmental concerns. They may be people who run competing businesses. We are all helpers or helpmates, and through our relationships we contribute to the development and growth of ourselves and others.

The last person we think of who embodies a helper is our direct competitor. Our competition just seems to come between us and the level of prosperity we desire. We can perceive this differently. With competitors, we have more incentive to improve the quality of our products or services. Competitors subtly challenge us to always better ourselves and to be more industrious. They are not the enemy. They're doing the best they can to make a living and offer value to consumers. Good intentions and actions are always rewarded in some way. Competitors are the influencing factor that makes growth not only possible but necessary. Because we have a competitive marketplace, we are personally required to stretch beyond our perceived limitations, and we have our competitors to thank for that. You needn't send them a thank you note. That's not what this is about. It's simply about recognizing the value of competition.

Investigating Summary

Take the following steps to access your hidden strength to invetigating.

- Be question-oriented.
- Look for clues.
- Use your resources.
- Investigate competitors' marketing strategies.
- Look at their benefits.
- Analyze your research.
- Find your advantage point.
- Win through creativity.
- Recognize the value of competition.

When Do I Take These Steps?

Before you do anything regarding a marketing campaign, investigate your competition so you have a complete understanding of what is already occurring in the marketplace.

If there is too much competition in your neighborhood, I strongly suggest you try another area where your opportunities are better. Some businesses find different opportunities through focusing on online retail efforts.

5

Identifying

Your Fourth Hidden Strength

After a long workday, you arrive at home, take off your shoes and sit down in your favorite, cozy chair that you use for reading, watching television, relaxing, or for thinking and meditating. During your quiet time, your concerns for the day dissipate, and you find yourself thinking about solutions rather than problems. You're wondering how a well-known, brilliant person you can identify might handle your situation. Perhaps, you consider Thomas Jefferson or John F. Kennedy. Maybe a top business woman comes to mind like Mary Kay Ash or Anita Roddick. An insightful spiritual leader might be the answer: Buddha, Jesus, Gandhi or others.

Business leaders are trained in creative problem solving. Perhaps Dale Carnegie, Walt Disney, or Thomas Edison could inspire you. Identify and envision one admirable person, living or not, whose biography you know or have read, who could bring a promising solution to your situation. Create him or her in your mind, ask questions pertinent to your situation, and listen to that person's words of wisdom. You are aware of their power, strength, and determination, which is what it took to develop their skills. You've just identified someone you can relate to who can help you solve problems and get something you want.

Many people are similar to you and are looking for creative direction and problem solving techniques. Identify those people who need the information, service, or product you have, and you have found your target market.

The hidden strength of Identifying focuses on discovering the distinguishing characteristics of your target market. Answer the questions in the *Action Step* sections, and you'll benefit by having a direct line to more customers and the prosperity they bring to your business. Focused attention always brings maximum rewards.

Example from a Top Marketer

Margot Fraser, President and Founder of Birkenstock Footprint Sandals, Inc., identified her target market when she needed relief for a foot condition in the 1960s. As with many company founders, Margot was a member of her target market. While on holiday in Germany, Margot came across Birkenstock sandals. Soon she founded the company that was originally known as Birkenstock Footprint Sandals, Inc. in Novato, California. Since the 1980s, dentists and nurses have favored the sandals, and in the United States, Birkenstock's clogs are worn with blue jeans in the winter. The sandals are usually worn during the summer. In the 90's Margot's organization became the #8 largest woman-owned business in the San Francisco Bay Area. Not bad for sandals that began as house slippers in Germany.

Your Objective for the Identifying Strength

Your objective is to reminisce, and identify the situations in your life where you used this strength to help you gain clarity. Apply what you remember to the area of identifying your target market.

Identifying as a Natural Strength

Just like your other natural strengths, you have years of experience and can easily transfer your ability to identifying new situations and circumstances. Psychologists discovered that human newborns just a few hours old can identify a picture of their own mother's face and prefer to look at it over any other picture paired with it.

Years ago, during the Holiday Season, I noticed that my young nephews easily identified presents they wanted to receive. From the massive amount of merchandise, they knew exactly which gift items would suit them, or fit in with the toys and things they already had. It's an inner knowing we develop at an early age and continue to practice throughout our lives.

As adults, we still identify with things that will either contribute to or distract from the quality of our lives. When buying my first computer, I was confronted with so many options that I realized some serious investigation was in order. To make an informed decision, I explored: (a) many available computers, (b) their cost, and (c) which computer would serve my purposes and still allow me to grow into it as my technical strengths improved. My research included talking to experts, quizzing salespeople, reading computer magazines, and taking classes. After analyzing all the data, I finally identified the computer that would best serve me. By using the first four strengths: envisioning, transforming, investigating, and identifying, I became comfortable enough to make an important decision and an expensive purchase with complete peace of mind.

You'll make more effective decisions by focusing on "Who is my customer and how do I reach them?" This can sometimes seem to be just as difficult a question as "What is the meaning of life?" Let's begin with practice examples, then you'll move on to identify who your customer is, what they need, and what motivates them to frequent your business.

Action Step

List two examples from your past when you used your identifying strength.

Identifying Your Target Market

My father practiced archery by first attaching a paper target to a bale of hay, which was a focus point for his arrows. For marketing to be successful, you need a focus point for your efforts, a target market. Imagine your product or service and associate it with the types of people who are now using those products somewhere else in your community. Specifically identify which clients might be interested in purchasing your products or services, in your location, and with your image.

Location is important. Suburban locations with a storefront attract clients from a 3-5 mile radius, and city locations attract consumers mainly from their immediate area. With the popularity of the Internet, many businesses are able to sell products to consumers anywhere in the world. Whether you market your business online or locally, you will identify potential customers through their buying habits, their demographics, and their ability to respond to your marketing messages.

> *Identifying your target market helps you focus your energy and resources where they will best serve you, your business and your community. There is an 80/20 rule which says that 80% of your business will come from 20% of your customers.*

Identifying can be a tricky strength because we often need to let go of biases in personal judgment. To accurately identify your potential clients requires you to be realistic and use good judgment. Jerry owned a budget-priced clothing store but wanted to target an upscale neighborhood for newspaper advertising. I advised him to take care about attempting to attract these clients because he could not deliver (at that time) in the areas of image, personal service or quality.

Many factors will determine who your real market is, such as: your position or niche (I'll explain this later), the demographics in your neighborhood, your business image, your goals and your objectives.

If you envision a business that offers low-end value to customers, you would target the neighborhoods where people with reduced incomes live. Your high-ticket items would require you to target another neighborhood clientele.

It can be costly to develop professional quality marketing products. Aiming those products (brochures, mailers, flyers, website) at the most receptive population greatly increases your chance of persuading them to use your business.

You might encounter a challenge if your neighborhood demographics change after a period of time. You may have to upgrade your image, so consider your financial state before you locate your business in an upscale neighborhood.

In certain cases you may have to lower your prices. Maria owned a small gourmet restaurant and came to me after she had made some mistakes: she had over-improved elements of the décor of her business and was unable to charge higher prices. The neighborhood people would not pay for her investment. I helped her to realize her errors and take action to dig her way out of her predicament. The solutions began with realizing the true characteristics of her clientele.

Business owners must make scores of decisions. Just think of these questions: What actions do I take to discover my true target market? How much time and money do I devote to uncovering my target market? How can I know that I have found my true target market? How much money do I spend to reach my target market? What do I do if I make a mistake and lose money?

What you need is a procedure for making good decisions. Now here is Brian Tracy's guide to making excellent decisions.

Confident Decision Making

Brian Tracy

Just imagine that someone gave you a simple but powerful computer that had the capacity to answer any question or solve any problem you would ever face. All you would have to do is properly program the problem into the computer. Then, at exactly the right time, it would bring you exactly the answer that you need; the answer would always be perfectly correct for you.

The fact is that you already have such a computer, and it's installed right between your ears. The only real difference between extremely effective men and women and men and women who are not happy with their results is the degree to which they use this amazing computer. The wonderful thing is that you can easily learn to use this computer, and when you do, you will immediately start to benefit by making better decisions and getting better results.

To begin, it's important for you to understand that your brain is divided into two hemispheres, commonly called the right brain and the left brain. Extensive research suggests that each part of the brain is responsible for specific functions.

Your left brain tends to be responsible for linear, sequential, orderly and organized functions. It is practical, analytical and skeptical. It is the part of the brain that deals with categories and concrete things. Your left brain deals with the verbal, the mathematical and the scientific. It is the engineering half of the brain, and it is primarily focused on processing facts in a step-by-step fashion.

Your right brain, on the other hand, is very different. Your right brain is holistic and spontaneous. While your left brain deals with individual details, your right brain deals with complete pictures and fully integrated ideas and situations. Your right brain is also in charge of your creative, musical and artistic abilities. It is responsible for dance and singing and laughter. Your right brain is also responsible for the intuitive processes of thinking, feeling, problem solving and decision making.

When you learn to harmonize the operations of both of these brains so they work together in cooperation, you begin to perform at exceptional levels. In fact, men and women begin to become great when they begin to utilize the marvelous capacities of the right brain, especially for making important decisions.

An intuitive decision, one that comes to you from within, is always superior to anything else that you can arrive at by simply considering the facts and details. An intuitive decision integrates all of your knowledge about a subject simultaneously and gives you an answer that is a superior synthesis to anything that you could have worked out in a step-by-step fashion. This is why the men and women who are at the top of virtually all organizations tend to be extremely intuitive in the way they solve problems and make decisions for themselves and others.

Ralph Waldo Emerson called intuition the "still, small voice within." This inner voice is like an unfailing guide or mechanism that always tells you the correct thing to do or say. The more you trust it and believe in it, the better and more accurately it works for you. And your ability to use your intuitive decision-making powers precedes and predicts your success and effectiveness in virtually everything you do.

To trigger your intuition and tap into higher levels of your mind on a regular basis, you need to have four mental qualities. The first, as I mentioned, is a complete trust and belief, almost a childlike faith, in your intuition, and the disposition to just "go with the flow" of your inner mind. Your intuition functions effortlessly and works best when you stop trying to make something happen and instead just "let go" and accept whatever solution comes to you.

The second mental quality that enables you to use your intuition more efficiently is a positive mental attitude. By this, I mean that you are simply calm, relaxed and cheerful about outcomes. A positive mental attitude has been described as a constructive response to stress and adversity. When you respond in a relaxed, easygoing way, you create the mental climate that enables your brain to function at its best, and this is what triggers your intuition. The third mental quality for enhancing your intuition is an attitude of confident expectation. The more positive and more confident you are, the sharper and quicker your intuitions and solutions will be. So confidently expect things to go well for you. Look for the valuable lesson in every difficulty and adversity. Seek out the advantage or benefit in each setback or obstacle that you face. Your conscious decision to keep your mind focused on the good parts of your situation, coupled with your refusal to dwell on the negative parts, will give you a mind that functions at its best to help you achieve your goals.

The fourth mental quality for intuitive decision making is listening. Women tend to be better at listening to their intuition than men are. This is probably why women's intuition is so much more respected than men's intuition is. However, both men and women have the same intuitive abilities. All they have to do is listen to them on a regular basis. Most of our mistakes in life result from ignoring our intuition or refusing to listen to our intuition because we think that by doing so, we will be better off. It always turns out to be a mistake.

There are three areas where you can use your intuition continuously to enable you to make better decisions and avoid costly mistakes. The first place where intuition plays a major role is in your personal relationships. Whether it is with your spouse or child or a friend, your intuition will always tell you the right thing to do or say. All you need to do, in any situation, is to quietly turn to your intuition and listen, and then say or do what seems to be the most proper and natural thing to do. In my experience, one of the major reasons for problems in relationships is that one or both parties are ignoring their intuition and refusing to listen to it or act on it. People get into, or out of, relationships, or make decisions in their interactions with others, even when, deep inside, they know that they are doing the wrong thing. And if ever you do the wrong thing from the standpoint of your intuition, you always create a problem that is bigger and more difficult to deal with than if you had made the intuitive decision at the beginning. Many people actually make themselves physically ill by refusing to follow their intuition and do what they know is the right thing to do.

A second area where your intuitive decision-making capabilities can be extremely helpful is in business. If you listen quietly, you will always get a good feeling, or intuition, about the right thing to do, or not to do, in every business situation. If you are in sales, when you are with a prospect or a client, you can rely completely on your intuition to tell you what to do and what to say, and when you follow it, you will always find that it is the right thing. Many salespeople have told me of their having a sudden impulse to bring up a particular subject in a sales interview, and later finding that it was exactly the right thing to say at exactly the right time. In fact, all top salespeople tend to trust their intuition and listen to it continuously in their sales work.

The third, and perhaps the most obvious, area to use your intuitive abilities is in the area of making choices. Whether you are communicating or negotiating or buying or selling, or accepting or leaving a job, you are always making choices of one kind or another. Some of these choices are not important, but many of them have potentially serious long-term consequences.

Accepting a job, or a salary, or going to work for a particular company, at a particular time, can have a significant impact on the whole direction of your life. Investing or spending or borrowing money for any reason can have significant long-term consequences. Any decision that has results that last long after you have made the decision is the kind of decision to which you need to apply your amazing intuitive powers.

Fortunately, there are some specific steps that you can take to hone your intuitive mind. Select any area of your life, any problem or situation that you are dealing with at the current time, and begin to program it into your mental computer by taking the following steps. First, define your problem or situation clearly, in writing if possible. Your mind cannot go to work to bring you the right answer if the question itself is jumbled up and unclear. Exactly what are you trying to achieve, avoid or preserve? Is it a single problem, or is it a cluster problem—a problem made up of several smaller problems? Whichever it is, take some time to think it out and describe it clearly on paper so that you know exactly what you are trying to do. This is the beginning of the intuitive process.

Once you have a clear idea of the problem, ask yourself, "What else is the problem?" Are you dealing with a real problem, or are you simply dealing with a symptom of a deeper problem? Many people try to solve a problem with their dissatisfaction at work or in a relationship, but often, the real problem is that they are in the wrong job or relationship altogether. There is an old saying, "There is a price that you can pay to be free of any problem, and you always know what it is." This is just another way of saying that if you listen to your intuition, it will tell you the right thing to do, although the right thing may not be the easy or convenient thing. But you must keep your mind open, in any case.

Once you have defined your problem clearly, begin to research and read and gather information about the problem. Has anyone else had this problem before you? What did he do about it? Don't try to reinvent the wheel. Sometimes a little research will turn up exactly the answer you are seeking.

For several months, two scientists at the IBM research laboratories in Zurich, Switzerland, had been intensely working on the problems of superconductivity. They knew what they were looking for but were making no progress, so they decided to take a break and come back to the problem later. During the break, one of the scientists went down to the company library and began browsing through a French journal on ceramics. One of the articles told of a new ceramic application that had just been developed. It turned out to be exactly the key that the scientist had been looking for. He immediately took the article back to the laboratory, and by applying the principle, they discovered the secret of superconductivity. It was such an important scientific breakthrough that these two men were awarded the Nobel Prize in physics the following year.

Once you have defined your problem clearly and researched it as thoroughly as you can, speak to people who may have information that you can use. It's amazing how much you can learn simply by asking questions of others who may have had similar experiences. If you ask enough people, you can often find yourself in the position of being informed than any one of them could be, acting in isolation.

A friend of mine, who is a management consultant, was employed by a large company to investigate the feasibility of placing a large sum of money in a particular type of real-estate investment. Company executives asked him to evaluate the possibilities nationwide and give them some advice on which direction to go.

First of all, he went to the library and got copies of several articles that had been written in this field over the past few months. After reading the articles, he phoned some of the people and companies mentioned in the articles, and told them he was thinking of investing a large amount of money in this industry. He asked them for their insights and their ideas and what advice they would give.

Over the next few days, he spoke to about 30 people in different parts of the country, all of whom specialized in this particular industry.

Most of them were quite open to giving him whatever information he required—sometimes sending it via Federal Express—because they looked upon him as a prospective investor.

By the time he was finished with his inquiries, he was one of the most well-informed people on this subject in the United States. He then summarized his findings and recommendations in a detailed report and submitted it to his client, along with a bill of $30,000 for consulting services. The client read the report and paid the bill willingly. And the consultant went on to his next assignment.

Your most valuable asset is your ability to think, and to apply your mind toward getting results. The more you utilize your mental capabilities, by doing the things that other successful people do with their minds, the more successful and prosperous you will be, and the faster it will happen for you.

Let's say that you have now defined your problem clearly, read and researched thoroughly, asked others for their advice and input, and written down every single detail of the problem or situation.

The very act of writing out all the details often stimulates intuitive breakthroughs that lead to ideas and solutions that are superior to those that are currently being used. Once you have written out the details, go over them several times, and let your mind soak them up so that your right brain is properly fueled to synthesize and integrate all the facts and respond intuitively.

If you still have no solution, your next step is to force yourself—discipline yourself—to write out 20 ways in which you think the problem could be solved. Quickly write out 20 solutions, or 20 answers or 20 courses of action, that might be possible. Forcing yourself to think in this way will often trigger your intuition and bring you an answer that will solve the situation perfectly.

If you have followed the previous steps and you still have not come up with a solution that satisfies you, take the next step in intuitive decision making, which is called "rumination" or "cerebration."

These words refer to the process of dropping all the information into your subconscious mind and then just forgetting about it for a while. During this period, your mind goes to work unconsciously to solve the problem while you are busy doing something else.

When they reach a dead end in problem solving or decision making, many people find it helpful to turn the entire matter over to their subconscious mind and simply "ask" for an answer. A good time to do this is just before you go to sleep. Sometimes you will wake up in the morning with the answer springing "full blown" into your mind. In other cases, as long as you keep your mind on other subjects, at a certain point the answer will emerge in its entirety, and you will know exactly what to do.

How do you recognize an intuitive decision? How do you know that this is not simply a decision or a solution that will lead to greater problems in the future? Well, there are four indicators that accompany every intuition-based solution or decision.

First of all, if the answer is truly from your intuition, it will come in a flash and be complete in every detail, answering every aspect of the problem, from beginning to end. The solution will integrate all of the various details and answer all of the concerns.

Second, an intuitive solution seems so simple that you wonder why you had not thought of it before. It feels like a "blinding flash of the obvious." You are amazed at how perfect it is, and you have the feeling that it was lying under your nose all the time.

The third indicator of an intuitive decision is that, whatever it is, the actions required are completely within your capabilities and your resources. The solution will be something that you can do right now, with what you have, right where you are. You can act on it immediately.

And the fourth indicator is that each intuitive flash or solution comes accompanied by a burst of joy and energy, a feeling of elation, that excites you and makes you happy and makes you feel eager to implement the solution. You will be excited, and you will feel terrific about yourself.

Intuitive problem solving and decision making is your key to the future. It is perhaps the most powerful faculty of your brain. And the regular use of your intuitive abilities will make them better and stronger and sharper, until you reach the point where you believe that there is really nothing that you cannot do if you put your mind to it. And you're probably right.

> Brian Tracy is the most listened to audio author on personal and business success in the world today. His fast-moving talks and seminars on leadership, sales, managerial effectiveness and business strategy are loaded with powerful, proven ideas and strategies that people can immediately apply to get better results in every area.

> BrianTracy.com

Now that we have covered Brian's procedure to making good decisions, it's time for you to get started with this next *Action Step*.

Action Step

Who do you think is your target market? Give details.

Most experts agree that entrepreneurs have better success by narrowing their target market to one or two markets. You may find that, after a significant time, you desire to expand your clientele and therefore aim for several suitable markets.

Four advantages of identifying your target market

Understanding these four advantages gives you a better idea of how you will benefit from this identifying process:

1. You are better equipped to direct your promotional and advertising efforts to that particular market.

2. Your business image will be more aligned with customer preferences.

3. Your prices will reflect what your target market is willing to pay.

4. You are better prepared for the future when you know pertinent facts about your neighborhood, such as what types of people or businesses are moving in or out.

Keep abreast of changes in your community by joining the Chamber of Commerce and attending Town Board meetings.

The four Identifying principles

In Chapter 4—*Investigating*, you learned that your competitors help to keep you on your toes. You also learned who "controls the ball." However, they don't necessarily control all of the customers. The trick is to discover who you can serve.

Customers are the main focus of your business; without them you don't have a business.

Apply the four principles to the people you want to influence and attract to your business.

They have …

1. Similar interests.

2. Needs that you can meet, or problems that you can solve.

3. A desire to be treated the same way as you or better.

4. Potential benefits from your products and services.

Explore Demographics

Begin identifying your target market through investigative research. Demographic research is, according to the *New World Dictionary* "the statistical science dealing with the vital statistics of populations." Demographic (statistics) and lifestyle factors are the two areas most often analyzed. This information will help you to discover which neighborhoods have the financial ability to support your business. Of course, you'll also take a look at the competitive situation, to be sure that ideal neighborhoods are not oversaturated with similar businesses.

1. Demographic research uncovers facts about your clientele and about the area in which you locate your business: age, gender, occupation, income level, education level, family status, geographic location and buying habits.

2. Lifestyle factors include special interest activities, philosophical beliefs, social factors and cultural involvements.

Make sure you identify why people buy. Research shows that people buy products and services according to convenience, price, and prestige.

How to Research Demographic Data

Use these four methods to research demographic data—to determine which method will help you pinpoint valued customers.

Your local Chamber of Commerce

Your Chamber of Commerce has clients' names, addresses, and phone numbers that they provide in a telephone directory.

Surveys

Surveys that include detailed and relevant questions give you fairly accurate results regarding your current customers. Do you really want to know what your customers need? This is the perfect time to ask. Here are three ways of conducting surveys:

1. Pinpoint who is currently walking through your door or calling you by doing a formal survey. It is still vital to do your research personally and discover the facts about your market. You can avoid spending huge sums of money building an overpriced or unnecessary

business that includes services no one wants; you can avoid hiring too many employees.

2. Hire an advertising agency to conduct demographic research. They will define your potential target market for you. Be careful with this step; call for price quotes.

3. Do an informal survey merely by eye-balling who is walking into your business on a daily basis. Interview customers and jot down pertinent information. You may notice a cross-section or a very specific group of consumers. This method is not as effective as the others, but is better than doing nothing.

Focus groups

Large corporations spend huge sums of money on professionally conducted focus groups. Focus groups are an organized and select group of people who give feedback on new products. They primarily benefit companies who focus on retail products. Group members' responses determine whether a company's new product or service is desirable to that market. You will hear opinions, thoughts or comments directly from consumers in their own words. This vital information can either assist a company in positioning their products in a successful way or cause them to abandon the product.

Focus group responses can be beneficial to you when developing your brochures and advertising copy. Participants may have some interesting comments that may not have occurred to you. However, most small and medium-sized businesses generally do not have the budget to conduct a focus group or pay for professionally designed demographic research. You may want to focus on surveys and other methods first.

Response marketing

If you are still uncertain exactly who your customers are, try response marketing. You'll implement various promotions throughout the year designed to attract a particular market. You will know your market by who responds to the advertisements. This may be a costly way to find out who your customer is or isn't, but it is much less expensive than hiring a firm to do your research.

Action Step

> How will you discover your target market? Which system or systems will you use?

Target market strategy

> 1. Do market research to find out what new product or service people want and what price they are willing to pay. Then start a new business line with that information in mind.
>
> 2. Do market research to find out specifically what consumers want, like or need in your product or service, and incorporate that information into a business that you already own and operate.

How to Make Sense of Your Demographic Research

Organize and tabulate the findings of your research so you completely understand who your largest customer group is, second largest, and so on. Separate the remaining data into information categories: employees, service, product, media, purchasing and others.

Action Steps

1. Write a descriptive analysis of who your current customers are.

2. Write a descriptive analysis of who your potential customers are. Include each of your target markets.

- **Target Market No. 1**—What are their interests, lifestyle factors, and where you can find them?

- **Target Market No. 2**—What are their interests, lifestyle factors, and where you can find them?

- **Target Market No. 3**—What are their interests, lifestyle factors, and where you can find them?

Produce a Customer Survey

Surveys help you collect statistical data, opinions and responses from a large number of people, usually by interview or questionnaire.

Keep most of your questions closed-ended. This means the customer will circle the answers you provide. Open-ended or comment questions give you a more personal response.

Produce your own formal business survey in order to determine demographics. Explain to your customers that the purpose of the survey is to help you serve them better. Your survey should not take more than 5-7 minutes to complete. In appreciation, consider attaching a 10%-50% off coupon or $2.00 off for a service or product. A discount could increase traffic for your business.

I used the following example as a survey for my business. You may add questions relevant to your personal situation. Keep your survey anonymous so customers will feel free to state their honest opinions.

Customer Survey

Date:

Are you ○ Male or ○ Female?

What is your age?   ○ 35-44
    ○ Under 18   ○ 45-54
    ○ 18-24   ○ 55-64
    ○ 25-34   ○ 65 or over

What is the highest level of formal education you have completed?
    ○ High school   ○ College degree
    ○ Some college   ○ Advanced degree

What is your marital status?
    ○ Single, never married ○ Separated or divorced
    ○ Married   ○ Widowed

How many children are currently living in your household?
    Under 18:   Over 18:

Do you own ○ Own or ○ Rent your home?

How knowledgeable are you about our products/services?
    ○ Very   ○ Somewhat   ○ Slightly   ○ Not at all

Which of our products/services have you used?

How often do you purchase our products/services?
    ○ Weekly   ○ Monthly   ○ Annually

Please rate the following, according to their importance to you.
    (1 is the most important)

Price	○ 1	○ 2	○ 3	○ 4	○ 5
Quality	○ 1	○ 2	○ 3	○ 4	○ 5
Attractiveness	○ 1	○ 2	○ 3	○ 4	○ 5
Brand name	○ 1	○ 2	○ 3	○ 4	○ 5
Dependability	○ 1	○ 2	○ 3	○ 4	○ 5

Availability	O 1	O 2	O 3	O 4	O 5
Customer service	O 1	O 2	O 3	O 4	O 5
Easy of use	O 1	O 2	O 3	O 4	O 5

When you think of our business, what image comes to mind?

In what way could we improve the appearance of our business?

What influenced you to come to our business?

Are our employees well trained, courteous, helpful? O Yes   O No

Are our employees knowledgeable? O Yes   O No

Would you consider referring your people to us? O Yes   O No

What additional products/services would like to see us offer?

Do you often use our sale coupons? O Yes   O No

If our business considered moving to a new location within 5 miles, would you continue your patronage with us? O Yes   O No

Which sources of information did you use to learn about our business and our products/services.

O Business publications O Radio/television
O Word-of-mouth   O Newspaper
O In-store displays   O Personal experience/knowledge

Which radio stations do you listen to and when?

Do you watch television? O No   O Yes, if so, what do you watch?

Which newspapers do you read and which sections?

Please indicate your household income

O Less than $30,000   O $50,000 – $75,000
O $30,000 – $40,000   O $75,000 – $100,000
O $40,000 – $50,000   O Over $100,000

I recommend asking where customers do their shopping. You can tell a lot about a person's buying power by where they shop. Be sure to thank the customer for taking the time to fill out your survey, and give them a coupon.

Action Step

Read the small business survey, and personalize it by adding questions relevant to your situation.

Do a "Best" Customer Profile

Another good place to start identifying is with your current best customers. Always talk to your favorite customers about their likes and dislikes, when they started coming to your business, what influenced that decision and what motivates them to return. Never underestimate the value of personal feedback.

Use surveys or questionnaires to ask more detailed questions. Knowing the attitude of your current best customers will give you some insight on how to attract more customers just like them.

Action Step

Create a profile of your "best" client.

How to Keep Customers

Business is essentially an exchange of energy: money for a service or product. But the real foundation of your business is the association of human energy, which is based on relationships. Business relationships are very much like personal relationships, without the level of intimacy that you create with children, parents, and spouses. There are three things people desire: to be recognized, appreciated and wanted. In my mind, this means people want your relationship with them to be a heartfelt one. We need to express sincere caring as we provide products and services to the public. When we relate from the heart, we give from a special place inside us that says, "We value you as a person, and our relationship with you. It's not just about taking your money, but providing friendship and solutions to your problems."

When you give, you always receive—not always from the person you gave to, but a return always comes from somewhere or someone else who is capable of giving to you. The universal law of cause and effect always prevails. The main idea is to avoid setting conditions for the relationship. Unconditionally give the support, encouragement, information, or guidance that your customer needs, and you will gain much more than if you had not contributed to that person at all.

We all know of customers who demand more than the normal amount of attention. They cause us to stretch and reach inside ourselves for answers to their individual problems. These are the customers whose extreme call for attention teaches us the real possibilities of giving from the heart.

Create Rapport

Dale Carnegie, author of *How to Win Friends and Influence People* and *How to Stop Worrying and Start Living*, emphasized the importance of creating rapport in order to get new customers and keep your current ones. The relationship should always be established first before the service or product is introduced. Establish rapport first by developing a friendship and a sincere interest in the needs of the customer. Your alignment of common purpose will put you in the best position to be called upon when the customer needs your product or service.

Let's remember that it's less expensive to keep an old customer than it is to get a new one. A sincere interest in all customers, along with quality services and products at the right price and location, keep clients coming back for your brand of friendship.

Cardinal Rules for Building Relationships

1. Listen attentively.

2. Create the space for friendship.

3. Avoid judgments.

4. Be positive.

5. Always honor the customer's wishes. Try to understand their point of view.

6. Let go of your need to be right.

7. See constructive criticism as an opportunity to grow.

8. Keep smiling, even when you feel challenged.

How to Improve Customer Service

Knowing what makes customers quit using your business also gives you some insight on what you can do to make them stay. According to Earl Erickson, professor of marketing in San Francisco: 1% die, 3% move away, 5% develop other relationships, 9% go to the competition, 14% are dissatisfied with their product or service, and the largest majority of customers, 68%, leave because they were upset with their treatment.

Consumers are dissatisfied and upset because of poor customer service. Here we have a list of seven consumer complaints:

1. No business philosophy.

2. Employees who don't care (negative attitude)—related topoor training.

3. Perceptual differences of what they want or need.

4. Perceptual differences of what is provided and what is received.

5. Improper handling of complaints.

6. No company set of standards.

7. Employees not given authority to make decisions.

This list of consumer complaints vividly discloses the problems with small business today. Employees need to focus on both technical and people strengths.

It all goes back to you, and your ability to choose and train remarkable people who represent your business and reflect your philosophy. Take care of your business, and you won't have to be concerned about customers being upset and going elsewhere.

Action Step

To help you document vital information about your customers, respond to this list of questions regarding the results of your survey and demographic data:

1. How much money do customers spend on products or services at your business?

    1A. Female:

    1B. Male:

2. What percentage of your business is professional women?

3. What percentage of your business is retired women?

4. What percentage of your business is women who are homemakers? (There are also house husbands, so you may want to account for this.)

5. What percentage of your business is men?

6. What percentage of your business is retired men?

7. What percentage of your business is teenagers?

8. What percentage of your business is children?

9. Are the majority of your customers over or under 30 years of age?

10. Are the majority of your customers over 50 years of age?

11. In what income bracket would you place most of your over-30 customers (low, medium, high income)?

12. What are the most popular services?

13. What are the most popular and best-selling products?

14. Which media are reaching your target market?

15. What changes or additions are your customers requesting?

16. If your small or home-based business is located in a diverse ethnic community, are you and your employees prepared to speak various languages and realize cultural differences?

The following examples show how you might categorize knowledge about your clientele. Document exactly who your customers are and what is important to them. This information provides a clue on how to strategize your marketing efforts and proceed with changes to your business.

Example A. As you analyze your existing customers, you understand that 60% of your customers are women, 25% men and 15% children. You discover that 75% of your customers are between the ages of 25-45, and the balance are either under 12 or over 60. The group in the 75% range have an average income level of approximately $20,000 a year and have a low education level. Your marketing plan would take all of this information into account. Your target market is mainly women between age 25-45 with a low income level.

Example B. If you had a different customer base, 50% men and 50% women between the ages of 30-50, mostly college educated with an income level of $30,000-50,000 and up—how would you adjust? These upscale professional people would have different needs. How would you adjust your marketing messages to reflect those needs?

Realize that accurately identifying our target market and then assuring customers that they can trust that you will provide for their needs is a critical process for your success. Now, my co-author Tom Marcoux will discuss the process of creating trust.

Marketing Is Trust

Tom Marcoux

Good marketing gains trust. How do you do that?

Tell a story. Why?

If you say, "Best customer service in the country," the prospective customer reflexively thinks: "Oh yeah? Prove it."

But if you tell a story, it slips under the radar. How does that happen? Researchers theorize that it is because we are raised on stories as children. Every moment across the world, children are saying, "Tell me a story."

One of the most successful marketing websites I ever wrote began with:

> Dear Reader,
>
> I never expected to write *Darkest Secrets of Persuasion and Seduction Masters: How to Protect Yourself and Turn the Power to Good.* But I was angry and I had to stand up for you.

When I was a child, I was hurt badly. My parents could not protect me. As a young man, in one of my first business deals, I was hurt terribly.

Now, I'm 44 years old, with gray in my hair, and for 24 years I have been taking action to protect people.

And now is the time that I protect you with the countermeasures I reveal in *Darkest Secrets of Persuasion and Seduction Masters.*

Every human being needs to be able to break the trance that a manipulator will create. You need to make good decisions so you are safe and growing and not cut off at the knees.

This Darkest Secrets material is so intense that I am only releasing it by counterbalancing it with my most energizing and uplifting books *10 Seconds to Wealth* and *Nothing Can Stop You This Year!*

Now it's time, this very minute, for me to write this to protect you. I must speak the truth.

These darkest secrets of persuasion masters are … Wait a minute. Let's say it plainly: These are the darkest secrets of masters of manipulation.

As you can see, tell a story and you do four effective things: arouse curiosity, create tension, use suspense and prove the triumph. These 4 elements provide a good story.

And in effective marketing the fifth element is "Ask for the order" (that is, ask the person to buy).

Now you're on your way to *Full Strength Marketing*.

As you do the research related to identifying your target market, also think about what story (as Tom's above article points out) would be helpful. The right target market and appropriate story form a powerful combination for effective marketing.

Identifying Summary

Take the following steps to access your hidden strength to identify.

1. Identifying your target market.

2. Explore demographics.

3. How to research demographic data.

4. How to make sense of your demographic research.

5. Produce a customer survey.

6. Do a best customer profile.

7. How to keep customers.

When Do I Take These Steps?

Identify your target market before you open for business. You must also identify them before you begin your next marketing campaign. This identification process can be done at the same time that you investigate your competitors. You don't necessarily need to identify your target market every year, only when you notice substantial demographic changes.

Visit your local Chamber of Commerce to get demographic data. Look at online resources. Talk to mentors, other business owners and friends in the neighborhood where you plan to locate your small or home-based business. If you are already open for business, do a survey to get more information.

6

Positioning

Your Fifth Hidden Strength

Hot dog in hand, you sit in your hometown stadium, enjoying one of America's favorite sports, baseball. Using binoculars, you search the dugout for your favorite batter. Many people admire baseball players because they excel with certain abilities: a great long-distance hitter, a superb catcher, a dynamic pitcher, and a first baseman who plays with great style and ease. The secret to winning the ball game is that each player performs a unique function in his area of the field or position. He's deemed a valuable player by doing only what he does best. Apply this idea of "value determined by strength" to positioning your business in the marketplace. Do only what you do best, and you too will be admired.

Positioning is an extremely purposeful act. Focus on positioning your business so it performs a unique function, and therefore stands out in the marketplace. This strength answers the one important question, "What is the most valuable position for my business, and how will I express that in my community or industry?"

When Marketing Doesn't Feel Good to You

Tom Marcoux

Have you ever said to a friend: "I don't like marketing or selling"? I hear you.

This is a major opportunity to reframe the whole situation. I have worked with a number of clients and helped them transform the idea of "marketing" into being a "coach to action."

What does a good coach do?

"She helps you get done what you know you need to do," said my client Mirna. Yes! And whose agenda is it?

"The person getting the coaching," Mirna concluded.

So to accomplish this empowering reframing of the whole strong marketing process, ask yourself these questions (and write down your answers in a personal journal—or better yet—your Marketing Plan binder):

1. What do you like about your work?

2. What's the best part of your work?

3. How do you help people?

4. When you're feeling good about your work, what is going on?

(Question 3 is part of the process of positioning your business.)

Now from this framework, imagine that you're going to help people get the advantages of working with you. The new clients are going to greatly benefit from interacting with you. And if they are not a match, you're going to help them in some way (refer them to someone who can help, or send a helpful link to an article).

This leads to an empowering phrase: "It's all good."

Now, we can approach marketing as a benevolent process.

It's all good. That's better!

On completing the *Action Steps*, your benefit is the awareness that you have created something rare and valuable.

Example from a Top Marketer

Dottie Walters, co-author of *Speak and Grow Rich,* and contributor to the *Chicken Soup for the Soul* series, positioned her speaker's bureau as a very friendly, helpful service to meeting planners. Dottie said, "You need to think 'what have I done to advance my career today?' Write 20 thank-you letters."

Your Objective for the Positioning Strength

Your objective is to recall past situations where you positioned yourself to your advantage, and apply that knowledge to the area of positioning your business. Positioning means to be placed or arranged in the best possible situation. In business we use our positioning strength as a competitive strategy.

Positioning as a Natural Strength

Children demonstrate "positioning" at a young age. Checkers is a fun and easy game that teaches us positioning and strategizing strengths. We quickly learn how to arrange our red or black checkers into a position where we can jump two or more of our opponent's checkers and eventually win the game.

Years ago I read a book called *The Birth Order Book* that explains our traits and personalities according to our family position. Each individual is characterized by whether they were first born, a middle child, the baby, or an only child. This is an example of living your position.

Employees who learn new skills and meet key people in their company are purposely positioning themselves for a promotion, a raise, or a choice territory. They may eventually buy the company, or achieve whatever goals they desire. They are positioning themselves for success.

Envision the last time you attended a class or seminar. Where did you sit: in the front of the room near the speaker, next to the exit, by the window, or in the back of the room? You subconsciously positioned yourself to either tune into the speaker, make a quick getaway if necessary, daydream, or chat with friends. Your purposeful position in the room demonstrates the level of attention or commitment you directed to the subject.

These examples show how we automatically use our positioning strength. You'll now draw upon your experiences to position your business and place it at an advantage.

Action Step

List two examples from your past when you effectively positioned yourself.

Choose Your Position in the Marketplace

Positioning is a key marketing principle that produces specific purposeful results. Before you can choose your position, study the strengths and positions of your competitors to become aware of where you might fit into the picture. Then choose a position that focuses on the specific benefit which will attract potential clients to you.

Action Step

List at least two of your business's key benefits.

Dare to Be Different

Effective positioning is placing what's uniquely different about your small or home-based business into the minds of local consumers. You must get them to think that your business and its employees do something special or unique that no one else can do as well. That, plus the element of caring, will differentiate your business from similar ones in the same industry.

Your community probably doesn't need twenty similar "discount" businesses, and it wouldn't be wise to try to compete with the other nineteen. It also doesn't need fifteen upscale, high-priced businesses. It is important to determine exactly what position you intend to fill.

If you were playing baseball, which position would you want to play? Would you want to just hang out in the outfield, or play the infield and be part of the action?

In the book *Positioning: The Battle for Your Mind,* authors Jack Trout and Al Ries wrote that positioning is the key to success. According to the authors, there are four positions from which to choose:

The First or Leadership Position

The best way to get into the customer's mind is with a revolutionary idea. A strong marketer would take a leadership role and become first in the marketplace with new and innovative ideas, services or products. You'll create a new market with a new product or service. Otherwise you will be sharing part of an existing market. Vidal Sassoon is one example of a best, innovative and leadership position.

Tip: Be innovative.

Innovation is one of the most desirable and admirable traits. When it comes to promoting new products and services, make a real effort to be the first to introduce them to the marketplace. Getting into the act early will help you capture the market and grab those first profits. Be innovative by inventing something new and useful, or creating a handmade object. If you can't be first, then you must find creative ways to attract the attention of consumers.

For another alternative, consider writing an interesting article about your innovation in your enewsletter, trade websites, local newspapers, or trade magazines. Build a bridge from the product to you by associating the information with your name and business.

The Against Position

This position is created by businesses who claim to be second, but try harder. 7 UP created a unique position by developing "the uncola." Avis developed the "we try harder" slogan to compete with Hertz.

The New Position

Establish this position by creating a new category. Federal Express was once an example of this position by offering overnight service. Revolutionary ideas have an element of risk attached to them. Thorough market research could help you determine if the timing is right for your new idea, invention, or service. There's a fine line where you must determine if your idea is so far ahead of everyone that they are not ready (motivated or interested) to buy. Or perhaps the market is ripe for your new ideas.

The Niche Position

This position is created by aiming for a small portion of a large market. Later we'll discuss the niche position in depth.

Action Steps

1. What positions do each of your competitors hold? (identify details for 5 competitors)

2. What needs does your business meet?

3. In your community, what needs are not being met by any small or home-based business?

4. What problems does your business solve?

5. How will your services or products benefit your customer?

6. How will your services or products specifically benefit your customer's mental attitude?

7. What information could you gather in order to position your current or future business more effectively?

8. To add to your positioning awareness, review the *Action Steps* in Chapter 4—*Investigating* and Chapter 5—*Identifying* to find positioning clues.

9. What obvious position could your business pursue?

10. What revolutionary idea will spark an interest in your business?

Design Your Own Springboard

You need a position strategy that acts as a springboard for success. Your position in the community differentiates you from competitive businesses. Avoid repeating positions your competitors have successfully taken. Think of positioning as a unique starting point that launches you into first place.

Your unique position builds upon your recognition. Focus more on accessing your prospect's awareness rather than your promotional projects. Try to think like consumers think, and put yourself in their shoes. For instance, think about your retail products and the purposes they serve. Answer the questions in the *Action Step* section for more clarity.

One more important point: once you find a position for your business, you must be patient and commit to your plan for the long term. Use creative advertising and promotions to support your positioning objective.

Action Steps

1. What can you say in your promotional and advertising materials that will create awareness of your position and add impact to your marketing campaign?

2. How do your products serve your clients?

3. Why would consumers purchase your products and services?

4. Are retail products a major or minor part of your business?

5. Can products be displayed better, more efficiently, or with more impact?

6. Can you sell novelty items that other businesses don't have the space to carry, and be recognized for your retail area?

Write a Position Statement

Write a position statement for your marketing campaign. Here is an example:

Position statement: The purpose of Mabel's Beauty Boutique (a fictitious name) is to provide comfort and friendly service. The target market will be senior citizens who live in the immediate neighborhood and attend a large senior center. The salon will be positioned as a sanctuary exclusively for seniors.

Resulting marketing strategy: Mabel's Beauty Boutique will provide a convenient location that is wheelchair accessible. The value will be a one-stop shopping experience where quality personal service is offered regarding hair, skin, nails, beauty supplies and massage. Moderately priced clothes and accessories are available for purchase. This strategy will be made possible by considerate and attentive attendants and patient employees. Marketing tools to be used are flyers and posters within the senior center, flyers in the local grocery stores, local newspaper advertising, printed door hangers, a cross-merchandising promotion with other businesses in the neighborhood (physicians in particular) and a business referral contest. Free monthly seminars will be implemented at the Senior Center.

Action Step

> What is your position statement? Keep it simple, focused and brief. (Refer to Mabel's example if you need to.)

According to Al Ries and Jack Trout, authors of *Positioning*, "To succeed in our over-communicated society, a company must create a position in the prospect's mind, a position that takes into consideration not only a company's own strengths and weaknesses, but those of its competitors as well." Effective advertising heightens expectations. The objective is to create 'a sense of expectancy' that your product or service will perform the results they expect.

Now Raleigh Pinsky shares how to use public seminars in marketing. As we'll notice, she says that public seminars help you effectively position yourself and business in the marketplace.

Why Presenting Public Seminars is a Great PR and Marketing Tool to Promote and Prosper

Raleigh R. Pinskey

Imagine receiving a glowing introduction just before you step in front of an audience. You're greeted with a warm round of applause.

Now imagine that such a process brings you business opportunities immediately and for years to come. Just today, I received a phone call in which someone remembered my little stage method of giving myself that introduction! He remembered me 15 years later.

How do you get the business? You need to be memorable and you need to be perceived as an expert.

How? Present a public seminar. Here are the benefits:

- It is a highly effective means of positioning yourself or your business in the marketplace.

- It is a promotional vehicle that increases awareness of what services you offer

- It shows your expertise on the subject matter

- It establishes you as a spokesperson in your field

- It provides you with name recognition

- It sets you up as a consultant on the subject matter

Case Study 1

A friend from New York city, where she was a household name in the fitness and personal growth for many years moved to Los Angeles. There she was " just another expert in the Personal Growth industry." Advertising was expensive, so to rev up her engines in a new community I educated her on using social media and creating her 8-Second Power Pitch for introducing herself at business social functions. I helped her to get interviews on radio and in the local area papers to announce her public seminars/gatherings at her home. In no time at all she had herself a name and a lucrative consulting and speaking business.

Case Study 2

A friend who became a corporate down-sizing casualty became a nutritional products distributor. Pressed for time and financial resources she chose to showcase her product not by joining organizations, but by giving public seminars on "How To Create A Successful Home Based Business With $39 Down." With that hook, social media, electronic and print media she attracted audiences like flies, advancing up the quota ladder in no time.

Case Study 3

I held a public seminar at the library's free community room. Attendance was thin, but I didn't mind. I knew between the library's efforts, social media, my electronic and print PR marketing efforts, and my outreach through PromoteYourself.com that hundreds of local people would get to know me. That one hour event with six people brought me several meaningful consulting opportunities.

The point is that public seminars can lead to all kinds of wonderful opportunities that can bring you fame and fortune. So conquer your fears around public seminars by remembering that what you are doing is pure business.

Do what Raleigh Pinskey says: "Go for it ... Promote & Prosper!"®

Raleigh Raleigh R. Pinskey, speaks on *The New Rules of PR, Brand Blending, 8-Second Business Motivators*, and *Visibility Strategies*. Raleigh is a high content speaker, seminar leader, facilitator and self-promotion coach, Her expertise is drawn from thirty years experience at the helm of The Raleigh Group Communications, a visibility marketing company. Raleigh began speaking in 1993 promoting her first book, *The Zen of Hype*, followed by *You Can Hype Anything, 101 Ways to Get On Talk Shows, 101 Ways to Write*

Results Producing Media Releases, Your 8 Second or Less Benefit Driver, and the international best selling *101 Ways to Promote Yourself*™.

Raleigh has over 2,000 presentations to her credit. Platform colleagues include Susan Rowan, Mark Victor Hanson, Jack Canfield, Brian Tracy, Dan Kennedy, Jay Abraham, Arnold Sanow, and numerous National Speaker Association notables. Speakers Platform nominated Raleigh for the Top5 Speaker in Marketing for 2010.

The Raleigh Group Communications client history includes Sting, McCartney, KISS, Blondie, the $5,000 Marilyn Monroe Doll, Soap Opera and Broadway stars, the original *Chicken Soup for the Soul* authors, speakers, entrepreneurs, associations, non-profits, and the Bronx Zoo's a *Great Snake Named Jake*. Raleigh is the host of a blog talk radio show, and the writer/performer of the comedy solo show "*SPLAT! The Evolution of Soul 685.*" Raleigh R. Pinskey's motto is "Promote & Prosper!®"

PromoteYourself.com and RaleighRPinskey.com

Find Your Niche

Niche marketing is filling a gap in the marketplace. You must find a hole in the products and services currently available. It must be something no one else is doing, so you can do it. Your niche may be in the area of: price, quality, speed, specificity, newness or another area. To find a niche, you need to be alert, inquisitive, shrewd and "street smart."

First discover the needs of your target market (that haven't been met). Then find what needs your competition isn't filling. The result of those two answers becomes your niche. Provide that niche service to stand out from the crowd and be noticed.

Here are two examples from the cosmetology industry. At one time full-service salons were the standard, then came discount salons, or what we now call quick cut salons. It was a novelty that many consumers loved, especially for those who wanted quick service for themselves and their children. At that time haircut-only salons had a niche. The shampoo, blow dry and personal service were eliminated. They stood out because they were doing what no one else was doing—cutting hair fast at a lower price to the customer. Once it caught on, and more salon owners found it profitable to run their businesses that way, it became a standard, too. It isn't a niche any more because too many salons are offering quick cut services.

Years ago, nail care was done only in the salon, and was just a minor service. With the advent of artificial nails, many nail care businesses sprouted up in the marketplace. Salons devoted exclusively to nail care became a booming industry. Savvy entrepreneurs found a lucrative niche—career women with disposable income who desire specialized services such as manicures, pedicures and various nail extensions. It's a low-overhead business. A good location and employees who work quickly put nail care entrepreneurs on the fast track to success.

Be a specialist

In finding your niche, you must be a specialist rather than a generalist. In the medical profession, some doctors specialize in cardiology for heart patients; obstetricians for the birthing process and gynecologists for women's health. The advantage of going to a specialist is their additional education and expertise in a particular field. If you are a specialist, you can blow your own horn and accumulate wealth and prestige.

Similar to focusing on being a specialist, you need to identify and communicate your personal brand. Mark Sanborn now shares with us helpful strategies about developing your personal brand.

Personal Branding Makes Marketing Easier

Mark Sanborn, CSP, CPAE

Your brand is critical.

It will either supercharge your marketing—or kill it.

If you want your marketing to be easy and effective, consider your personal brand and whether it is helping or hurting.

I work with corporate clients in the area of brand development, and I've identified the DNA that makes up a good brand. This DNA, the basis which guides the development of a brand, also applies to individuals as well as to products and organizations.

DNA is, coincidentally, an acronym. To get you started on your journey of ongoing individual brand development, contemplate these three concepts, which form a similar acronym:

Dependability

A good brand is consistent. With a good brand, there are never any unpleasant surprises. You can count on a brand to help you quickly sort through an unlimited list of options to identify "a sure thing." In the old days, there was a sales adage that went something like this: "Nobody ever got in trouble for purchasing IBM." If you aren't old enough to recall exactly what that meant, it alluded to the fact that IBM was not always the "best" or "most innovative" or "most anything" for that matter, but it was a dependable brand.

When applied to you, the question becomes: What can others—your customers, employer, and colleagues—depend on you for? What kind of "sure thing" are you exactly?

Whatever you decide distinguishes you in the marketplace of talent, make sure consistency is the bedrock of your brand. Nobody wants to buy from an individual or organization that is "hit or miss."

Novelty

OK, so what makes you different? It's not enough to be as dependable as everyone or anyone else. Brands always have substantive identifiable differences—perceptually if not in fact—in the mind of the marketplace.

Being a generalist isn't a bad thing, but being a generalist without any discernible specialized skills, abilities, or talents isn't a great thing, either.

Marketing requires capturing the attention of a potential customer. Nobody notices "sameness." Everybody notices what is different, especially when that difference or novelty is valued.

What makes you different (or better)? While weird may work for celebrities, it is seldom a desirable attribute for the world of commerce. For a difference to be valuable to the brand, it must be valuable to the customer.

Attitude

This is the most nebulous part of a brand. It is more than a combination of novelty and dependability. I call it the brand's predisposition to the world. It is about the vibe a brand puts out. It's about the demeanor and flavor and orientation.

Attitude is how the brand—"you, inc." or "organization, inc."—presents itself to the world. I believe that all brands have a boldness about them. Even if a brand is quiet, dependable, and safe, those attributes are expressed to the marketplace boldly and definitively.

What is your attitude? Have you considered it and identified it? Is the attitude of your brand something that draws others to it, or puts them off?

Think Apple, Harley Davidson, Nike and MTV. Hate 'em or love 'em (and most people love 'em), they're brands with attitude.

DNA. Dependability. Novelty. Attitude.

As a first step toward marketing yourself better, take some time soon to write out the DNA of your brand.

For more ideas about personal branding, check out the book *The Brand You 50* by business guru Tom Peters. This handy little book presents 50 specific ideas you can use for distinguishing yourself as an employee or potential employee.

Mark is the president of Sanborn & Associates, Inc., an idea lab for leadership development. Leadershipgurus.net lists him as one of the top 30 leadership experts in the world. Mark has authored 8 books and more than two dozen videos and audio training programs. He has presented over 2200 speeches and seminars in every state and 12 foreign countries. His book, *The Fred Factor: How Passion in Your Work and Life Can Turn the Ordinary into the Extraordinary* has sold over 1.1 million copies. His latest books are *You Don't Need a Title to be a Leader: How Anyone, Anywhere Can Make a Positive Difference* and *The Encore Effect: How to Achieve Remarkable Performance in Anything You Do*. Mark is a past president of the National Speakers Association and winner of The Cavett. In 2007

Mark was awarded The Ambassador of Free Enterprise Award by Sales & Marketing Executives International.

MarkSanborn.com

Look at the Big Picture

Don't get caught up in the details, look at the big picture. Review your vision and mission statement. Stay focused in your efforts and align your niche with your vision.

Is there something that you're already doing or have which the public is unaware of because you haven't promoted it? Also, when you become aware of an available niche, grab it before a competitor does.

Your real objective in niche marketing is not necessarily to compete, but, if possible, to do what other businesses aren't doing. Then, you don't have competition, at least not for a while. When you are the only business filling a need, then you corner the market for that need. Otherwise you must take a smaller share of the existing supply of customers.

Action Steps

1. What slogan or philosophy best describes your business and its attitude?

2. Which specific social groups does your business service?

   (*Examples:* certain minorities, professional people, travelers or tourists, a college clientele, church members, politicians, handicapped individuals such as speaking and hearing impaired.)

3. What obvious niche could your small business fill?

4. What service or product could you expand upon (a springboard) to develop a niche market?

5. Will quality be a factor, and if so, how will it set you apart from the competition?

6. How does your niche align with your vision?

Tip: Have a key item that puts you on the cutting edge

Become an Infopreneur

Become a professional information organizer and manager. Create opportunities for yourself by gathering information from customers, friends, relatives and employees. Listen to your own ideas, intuitions and experiences for clues.

Use your resources to position your business:

1. Use your own surveys to discover what consumers don't already have.

2. Review the results of your demographic research.

3. Read trade magazines, newspapers, catalogs, and entrepreneurial information.

4. Attend conferences and tune into the trends.

5. Watch the news.

6. Talk to suppliers.

7. Look around you and notice what noncompetitive businesses are doing and what niches they are creating.

8. Review your business plan for inspiration.

9. You must know your industry and know what people are open to or looking for before they know it.

Action Step

Where could you get vital information on trends and industry news?

Initiate the Four Principal States of Presence

Marketing will let customers know your business exists; positioning will let them know how you are different from your competition; and presence lets customers know your business's individuality. There are four principal states of presence:

Give: Giving encompasses how much we give of ourselves; our encouragement, compassion, support, knowledge and enthusiasm. Many of us get so caught up in our day-to-day circumstances that we forget to give back to others, and to the community. Giving establishes you as a humanitarian, who selflessly gives for the benefit of others. Giving goes beyond the typical donation to a worthy cause, or discounting products and services.

Comfort: People will instinctively measure their comfort level when utilizing your business. Customers notice comfortable furniture, ambiance, lighting, and cleanliness. A careful study of the human comfort zone will aid you in projecting an atmosphere that is conducive to satisfied repeat customers.

Cheer: A Chinese proverb says "A man with an unsmiling face should not open a shop." A new gift shop opened in my neighborhood, so I went in and explored the store for unusual treasures. I was excited about a classy new store in the neighborhood and eagerly greeted the store owner, asking particulars about the store. He answered solemnly, without a smile, and quickly diminished my enthusiasm. After browsing for a few minutes, I left the store without making a purchase. It appeared that he didn't care whether I bought anything or not, so I didn't. A cheerful attitude and a smile from the owner and employees go a long way in making customers feel welcome, comfortable, and in the mood to buy products or services.

Style: What is the manner in which you present yourself or your business? The most profound presence is made when a business is stylish or fashionable. The furniture, floor coverings, paintings, decor and ambiance make a contribution to the overall presence of a business establishment.

One business owner wanted his target market to know that his methods of service were cutting edge, yet his worn-out furnishings and run-down signage gave his business the appearance and feeling of being obsolete, sending a mixed message to the customer. They don't know whether to stay or run the other way. A stylish business presence gives every indication that someone cares, about the customer and about a pleasant shopping experience.

Positioning Summary

Take the following steps to access your hidden strength to position.

1. Choose your position in the marketplace.

2. Dare to be different.

3. Design your own springboard.

4. Write a position statement.

5. Find your own niche.

6. Become an infopreneur.

7. Initiate the four principal states of presence.

When Do I Take These Steps?

Use your positioning strengths directly after you have researched your competition and your target market. Niche marketing is a form of positioning. If you find no niche for your business, then you may want to consider another neighborhood or even another type of business.

7

Defining

Your Sixth Hidden Strength

Imagine that you're giving a heartfelt speech and you breathe easy as the audience enjoys your presentation. Your audience, fellow students in a public speaking course, all prepare a weekly short speech about a personal life experience. Your speech topics cover lessons you've learned, successes you've experienced, or challenges you've endured. Continue to envision yourself confidently standing up and giving the compelling speech in front of the class. Your personal image and your unique message define who you are as a person and as a speaker. Certain audience members will identify with you and your experiences. You have stories to tell and they make up the rich tapestry you call your life. Likewise, every business has a story to tell. Your business has its own image, life, and history. Many customers will identify with its unique image and therefore define themselves by their association with your business. A closer definition means a stronger loyalty.

The defining strength focuses on your ability to create a magnetic definition for your business through its unique image, location, employees, and target market. You'll answer the one main question, "What is my image and how do I project it to consumers?"

Complete the *Action Steps*, benefit by effectively developing your image, and make lasting impressions on your target market.

Your Objective for the Defining Strength

Your objective is to remember times when you defined something to yourself, it became clear and thus you better understood its components. You were then able to effectively use the information and share it with others. You'll now apply the defining process to your business image.

Defining as a Natural Strength

During Halloween we, as children, defined ourselves by our costumes: spooky skeleton, wild cowboy, fearless pirate, or pretty princess. Children define themselves by what grade they're in, their grades, where they go to school, and the neighborhood where they live. Teenagers define themselves by the clothes they wear, the music they listen to, and who they hang out with.

Our car, clothes, and possible college education are three common areas by which adults define themselves. Think about the distinguishing characteristics of these examples. Someone who drives a Mercedes wants comfort, elegance, and prestige. A Porsche owner wants speed, size, and precision handling. Look into your closet and you'll become aware of how you define your appearance. The quality and quantity of items say something about your values and economic situation. Someone who graduated from an Ivy League college will define themselves differently from one who graduated from a community college or a trade school.

～～～～～～～～～～～

Here's an example of someone who clearly defines his image. Years ago, I met David Copperfield, the world's most successful magician. David successfully defined his image as a performer with grace and style. I found it present even in his handshake—when he made my hand disappear (… just a bit of humor). What's significant about David's present smooth style is that, according to a television documentary, he began as a gangly, awkward teenager. Evidently, he set his sights on becoming a polished performer and his graceful gestures on stage hint that he studied movement with a dance choreographer. The second vital thing we can learn from David is that his definition of himself is broad enough to include changing with the times.

At the time David was developing his style, another magician, Doug Henning, came to popularity with his long hair, mustache, and bell bottom trousers. Unfortunately, Doug did not take action to change with the times and he is no longer a popular performer. Instead, David Copperfield always dresses at the height of tasteful fashion. He makes a lasting impression.

Likewise, lasting impressions generally begin with your image: how you present yourself and your business associates.

Impressions are made by how you operate your business on a daily basis. Customer satisfaction is created by your code of ethics, integrity, attitude, friendliness and willingness. Customers become impressed that they are important, appreciated, and valued.

Action Step

List two examples from your past when you used your defining strengths.

Win with Clarity

According to *Webster's New World Dictionary*, "define" means "to set down the boundaries, state the extent and nature, and give distinguishing characteristics." Defining your business's image requires you to be clear and concise. State your distinguishing characteristics and you'll stand out from the crowd.

Be concise, and win in four compelling ways as you ...

1. Design your business's interior and exterior.

2. Write the copy for your marketing materials.

3. Talk about your business to potential customers.

4. Attract customers with your style of business.

Position first, then define

You practiced your investigating and identifying strengths by making inquiries into your competition and targeting specific consumers. You also found your niche and are now able to position your business effectively in your community. The results of that information will provide the basis for creating the image that will best serve you. Your position determines your image.

Determine your position or niche before you establish a lasting image for your business. Because a position or niche has a specific audience, an effective marketer will need to tailor the business's image to that audience's preferences. Narrow your focus to become a magnet for those customers. Here are two examples.

A large department store in your neighborhood offers a variety of products. In one section of the store they offer CDs and DVDs. Due to buying restrictions, policies, and space, the store is limited to current popular titles. They don't carry the classics and used, 'hard to find' merchandise. You consider opening a specialty store that offers that merchandise. You position yourself as the specialist offering those unique products. But before you begin your business, you investigate your competition to ensure that a similar store is not in your area. If there is already one or more such stores, then you must research the demographics and determine if the market is saturated. Or you could choose another type of product and incorporate that into your store.

Let's say, after investigating the competition and researching demographics, you decide that you'd like to open a Country and Western clothing store. There is already one Country and Western store in your community, and they offer a variety of casual jeans, shirts, and dresses. As an alternative resource, you could offer dressier clothes, more boots and hats, a selection of dance instruction DVDs and popular C&W music. You'll write an e-newsletter and blog to establish yourself as the No. 1 resource for the Country and Western scene. Your mailing list will come from customers who purchase products. You've just positioned your business as the Country and Western resource for special occasion attire or C & W nightclub scene specialist.

Defining strengths help you to concentrate on one specific image, as opposed to being scattered. This may or may not have been obvious in the initial phase of developing your vision or business plan. Let's learn more about defining your image.

Action Step

> Does your business name convey the type of business you're in?

Define Your Business Image

As a strong marketer, you'll find four advantages to defining your business's image to yourself, your employees, and the public:

1. Differentiate your business from other businesses.

2. Attract customers who are seeking what you have to offer.

3. Assimilate all the features of your small business into one integrated image.

4. Create a more professional marketing presentation.

Whenever we meet someone for the first time, we immediately respond positively or negatively to that first impression. We usually notice a person's physical characteristics first, such as hair style, facial features, the colors and style of their clothes, jewelry or accessories, and choice of shoes. We also become aware of that individual's posture and demeanor. A person's image is a complete visual package. After the first impression is made, and a personal interaction has begun, we then discover that individual's personality, character, attitude and intelligence. Now, we have a well-rounded idea of who this person is, which helps us decide on further interaction.

A business entity has a visual image very much like a person. Consumers who visit your small business respond to this visual representation you have prepared for them. Consumers either identify with it or they don't. That's why it's important to thoroughly research and identify your target market, so your business image will appeal to them.

In order to effectively express your image to the public, you must be really clear about your image, remembering the direct relationship between your vision, target market, niche, and image.

The type of products or services you sell may well determine your image. A different image and ambiance would be required for a children's store, an exclusive gift shop, a restaurant, a clothing boutique, a dental office, or a sporting goods store. Study your competition, read trade magazines and attend trade shows to find innovative ideas.

Action Step

Your Small or Home-Based Business Image

1. What are some of the outstanding characteristics of your target market, and how can your business successfully align with them?

2. List characteristics of the image your business now has. Do you want this image?

3. List characteristics of the image you want in your future business.

4. Explain the advantages of your current image.

5. Explain the disadvantages of your current image.

6. Describe ways in which your image could be improved upon.

7. Describe the image you would like to project if not happy with the current one, and why?

8. Is your small or home-based business perceived as utilitarian, prestigious or other? What makes it so?

9. When presenting (marketing) your business to the general public in the form of advertising, Internet or other media, you need consumers to get a clear understanding of what your business is as a business entity, and what it has to offer the public. In other words, why are you in business?

Create a Synthesis

A synthesis is created when your business name, your marketing materials, your products and services, and your employees combine to form a complete image.

Does your business name reflect your image? A fancy French restaurant would not refer to themselves as Charlie's Bar and Grill. A full service hair salon and day spa wouldn't call itself Kuts are King, nor would a small town motor lodge call itself the Ritz.

In order to make your whole image much stronger than its parts, be certain that your employees understand the image you want to project. Employees play a major role in expressing your image, and their cooperation and support help create a total look.

Create a unique synthesis by keeping your business image and a complimentary employee dress code in effect. I consulted with an elegant restaurant whose ambiance was that of chandeliers, soft lighting and extensive personal service. The owner stipulated that the dress code was casual elegance, so the employees dressed accordingly. A synthesis was created.

Another definition of your image is the sum total of your employees' experience, strengths, attitude, and desire to serve. You and your employees define your business's image every time you interact with clients in a positive or negative way.

For instance, you would lose credibility if your marketing materials promote your public image as a friendly small-town business, then you hire an impatient or a painfully shy receptionist or team member.

Always look at the whole picture, just as you look at a painting. Does the frame compliment the painting, or does it distract from the feeling or mood that the artist wants to project?

Action Step

How will you create a synthesis for your business image?

Building your image is a process. It will require many hours of your time, but intensive planning in the beginning stages of your small/home-based business career will influence your success for years to come.

Establish Your Image Package

Your image package consists of a public and personal image. Both of your images, public and personal, need to be aligned and convey a single message to the clients as to how they will be treated in your business.

Your personal image

Your Personal Image is based on an "intuitive feeling" and is enhanced by the ambiance of your establishment, and the friendliness and professionalism of you and your employees. People notice attitude, caring, and integrity.

Your public image

Your Public Image creates a lasting impression based on your location, exterior/interior decor, business policies, cleanliness, prices and reputation. Many home-based business owners receive clients in their home office or residence, and in that case, a positive or negative image could have an impact on the consumers' purchasing decision.

If you have a retail location, consumers will have already formed expectations according to word-of-mouth information, previous advertising or by just looking through your door or windows.

Whenever I'm shopping for clothes, shoes or anything, I'll pass in front of a store, glance in, and become aware of the image the store projects. In a moment's time, the decision is made to either go in and look around for what I need or move on to another store. You have only a few seconds of the consumer's attention to make an impression, so it's important to make the right one.

Your marketing materials and your media package are two important parts of your public image. Make them distinctive, and people will remember you.

Marketing materials

The visual appearance of your marketing materials: business card, brochure, and letterhead, quickly send a message to the reader about your image. What comes across is quality and polish. Visual design elements will establish a strong voice for you through color or lack of color, paper quality, typography, and use of photos or illustrations. More information on this topic is given in the Energizing Strength.

Media package

Your media package consists of Internet elements (website, downloadable audio/video, downloadable PDF files) radio, television, newspapers, newsletters, flyers, and more. You are distinctively associated with the media you choose. Expensive billboard, television, radio and magazine advertising will give you a specific public image. Coca Cola, Microsoft, and Mitsubishi would use these media. Handing out flyers on the street, nailing posters onto telephone poles, and putting coupons on windshields will give you an entirely different image. A neighborhood saloon or local psychic would use these media to reach consumers. Flyers can be just as effective as a more expensive medium for many businesses. The important thing to consider is what media reaches your target market and effectively expresses your image. More information is given on this topic in strength 7—Strategizing.

In recent years, your image needs to be broadcast via social media marketing. Now Karmen Reed alerts you to the advantages of being appropriately active with Facebook and Twitter.

Becoming the Conversation on Twitter and Facebook

Karmen Reed

The two social networking tools everyone is talking about, Twitter and Facebook, are not just social networking tools, they are "conversation tools" of the new millennium. How they change the way businesses go to market today and communicate to their prospects is what makes them worth a mention.

Think about this for a second: how do your customers find information about products and services today? Are they reading magazine ads, watching TV commercials, or are they searching the Internet and asking their friends for opinions and about their experience? The new way of finding the answers to their questions is through Internet search engines like Google and Yahoo, or on social networks. So, will you be there to answer those questions?

The new way of online marketing called Social Media Marketing, formed a new way of building relationships by encouraging a two-way dialog. Social Media tools provide businesses with the unique opportunity to have a direct transparent relationship with their customers by having an open conversation.

Having a conversation means: first listen, then talk. Learn what your community needs and then share good content, provide value, and offer a solution, wherever and whenever you can.

How to become a conversation on Twitter

Social Media tools like Twitter, allowed for a new way of spreading your message in a relaxed, conversational way. Twitter is becoming one of the most powerful business communication tools on the Internet, used for networking, word of mouth marketing, promotion, traffic generating, learning, and teaching.

With Twitter, you will have the opportunity for fast and direct conversations with your customers, and will be able to reach a new base of prospects. You connect with people by "following" them, and engaging in conversations.

Why is Twitter an important online place to engage with your community? Twitter is a social networking tool that uses 140 characters or less for online communication. Messages you post on Twitter are called "tweets". Tweets are actually nothing more than a mini blog posts. And this is great news, because all blog posts are indexed by Google search engines, and considered "content". This means that your tweets are also indexed by Google and Yahoo and Bing search engines, and will be showing up in the search results. Word of advice: do not tweet anything you would not want to see on the front page of a newspaper.

Remember, even though it's such a simple concept, Twitter is one of the most powerful connection and conversation tools on the Internet today. Do not underestimate the power of words and the speed information spreads these days.

"What you say on Twitter may be viewed around the world instantly. You are what you tweet."—Twitter Tip

Top 10 reasons you should use Twitter for business:

1. Build relationships with transparency and trust.

2. Drive traffic to your blog or website.

3. Market your brand and your business.

4. Share your expertise (answer/ask questions).

5. Learn from experts in your field and expose yourself to new ideas.

6. Connect with conferences by watching the real time chatter thread.

7. Learn more about social media marketing.

8. Stay current with the latest news and industry trends.

9. Improve your search engine rankings.

10.It's free!

How do people use Twitter? To share news and ideas, ask for opinions and advice, collaborate, research products and services, and build relationships with people they wouldn't have an opportunity to meet in any other way.

This is how you create brand awareness and visibility on Twitter:

- Learn to use Twitter properly and regularly.

- Be strategic with your messages.

- Connect with customers and prospects.

- Develop business opportunities and partnerships.

- Become a resource of valuable information.

- Be conversational.

People really appreciate openness and honesty, and that will make people more personally connect with you and your brand. Here are some tips on how to successfully engage with your followers:

- Embrace transparency, tweet regularly, and stay positive.

- Do not make your tweets "me focused".

- Make somebody smile: share a funny story.

- Inspire by sharing an inspirational quote.

- Enrich by sharing a link to a good article.

At first Twitter may be a confusing tool in which you are limited to only 140 characters or less per tweet. How can this restricted communication help your company? It teaches you how to condense your thoughts and compress your words in order to create a meaningful, strategic message.

Is it worth the time and money to invest to get familiar with Twitter and to start tweeting like a pro, so you can grow the visibility for your business, show expertise and become the conversation everyone craves? You betcha!

How is Facebook relevant to your business?

Facebook is one of the most popular and vastly used social networking tools today. Facebook is not just for college students anymore. It may have started that way, but many joined after college to keep in touch, exchange photos with family and create conversation online. Why does this matter to you or your business? Why do you need to establish your presence and create a community on Facebook?

Take a look at some valuable facts about Facebook:

- Facebook has more than 500 million users world wide

- It is the number 2 most trafficked website on the Internet

- Most rapidly growing demographic on Facebook are adults ages 35 and over

- An average time a user spends on Facebook is over 30 minutes per session

Wouldn't you say that some of your market lives here? Mature audience, with college degree, with time to network, and money to spend. As Facebook recently evolved into this new marketing tool everyone is talking about, businesses and professionals realize they need to be a part of it.

You can use Facebook to gain new clients, stay in touch with current ones, promote new products and services, share the news about your industry, and establish yourself as an expert.

Be on Facebook for these 5 reasons:

1. Reach: large user base

2. Search Engine Indexing for Pages: get found by people who are searching for your services or product

3. Users are spending significant time on Facebook: connect and engage with your customers and prospects

4. User demographics are working professionals eager to network

5. Facebook continues to grow fast and steady: take advantage of this

On Facebook, profiles are for people, and pages are designed for businesses. Pages are by default public and will start ranking in public search results (i.e. Google search). Profiles have permission based "friends", while all users can become "fans" without asking for permission. There is a limit of 5000 "friends", while the number of "fans" is unlimited. Pages are similar to Profiles, except that they are public and visible to all Facebook users, as well as to general public.

To begin creating your presence on Facebook, create your Profile first and start making connections and sharing information. Having your personal Profile on Facebook allows you to fully engage and leverage Facebook features for Pages.

Facebook offers many tools you can use to market your business, and in order to be successful, you must have an understanding of these tools and learn how to use them to your best benefits.

The buzz about Facebook, Twitter, and other social media platforms is getting so loud you cannot ignore it any longer! You hear about it on the news, from your friends, colleagues, clients, and vendors. Although you may feel too busy, overwhelmed, discouraged, or frustrated, do not be the one to miss the opportunity to grow your business because you lack the knowledge and understanding of social media marketing. In today's world of online business presence, using social media tools is necessary for every company. Take time to learn it and embrace it.

Karmen Reed founded Kickoff Topic, a social marketing and online visibility solutions company that focuses on maximizing the power of social media for professionals and small businesses and creating solid online presence and visibility. She also recently cofounded Supreme Social Media, a social media product and training company. Karmen's product marketing expertise in electronics industry where she also coordinated relationships between vendors and sales teams, combined with more than a decade of experience in the publishing industry managing projects from editorial to post-production marketing, position her to help clients attain their goals from concept to market. Karmen is a passionate advocate for the power of social media relationships in building brand currency online and was named by Forbes.com as one of the top 20 women for entrepreneurs to follow on Twitter.

Facebook profile: facebook.com/karmenreed
Facebook page: facebook.com/kickofftopic
Twitter: twitter.com/kickofftopic
Linkedin: linkedin.com/in/karmenreed
Website: kickofftopic.com
Email: Karmen@kickofftopic.com

Karmen has revealed the process of getting started with social media marketing. Now, we'll discuss the value of integrating images.

Integrating the two images

The public easily defines your business when both your public and personal image are integrated. I consulted for a business whose public image was poor, but the personal image, quality of work and professionalism were above average. This business constantly stayed in a slow growth stage. The owner was resistant to upgrading the business's image and customers were not attracted to a poor public image. The result is that customers eventually become aware of the personal image, but the business never really booms due to the lack of integration.

Action Steps

1. What is your 'personal image'?

2. How can your image be improved upon?

Products and Services

1. How do your services and products align with your image?

2. List (new) services or products you would like to offer and why.

Your Business Location

1. Describe your location and how it does or doesn't support your image.

2. How does your location place you at an advantage—a disadvan tage?

3. What will make your location more desirable?

Adopt the 'Mirror' Concept

How do you want the public to perceive your small business? Your answer to this question may be the key to your success. Do you want your small or home-based business to be considered professional, powerful, classy, respected, trendy, innovative, friendly or low key? Whatever it is, you need to define it to yourself first, then use the mirror concept and take the steps to reflect that image into your decor and promotional materials. Remember that your image should be a realistic reflection of what you can do for the client. Then you will attract the consumers who identify with your image.

People tend to gravitate towards service businesses which:

1. Appeal to your customers' comfort zone. Offer the creature comforts that would attract your target

market. Your market research will guide you in the right direction.

2. Offer prices your customers can justify and are willing to pay.

3. Make your customers feel good about themselves.

4. Provide innovative products and services.

Action Step

Define Your Uniqueness

1. What special needs does your business meet: ethnic services, foreign language strengths, services for handicapped customers, a children's area, others? How does this contribute to your image?

2. What can you do or offer that will make your business unique?

3. What is outstanding about your employees that aligns with your image: special training, foreign language strengths, award-winning employees, others?

Define Customer Benefits

1. How will your customers benefit psychologically

   (feel relaxed, enjoy quick service, feel pampered, others)?

2. What are your specialties or areas of expertise, and how will your customers benefit from this?

The Small or Home-Based Business 'Difference'

1. Describe the unique features that distinguish your business from others. Include attributes such as employees' experience, variety of services and techniques, location, and management abilities.

2. What specialty products do you use or sell that other businesses don't carry? Specify the types of customers who purchase those products.

3. What services or products do you offer in your area that are not available anywhere else?

4. Which specific problems does your professional team solve that neighboring businesses do not?

5. What unique promotions does your business offer that no one else does?

Employees Who Make a Difference

Give three examples of what your employees can do to make a difference and establish customer satisfaction.

Define Your Spirit

Determine the spirit in which you will participate in the competitive marketplace. Will you express your spirit in a positive, inspirational, or enthusiastic manner? Or will it be a critical and derogatory expression? Will you be generous to the public, or will you think only of yourself? Define your spirit first to yourself, then to your community through your media messages.

I remember when Herb Caen, the beloved San Francisco Chronicle columnist, passed away. A street in San Francisco was named in his honor. There was also a huge memorial service for him in which thousands of people participated. Many of them turned out to visit his regular social spots and to celebrate his life in the same spirit by which he lived. We are remembered for the spirit, character, and integrity we bring to the world.

Where Do You Get Your Inspiration?

Tom Marcoux

Until now, I have never written about this personal detail in any book.

Do I have your attention?

My close friends have seen that I have a couple of items that have the "S" shield of Superman. No, I don't wear t-shirts with a comic book character on them. It is the "S" shield that inspires me. To me it means: hope, compassion, nurturing, strength—oh—and flying.

Your marketing needs to inspire you! When you hand out your business card, there must be no hesitation. We need you to make your marketing materials into things that fill you with good energy.

For example, more than ten years ago, I wrote a book and a dear friend suggested I call it *Communicate to Win*. I felt okay about the title.

Later, I renamed the book *Be Heard and Be Trusted* (now in its third edition). Now that inspires me! I help people be heard. And

I support people expressing how positive and trustworthy they are. (You can see the helping and nurturing aspect as mentioned with the "S" shield above.)

So ... Where do you get your inspiration?

Make a Lasting Impression

Similar to our unique fingerprints, anything we touch is embedded with our own individual impressions. Whether we are touching objects or lives, we do it in our own unique way. You would handle a priceless object with great care, making certain not to harm or damage it in any way. People are just as fragile as a priceless object, if not more so. Lasting impressions are created by exercising care in the way we influence another individual's life. Make a real impression by communicating in a clear, concise way and with authenticity. Of equal importance is listening to the needs of others. People have a real need to be heard. Whatever you do or say becomes something they will distinctly remember. Since we all want our businesses to be remembered, let's take into account that impressions are only valid when they're clear.

Action Step

> Review the previous Action Steps to make certain that your image is clearly defined.

Defining Summary

Take the following steps to access your hidden strength to define.

1. Position first, then define.

2. Define your business image.

3. Create a synthesis.

4. Establish your image package.

5. Adopt the 'Mirror Concept'.

6. Define your spirit.

7. Make a lasting impression.

When Do I Take These Steps?

The best time to define your image is after you have positioned your business or found a niche. That particular information, based on your competition and target market, will determine the image, character and ambiance of your business. Your small business image should reflect the tastes of your target market.

If you choose against niche marketing or find that the concept will not work for you, then you need to find an alternative solution. For optional choices, you could define your image by the characteristics of your target market, the image of the area where your business is located, or whatever appeals to you personally.

Walk around the area where you plan to open a business, and talk with merchants. Notice what type of people are around during the day or hours when you will be open for business.

8

Strategizing

Your Seventh Hidden Strength

You stand to address your advisors and team members gathered around a long, dark table in a large prestigious, conference room. "About our business—it's time," you say, "to put our heads together and devise strategies to get control of that ball. We know our competitors' strengths and weaknesses, and we know our own. So let's find a winning strategy." Each member of the group has all the information from the *Action Steps*. For the next two hours or more, you and your advisors roll up your sleeves, review the facts and choose strategies based on your primary objective.

Strength 7—Strategizing focuses on planning and directing winning strategies to use in your marketing campaign this year. You'll answer a significant question, "What strategies can I use to attract my target market?"

On completing the *Action Steps*, you feel good about your efforts. Winning strategies are created with intelligence, insight and determination.

Example from a Top Marketer

Ms. Marty Rodriguez, repeatedly the #1 Real Estate Agent in the world for Century 21, uses a strategy to convert prospects to clients. She says, "We offer a process for people trying to reduce their taxes. It's a free service, that some [competitors] don't bother with."

Your Objective for the Strategizing Strength

Your objective is to remember the many times in your life when you strategized to get something of prime importance. You'll remember how much you wanted it and the necessary effort involved. You'll take that information and passion, and use it to realize a winning strategy for your business.

Strategizing as a Natural Strength

Every day, we strategize on some level. Planning and directing form a crucial part of our lives, whether it's planning and directing our dinner menus and grocery shopping for the week, or scheduling weekly appointments. Babies know how to strategize and do something to get what they want. They cry, knowing they will be fed or get their diaper changed. When they coo, chatter and smile, they get more attention. Children strategize with each other and their parents. They strategize about playtime, household chores, and who gets to watch a certain television program. It's natural for us to strategize by planning and directing our day, an evening on the town, our education, our career, our investments, and our vacation time. When I was in college, I strategized my activities by planning and directing my classes, work schedule, social dates, relaxation and study time. There's really no end to the amount of strategizing we do on a daily, weekly and yearly basis.

Strategizing benefits us in several ways by saving time, getting things done quickly and easily, and giving direction to our lives. Strategies help us to influence each other and the mass population. It's done everyday on the Internet, television and radio—and in books, magazines, newspapers. A strong marketer is more effective and accomplishes more by applying strategizing strengths to a marketing campaign.

Action Step

> List two examples from your past when you used your strategizing strengths.

Market Strategies

Remember that marketing is not an exact science. Your financial resources, market research, human resources, and size of your business are variables that will influence how much energy you can put towards marketing your business.

In this section you'll learn how to create specific marketing strategies and how they can improve your position in the marketplace. You need to go into action and pull together a marketing strategy. Now, Noah St. John discusses the essential ingredients for real success.

The Real Secret of Success

Noah St. John

You sure you're ready for this?

OK, here goes …

The Law of Attraction (LOA) does not work the way they told us in [the video] "The Secret". The irony is, it ALMOST does.

But the difference between "almost works" and "actually works" is the difference between poverty and riches, happiness and stress, getting what you want and not getting what you want.

Here's what they told us:

"When you think about something, you get it."

Okay, that is sort of true.

For example, I teach people to come from "enough" instead of "not enough". And one way—ONE way—to do that is to think about coming from "more than enough."

But here's where they missed it …

Merely THINKING about "enough" or "abundance" or "prosperity" will NOT make it manifest.

For example, what if I had just THOUGHT about writing you this article. Would you be reading it right now?

Nope. I had to take ACTION and actually write the thing and send it to you.

Now, here's another thing I feel I must tell you … I hang around really rich people all the time. Not one of them sits around thinking about "abundance".

What they do is take ACTION. Even if they don't know exactly what they're doing, they're following a formula to live a rich life. I really feel bad that so many people took LOA so literally. That you thought there was an "abundance button" you could push to magically make money appear. It simply does not work that way.

I've said it before and I'll say it again. I want you to write this in big letters and put it where you'll see it every morning when you wake up:

➠ ONE POSITIVE ACTION BEATS 1,000 POSITIVE THOUGHTS.

Money, abundance, prosperity, riches—all of these follow the same formula they always have. There is a formula for living a rich life.

The sad thing is that so many nice people have been shut out of being shown how this formula really operates. In my book *The Secret Code of Success* I reveal a method I invented called AFFORMATIONS.

Rather than "affirmations"—which are statements we don't believe—Afformations are empowering questions that immediately change your thought patterns. As I mention in my book: "I realized that we first need to form questions that would change the thought-seeds we were sowing, which would change our lives."

Noah St. John is the author of six books including *The Secret Code of Success* and *The Book of Afformations*. Founder of SuccessClinic.com, he's been in over 1,000 media outlets including CNN, ABC, NBC, Fox and *The Washington Post*. Since 1997, Noah has taught thousands of people in over

50 countries the simple steps to enjoy more wealth faster, easier and with less effort.

Get a free sample of his books at NoahStJohn.com

Now, encouraged by Noah to take action, we'll pause to put his idea of "Afformations" into practice. My co-author Tom Marcoux will guide us.

Create the Energy to Manifest What You Want

Tom Marcoux

Anything you want can be accessed beyond a simple affirmation. If you say, "I want to be rich"—or if you state the affirmation "I am rich"—part of you automatically can respond: 'You're not rich.' That causes trouble. Two parts of you are fighting each other. Instead, follow Noah St. John's suggestion: ask a question. Noah calls empowering questions "afformations."

Ask yourself, 'Why am I rich?' What I do then is respond: "Because I have great team members that help me be more productive"; "Because I get from Higher Power, through intuition, good ideas to expand how I serve;" "Because I am serving people benevolently, the Universe helps me increase prosperity for my customers, team members, me, and my family."

Now, write down something you want:

____ .

Turn it now into an "afformation":

Why am I ____ ?

Now add your "Because" statements.

Because ____ .

Because ____ .

Ask yourself a question and truly engage your heart, soul and mind. Find your true answer—your 'because' statement. Then discover a vital source of personal energy.

Our next step is to delve into your process for creating a marketing strategy.

Three benefits of a marketing strategy are:

1. To unify your business's public and personal image with your marketing materials, resulting in a balanced and magnetic public appeal.

2. To link a business with its target market.

3. To become a strong presence in your community and within your particular industry. It positions your business in front of your competition.

Basic human motivators

Before you begin your strategic efforts, you need to determine what motivates consumers to buy. Knowing this information gives a strong marketer a better chance of appealing to his ultimate needs. My co-author Tom Marcoux will explore this topic.

What Do People Really Want? And How Can You Get 'Em to Buy?

Tom Marcoux

What is the "holy grail" that marketers, for hundreds of years, have been reaching for? It's the real reason people buy.

Many theories of people's true desires have arisen. Here are a few:

Psychologists at the University of Rochester conducted research about what keeps video game players playing. The researchers discovered that video games provided opportunities for achievement, freedom, and even a connection to other players. Lead investigator in four studies, psychologist Richard M. Ryan said, "It's our contention that the psychological 'pull' of games is largely due to their capacity to engender feelings of autonomy, competence, and relatedness."

Blair Warren, known as a "master influencer" wrote: "People will do anything for those who encourage their dreams, justify their failures, allay their fears, confirm their suspicions, and help them throw rocks at their enemies."

Author Joe Vitale wrote: "Our goal as marketing and business people isn't to tell people what's wrong with them or to remind them of their pain, but to help them imagine and then experience the pleasure they long to have. It's noble, yes, and it works. Love moves everyone. Love is the great motivator. Love is the great pleasure trigger."

I'll add a few of my own. People want:

- To stop pain

- To feel good about themselves

- To feel appreciated and admired by others

- To feel powerful (some say that money and sex are part of this desire)

- To banish feelings of powerlessness

- To feel a spiritual connection

- To make a contribution—and to help others

- To be loved and to express their love—and feel connected to others

I invite you to find how your product or service fulfills the desires that I have noted above. Here's a secret: find something good, kind and wholesome that you help people with. This is the secret method to eliminate any hesitation you might have about marketing or selling. As I say with my clients: "Become a coach to action. A coach helps people do what they truly desire to do." Touch people's hearts and minds, and you'll get 'em to buy.

Now, that we have covered basic human motivators, we can look at the opposite. Lack of energy can feel de-motivating. Tom now shares with us methods to gain energy.

Gain Energy so You Do the Rough Parts of Marketing

Tom Marcoux

Imagine that you need to write some material ("copy") for a new website—and you're really not in the mood!

Here are three methods to get going:

Call a friend

You can say: "Is this an okay time to talk? (she says 'yes') I've got to write something for a website. Can I throw a couple of ideas around for 2 minutes with you?" Then you start talking about the material. You can take notes, or some of my clients prefer to record their side of the conversation.

Draw "balloons"

Draw five balloons and then place ideas in them. You will draw lines to connect them later. For example, you could write: "how to overcome procrastination"; "pain"; "help"; "solution"; and "relief." You can also number the ideas in order of importance. You might come up with a headline like: "Would you like to stop procrastination from causing you pain?"

Ask, "Where is the joy?"

So many times we get caught up in the pain of the moment—or avoiding imagined pain. Instead, target what good feelings your effective marketing efforts will create. For example, some of us enjoy getting a "thank you" email for a job well done. Or an author may relish signing books and shaking hands with happy workshop attendees. Ask yourself: "Where is the joy?" And then you may discover a spark of renewed energy.

Marketing is accomplished by placing one foot in front of the other. Just take the next step.

Determine Your Approach

Determine your own unique approach in order to unify your image, link up with your target market, and become a strong presence in the marketplace. Let's look at the word approach, which means to 'deal with' a situation or 'come closer to' an object or situation. A strong marketer approaches his/her marketing strategy with an acute awareness of many factors, such as:

1. Your vision or primary objective.

2. What your competition is promoting.

3. What consumers are buying.

4. The overall economic situation.

5. Your own economic situation or budget.

6. What's new in your industry.

7. Your position or niche.

8. Your timeline.

9. An eye to the future in terms of trends and upcoming changes.

10. Your comfort or aversion to taking appropriate risks.

Understand these factors and then determine your approach. There is no specific strategy that will work for every business. Look at the details and then the whole picture.

Do Your Homework

In a previous strength, I talked about coaches who desire a winning play, so they study their competitors' weaknesses and focus on the strengths of their own team. Strategies work best if you have done your homework. Develop the other necessary strengths: envisioning, transforming, investigating, identifying, positioning and defining. They lay the groundwork for your approach. If any area was weak or not thought through, then you have a hole in which the entire campaign could slip through and be lost.

For example, you use a plan to build a home, go on a vacation or start a business. What's called for is either a blueprint, a road map or a strategy. All of these are critical to accomplishing your goals and objectives. Without these directional tools, strategies or plans of action, your home might not be as functional as you need it to be, you may drive many miles farther than the map estimated, and your business may not evolve the way you visualized in your mind. Your strategy is a detailed visual representation of your successfully organized venture, while still allowing room for changes and growth. Doing your homework helps you to be prepared and move forward with courage and confidence.

Corporations spend millions of dollars to create public awareness of their name or product. A small business owner can spend much less to make a gigantic impression in their small community.

Pull It Together

Now, let's pull together everything that applies to your vision to accomplish your objective: get control of the ball (marketplace), increase name recognition, get control over the evolution of your business, and establish a magnetic public image.

Remember your narrow focus, niche, and position. Your marketing strategy increases your name recognition. Every strategy that you implement needs to be in alignment with your vision.

Set the Direction

Public awareness of your business rests on the owner or manager's marketing abilities. You create a particular dynamic for your business, and you consciously or unconsciously set the direction of its future prosperity. You made a substantial investment in the start-up phase, and supporting it in the media with clear strategies increases the worth of that investment.

You may not have to do more marketing, but if your client base is not increasing and your profits are not growing, then you may have to do "better" marketing than before by doing it differently. When the specifics (target market, competition, position, image, benefits) are more accurate, then your direction becomes clear.

Make a Balanced Decision

A strong marketer who is a great strategizer knows when to make a critical decision. He or she uses a balance of four powerful factors: intuition, past experience, the right timing, and reliable research.

Sometimes, the best strategy or approach is to move quickly: into certain markets, take on a new product or service, establish multiple locations, or broaden your territory. Other times it's best to do nothing. Use a balance of these four factors to make powerful decisions.

Action Step

1. Which new products or services could your small or home-based business be the first to provide?

2. What new products could you package together?

3. What unique promotion could you develop around those products?

4. What unique approach would put your business in first place?

Begin by implementing your market strategies as a consciously directed effort, rather than as a hit-or-miss operation. Implement a strategic plan in the present, so the future will be more prosperous. If you are just starting out in business, you may be spending as much as 25-50% of your time designing and implementing promotions. You will spend slightly less time once your business starts gaining momentum.

Create a Sense of Expectancy

A strategy includes any marketing effort done more than once. Base your strategies on the relationship of three factors: position, niche and communication messages. Everything you do in your marketing campaign must attract the consumer, appeal to the person's sense of necessity, and create a sense of expectancy.

Many small business marketing campaigns are set up around events on the yearly calendar; consumers expect these social events to happen and look forward to the experience. It's your role as a community business owner and participant to help create the excitement, the benefits, the atmosphere, and the whole whirlwind hoopla around these events. The popularity of those events attract public attention, which in turn attracts the public to what you have to sell. Consumers are conditioned to look for new products and services at certain times of the year and have a sense of expectancy.

For instance, the motion picture industry generally releases their blockbuster movies during the summer and around the Holiday Season. Hollywood releases the movie most likely to win awards just before votes are cast for the Academy Awards. Their strategy is that Academy voters are more likely to remember the qualities and merits of the prospective movie at that time of the year, as opposed to it being released earlier in the year, when it is likely to be forgotten or overlooked. The big media blitz draws thousands of moviegoers to the cinema each weekend. Film makers and theater owners reap huge profits during these peak times. They create a sense of expectancy.

Action Step

How will you create a sense of expectancy?

Slice the Pie

Use my Slice the Pie strategy to defer risk. Instead of having one whole pie, slice it into several pieces to serve and attract customers. Divide your marketing efforts into pieces such as: relationship marketing, network marketing, niche marketing, promotions, public relations, advertising, and online marketing. The size of each slice is determined by how effectively it reaches your target audience and fulfills your objective.

Action Step

How will you slice your pie and defer risk?

Get Ahead of Your Competition

For your marketing campaign to be effective, you'll develop methods for getting ahead of the competition. You know who your competitors are and what they're doing. This gives you the option to do something different, do it well, and clearly get that across to the people who buy your product or service.

Review

Review the reasons why you went into business in the first place. What did you envision you could do better, faster, or less expensively than others who were currently doing it? Look back over your business plan to get ideas. It also helps to stay abreast of trends in your field and current technology.

Campaign

Keep campaigning for your business. Remember that to be consistent, you must advertise often and use the media that attracts your target market. One or two random advertisements won't do it, because just getting by is not the goal, the objective or the way to profitability.

Communicate

Marketing fulfills consumer needs by communicating information pertaining to those needs. Organize a campaign and use marketing strategies, and you're doing a service for yourself and your community. You provide a particular service or product to consumers; let them know about it through your marketing strategies and distribution methods, and they in turn pay you for your services. As you are more on target with your strategies, you attract more customers, and thus more profits.

Action Step

1. What were your reasons for starting a business?

2. How will you communicate with consumers?

Choose from Sixteen Strategies for Better Marketing

Choose either message or position strategies for your marketing campaign. A message strategy uses your media communication messages to reach consumers. A position strategy is based on how your business is positioned in your community, your industry or the general marketplace.

Network Your Way to Success

Build a network of allies who can open doors and help access resources. I know of one small business owner who wanted to add a day spa to his current location and enlisted the help and finances of loyal customers to achieve his objective.

Action Step

Who will you include in your network of allies?

Make a BIG Deal out of Seasons, Holidays, & Events

A large part of the population loves to attend stimulating social events. Take advantage of these opportunities to increase your business. Notice how large corporations sponsor events. Specialty Brands, a former San Francisco-based manufacturer of popular spices, seasonings and specialty foods, sponsored a National Cooking event in Northern California. The company brought in famous chefs for a cook-off. The company received coverage in a popular gourmet foods magazine.

A small business may not be able to sponsor a "national event," but it can create an event on a smaller scale. You can still make huge profits and gain extensive exposure. Enlist public relations and a media campaign to attract consumers' attention. Develop themes and make holidays, seasons and events a fun experience for people in your community. You must narrow down the choices and make your decisions regarding promotions. Choose the promotions that are 1) the most important, 2) most profitable and 3) most logical.

Review your primary and secondary objectives for the year, then plan enough promotions to attract the customers and sales to attain those objectives.

Action Step

> Which seasons, holidays, social events or themes would you be willing to promote in a BIG way?

Diversify

Any good financial investment counselor will tell you to diversify your investments. When you spread your money around, your risk is less. It's safer to use a variety of media and marketing techniques than to put all your eggs in one basket. If one promotion or advertisement doesn't bring in the results you expected, then you still have several others working for you. Your overall performance is better when you diversify your investment marketing.

1. **Test your advertisements.** Diversify by testing the marketplace. Use different wording and images in various advertisements to find which one attracts the most responses. Include a password or number that the customer must use to get a discount so you know which ad was effective.

2. **Use a combination of media.** When choosing a marketing strategy, be sure to spend a variable amount of money and effort on many categories. A variety of marketing approaches will prevent the public from becoming bored with the same old promotions.

To best attract your target market, use a combination of media: perhaps local newspapers and radio, or a large yellow pages advertisement and direct mail. Use a combination of flyers, the Internet, and school newspapers to reach students at a nearby college. Flyers and posters at a Senior Citizen Center can attract the older group.

Your fax machine or e-mail is a good way to quickly reach a specific client list. It's best to get permission from the recipient before you send a broadcast fax or e-mail.

Test your efforts by using a variety of media for various promotions to find which one best attracts your target market. Remember to include key words on your website so searchers will find your business.

3. Seek interesting promotions. Seek out new and innovative ways to catch the customer's eye and curiosity. Remember to coordinate all activities so they don't conflict.

Make time to read many different types of literature, visit your local library and network with other business people. Engage yourself completely in what you can do to make your business more prosperous.

Action Step

1. List three ways to diversify your marketing campaign.

2. How will your marketing strategies enable you to succeed?

3. What are some of the areas that require special attention?

Choose Your Opportunities

A strong marketer will choose products and services that have the best opportunity for profit. Secondly, focus on market areas which hold the most potential for development. Remember customers who are merely "bargain hunters" often do not demonstrate loyalty. They will jump from vendor to vendor in search of the best discount. However, your customers who buy high-ticket items and value good service will likely return to your business again and again.

Seek promising opportunities:

1. Find a brand new product from your suppliers.

2. Find an imported line that is exclusive to you (Tread carefully about the process of importing products. Studying appropriate resources and learning how to negotiate and verify the actions of other companies are necessary.)

3. Develop and promote a specific product for your target market.

4. Create a private label line.

5. Sell on clearance any overstocked products or merchandise.

One client of mine, Jennifer, wanted her own skin care and cosmetics business. She purchased the necessary products and equipment, trained her employees and launched a small campaign. A few customers enjoyed the service, but not enough to warrant the effort. She spent good money after bad, then eventually gave up on the idea. She finally realized that her small town was not sophisticated enough to supply a profit for skin care services. She was able to absorb her losses and learn a valuable lesson.

In hindsight, she could have done a survey first, received opinions from employees on the idea or networked with other small business owners. It's great to add new services, but do some research first to make sure there is a demand.

Action Step

> Which of your services and products have the most potential for profit? Describe how you know this to be true.

Solidify Team Spirit

Promotion is critical, but promotion alone won't make your business prosperous or successful (in the way you define it). Create balance in your business climate by energizing your human resources. Choose well-educated, talented and compassionate employees who are motivated and willing to go the extra mile to please customers. They must also be team members and work well together.

All promotions will directly affect your employees, so it is critical to get their comments and their support. Delegate certain tasks, thereby stimulating a sense of inclusion. Include them in the decision making process by letting them help you brainstorm for ideas. Support their efforts by using all valuable and applicable suggestions. Give an award or a bonus for the most profitable, innovative, or valuable ideas.

Here's the clincher: explain the benefits to all employees, so they become motivated by the possibility of additional clients, more profits, more commissions and other advantages. Confirm that they "got the message" by asking for feedback. When employees verbalize your explanation, it feels clearer to them.

Action Step

How will you solidify your team's spirit?

Use Creativity to Your Advantage

Mark Henricks wrote, "Creative thinking is all about putting things together in unexpected ways. The obstacles to creativity include experience, success, rigidity and conformity. To be creative, you may have to ignore what you know, what has worked in the past, what feels comfortable, and what everybody else is doing." He says that most creativity tools and techniques are all about breaking rules.

Action Step

1. How will you be creative by breaking from the past, and "break the rules"? (Be sure to abide by all appropriate laws.)

2. Does your small business (or you) have an interesting history or a fascinating story to tell? Write it. (For example, perhaps you are from a foreign country, and are now realizing a dream come true, or your family

has a history of business owners, or your location is a historic landmark. Maybe you personally furnished your business with heirloom antiques. Any interesting story will add zest to your campaign and give it individuality.)

Make a Splash, and Follow with Ripples

Make your first campaign grand enough for people to really notice you, then continually follow up in a smaller way. This is a better strategy than to periodically place small advertisements where they won't make an impression. Remember that repetition aids retention. Successful advertisements and promotions should be repeated, repeated, repeated.

Action Step

How will you devise a splashing strategy for your business?

Build a Professional Reputation

Give clients great things to say about you and your business to build a great reputation. A professional reputation is not built overnight, but over a period of time with effort, patience and perseverance.

Build your reputation on two factors: quality and integrity. Express your assurance of quality and integrity through your marketing materials. Take the time to develop a fact sheet on your company history, your philosophy, slogan and mission statement. Enhance your professional credibility by adding this information along with testimonials.

Get testimonials by asking for them. Whenever a client expresses their joy with you, your employees, or your products and services, take the initiative and ask if they would be supportive of your efforts. Ask them if you can type up a draft of their comments and have them approve it. Ask for permission to use their name. This is especially helpful when the client is a high-profile person in your community or industry. Let them know that you plan to use their personal recommendation in your brochures, newsletters, and advertisements. Also mention how their name, business and website will be promoted in your materials: a win-win situation.

When I practiced hypnotherapy, a satisfied client wrote me a beautiful note commending me on how I helped to create feelings of peace in her life. I used her supportive testimonial in my brochure. It gives readers a sense that you are effective in your occupation. It's all part of building your professional reputation.

Use testimonials as supporting material in your press releases, newspaper articles, brochures and other information about you and your business.

Action Steps

1. What measures will you take to build a professional reputation? List three or four.

2. Which high-profile clients can you ask for referrals?

Choose your Target Market Carefully

When choosing your target market, be single-minded; don't dilute your efforts by going in too many directions. Choose one target market, but no more than two. Direct different promotions towards particular groups, if you absolutely must target more than one market. Note which promotions work with different groups. Evaluate your successes afterward in your income and growth figures.

Action Step

> Who is your target market and why?

Be Focused

Keep your business, its image and your advertising all on the same wavelength. Be focused. Don't try to be all things to all people.

Action Step

> Write two things you can do to make your marketing materials more focused.

Emphasize the Benefits

Emphasize the benefits in your communication messages. Make a meaningful promise to the consumer. The promise is a summary statement that lists the benefits of the product or service. Jay Conrad Levinson, who wrote *Guerrilla Marketing* says, "People buy benefits, not features. Women do not purchase shampoo, they purchase beautiful, clean, manageable hair."

So, in effect, your customers are not purchasing perms, they're purchasing a lasting hairstyle. Customers who buy nail services are really buying glamour, and young customers who buy and wear multi-colored hair and punk haircuts are essentially buying a rebellious image. Clients who purchase perfume are actually buying romance. Buyers of automobiles are purchasing an image associated with that car. Furniture buyers are not necessarily buying comfortable, well-made furniture, but a lifestyle associated with the brand name. Understanding how this strategy works will help you to cross over from advertising features to marketing benefits.

Action Steps

1. What three benefits do you offer to the consumer?

2. What three features do you offer to the consumer?

3. List three ways to improve a former promotion that didn't result in a profit.

Meet Needs and Desires

Have what the customer wants or needs and distinguish between the two in your advertising materials.

For example:

Wants . . . . *versus* . . . . *Needs*
Impulse items . . . . Shampoo
Hair decorations . . . . Hair spray
Costume jewelry . . . . Rain hats/umbrellas

Action Steps

1. What customer needs does your business meet?

2. What customer desires does your business meet?

3. List three ways to create balance in your marketing campaign.

Provide Value

Attract sales by providing true value to the customer. Recognize that value is a three-way combination of price, quality and service. If you have a particular philosophy regarding value, add it to your communication messages.

Action Steps

1. List three ways your small or home-based business will provide more value to consumers.

2. How will your potential customers recognize the difference between your business and one around the corner?

3. What is your philosophy on value?

Make Changes When Necessary

Since change is inevitable, our best strategy is to take action daily to prepare ourselves for new beginnings. It comes when you least expect it, so be sensitive to changes in the marketplace, and continually revamp career plans when there are major changes in your industry.

The graphic design industry changed dramatically in the last twenty years. For many years, publications were designed by hand, employing many people. With the advent of desktop computers, everything changed almost overnight. People who resisted learning computer technology were left without jobs.

Always keep up with new technology and notice how it can improve various areas of your industry. Become friendly with IT professionals whose job is to be knowledgeable; subscribe to industry resources (for example, a number of enewsletters are available).

Keep abreast of changes by following this list of procedures:

1. Change your services and products when necessary.

2. For example, if your products are gender-specific, and your clientele changes from mainly female to male, then remember to carry products which appeal to men.

3. Review your neighborhood/online demographics.

4. Attend trade seminars to keep your training current.

5. Read your trade magazines (and online sources) and get new information from sales representatives.

Overcome Resistance

There are four reasons why consumers may be resistant to your business: cost, needs, habits and belief.

Cost

When cost is a factor of customer resistance, explain your higher prices—especially when competitive prices are substantially lower. State in your communication messages that you offer extra value, if that is true. Stress benefits in your marketing materials. Ask your receptionist and employees to support your claims when they interact with customers. A prestigious location, a high quality image and a successful reputation always warrant higher prices. Before you opt for the prestigious location and award-winning interior, be certain your target market or neighborhood will support your prices.

Notice possible reasons why consumers won't purchase certain products. Neighboring businesses may be selling the same line of products, so customers can purchase them anywhere. You and your employees may not be educating your customers on the products. Customers won't buy what they don't know about. They may prefer less expensive products from discount stores. Again, education is the key. Spend your money wisely by getting additional education and attending product training seminars.

Many companies print brochures that explain their products in detail. Buy them in bulk and offer them free to consumers.

Another way of educating clients is through video presentations. Purchase a small television and DVD player, and run client training videos in your reception area. Keep plenty of retail products nearby.

Needs

Thoroughly research your target market so you can pinpoint customer needs and address them in your marketing materials. Your advertising materials must clearly communicate the reasons consumers should use your services and purchase your products. For instance, seniors need hairstyles that are either easy to care for or that hold in place for a week at a time. Most women want hair color. Clients who are business people generally need to get in and out fast, especially if your business is a cafe, restaurant, hair salon or another business that caters to people on the go. Consumers in a low-income area need more value for their money. Research the demographics in your neighborhood for clues.

Habits

Many people are reluctant to change where they do business. They fall into the habit of going to the same place. Some people have developed a fear of trying a new service business or product. They may have had a bad experience in the past, which may keep them from experimenting, even though they're not totally happy where they are. A word-of-mouth recommendation is usually the best solution for this problem. Another way to overcome the "trust" issue is to use testimonials in your printed materials. Perhaps a high-profile customer or two could give you endorsements for your brochures.

Belief

The statements made in your advertising materials must be believable. You and your employees must be able to deliver on the message. When your message says you are an expert, then someone who works for you must be able to prove your claims.

Action Steps

1. How will you overcome customer resistance?

2. List all your products or services and their prices.

3. List the amenities to be absorbed in pricing: informational materials, samples, supplies, etc.

4. Describe your competition's effect on pricing.

Start a Sideline Business

Nurture one or two other aspects of your business. Let's say your service business traditionally slows down several times during the year. You could start up and promote a small retail sideline, which could potentially bring in substantial profits. By the same token, if your main business is retail, you might consider adding a service-related business. For example, let's say you own a shoe store and sell shoes, boots, socks, and handbags. You might consider adding an area where an employee could repair leather shoes and handbags. In my city, several laundromats have added a bookstore or a small cafe. Sideline businesses attract additional customers and add to your profit margin. Of course it is also wise to investigate the market and identify your sideline's potential for profitability before you spend a great sum of money.

Calendar Strategy

The biggest secret is that he largest profits come from organizing your marketing campaign around the Yearly Events Calendar. Marketing campaigns tend to be more successful when they tie in promotions with social events. Consumers are generally in need of extra personal service or products because of the significance of these events. As you know, a small business provides consumers with year-round support. Consumers may not have a favorite service or retail business, so your advertisements could attract them at the right time when they are needed. Consumers are going to go somewhere, so why not to you?

Marketing tools

You'll need a variety of marketing tools to help you strategize and increase your market share. Earlier my co-author Tom Marcoux and I advised you to place marketing ideas into a personal Marketing Binder. As you go through this book, you may find a good idea and make it better by adding your own personal and creative touch.

Plan a Calendar of Events

Before each new year begins, make it a priority to sit down with this book and figure out your marketing calendar of events. I suggest that you do this every November for the following year.

Do it before you get busy with the ever-hectic Thanksgiving and Christmas holiday seasons.

The best way to promote your small business for the year is to lay down the calendar in front of you, determine the busy times of the year, and mark those events for particular promotions. This gives you the ability to see when the slow times exist and plan specific promotions for those times as well.

The Five Advantages of Advance Planning

1. Prevents you from forgetting to do it during busy times.

2. Provides a simple and direct timeline to follow.

3. Frees up your time to take care of details, meet with employees and get your customers excited about your projects. You'll feel a sense of satisfaction and readiness.

4. Helps you manage your time effectively and assures that each step in the process flows smoothly.

5. Gives ample time to correct any errors which might occur. Remember that nothing is written in stone, so if you unexpectedly hire a new employee with special strengths, or find a new product, you can always substitute one promotion for another if necessary.

The last thing you want to do is throw a promotion package together quickly at the last minute without much thought as to its content and effectiveness. Mistakes can occur, costing you both your money and your reputation. Mistakes can turn off your potential customer; she may think, "If the person is sloppy with an ad, then he'll be sloppy with my needs."

Also, make sure you devote the time to shop around for the best-priced media package.

When choosing which events to promote throughout the year, remember your vision or objective and your marketing strategy.

Events Calendar Process

The Events Calendar is a focal point of this system. Use the Events Calendar to pinpoint events that help you reach your primary objective for the year.

1. First write in all the holiday events that you will promote.

2. Add special events like your business's anniversary, any local fairs or festivities, or themed events.

3. List seasonal events such as proms, graduations, the wedding seasons and back-to-school.

4. Mark the obvious slow seasons for themed product or service promotions.

Maintain Balance

Create a balance in your calendar events schedule to allow your campaign to make consistent progress. You'll also need adequate time to rest, renew and resume. Resist the urge to do too many promotions all at once. It will confuse your employees and your clients. A balanced schedule throughout the year is easier on your budget, too. Too much down time between promotions is also not helpful. Keep your messages consistent.

Choose Social Promotional Events

Here are ten possible promotional events:

1. Holiday events

2. Vacations

3. Community social events (festivals, fairs, parades, theater events, concerts, symphony or opera opening nights, and black tie affairs)

4. Personal rites of passage (weddings, graduations, proms, birthday parties, baptisms, religious confirmations, wedding and baby showers)

5. New products

6. New services

7. New employees

8. Your Grand Opening or Anniversary

9. Business renovations or change of location

10. When business needs a boost (an annual event specific to you)

Marketing experts recommend that you keep your business's name consistently in front of the public all year round.

Remember your primary objective

You'll be choosing important promotions that support your primary objective. Study this list of secrets to help you stay on course.

Six success secrets to event planning

Secret 1: Choose events that do the most for your business's image.

Participating in charity events, festivals, and parades are great for upgrading a business's image. There are other effective ways, depending on your location and your target market.

For example, your upscale business will find a more lucrative market by promoting to area hotels during the summer or winter tourist season. Your budget-minded business will find more profit potential by marketing to a local college crowd during a Back-to-School sale. A designer clothing store would get more value out of a promotion directed towards convention attendees as opposed to a Country and Western Jamboree. Always remember the image you want to project.

Secret 2: Select events that help you to establish your position.

Choose a position strategy for your business (the first and most important strategy). Decide which events and promotions clarify your position and distinguish you as the market leader. For example, a speaker who guides people to get jobs could hold a "job-a-thon"—that is, she could coach twenty participants and see how many gain job interviews in one month. This process could help her gain a position as the Job Seeker's Coach.

Secret 3: Embrace events that attract your target market.

Tailor your promotions to your target market, which will desire and purchase your products and services. If your target market consists mainly of senior citizens, then avoid advertising your services related to the prom, wedding services, or back-to-school seasons. Local health fairs or a Seniors' Center would be better. You might trade Appreciation Certificates with businesses that seniors frequent: doctors, health clinics, cafes or coffee shops, health food stores and others. Focus on clothing or department stores that appeal to seniors.

Secret 4: Determine which media will support your purpose for each event, and your primary objective for the year.

Inexpensive flyers and coupons will work fine for many events. Sometimes newspapers and radio will do the best job. Perhaps direct mail would be most effective in establishing the intimate contact you need. When I owned my salon business, local newspapers would offer special advertising rates to all merchants who participated in an event. Our Merchants' Association would buy a half page or full page advertisement at a better than usual rate. Invite other local merchants to join you in buying advertising space and save money for everyone.

Secret 5: Decide which events/media will be within your budget.

No doubt about it, experience helps you effectively gauge the right budget and which media to choose for promotions. Your decisions will depend upon the extent of exposure you want and which media reaches your target audience. If flyers and coupons reach your target market most effectively, that is the media to use. If your experience demonstrates that the Internet or direct mail works best, then stay with that medium. Here's the important point: if a more expensive medium or event brings in the business you want, then it's worth investing with it for that promotion. The money will return to you. Don't bother wasting less money on an affordable promotion that does nothing for your business.

Secret 6: Network your way to success.

Network and ask other business owners about their experience with printers, copy shops and direct mail companies. Cost, reliability, quality and results are what counts. Ask about their experience with different social events. Find out which media they used and the response rate. (Also, consider doing some form of "joint venture" or teaming up to target similar clientele.)

Action Step

1. How will you maintain balance in your marketing plan?

2. Which events will you choose for your campaign?

Remember that in the beginning, your promotions may be subject to trial and error. However, your groundwork here will help you to plan your future promotions and advertising more effectively.

Develop Your Media Plan

For every promotion, you'll need a media plan that includes how and where to promote your business. Add this information to your calendar of events.

Read the following information to discover which media will best reach your target market, stay within your budget, and allow you to reach your primary objective this year. There are four areas to develop: public relations, print, broadcast and digital media.

Public relations

Public relations is about keeping the public informed and interested in your business. It encompasses all the activities you do to obtain free exposure for your business. Some examples of public relations are announcements, press releases, feature stories, interviews, press kits and press conferences.

Local newspapers and radio stations are often open to interviews and feature stories, usually as personal interest stories. Send a light, human-interest story to the features editor of your newspaper. Remember to clip articles that feature your business. Save them for press kits and portfolios about your business.

Good public relations takes strategy. Now Gayle Murphy shares her secrets.

You Gotta Pitch It to Promote it so You Can Tell it to Sell it!

Gayl Murphy

"Your business pitch" is what's left standing after you've left the building. Fit the problem AND the solution in your pitch, and you've got them at "hello." You don't have to make your pitch perfect, you just have to nail it in "five seconds or less!"

Creating and delivering your business pitch is about who you are, what you do and what's next. This extremely effective networking tactic can often feel a lot like online dating to a newbie, like cyber lovers scouring the web in search of a special connection—it can be terribly daunting if you don't know what you're doing.

That said, when you are dating online, if you don't post a picture (preferably current), you won't get many dates because "one picture tells a thousand words", just like a "Killer Pitch can make you millions!" You've got to make that connection in an instant so people can "see you in action" just by meeting you.

A Killer Pitch can get you connected and in the door, clean and simple. Meaning, a good pitch will get you a two to three minute conversation; a Killer Pitch will book you a lunch with them walking you to your car!

An Elevator Pitch is about who you are and what you're selling. And, an "Interview Tactics! Killer Pitch" is whatever you need it to be in whatever environment you happen to be in at anytime. Making it the *right tool for the right time!*

Let's set the record straight right here and right now, you can have as many pitches for your business as you want. This is great news for those of you whose businesses are diversified over several markets. You can have a killer pitch that's three seconds, 30 seconds, 90 seconds, or three minutes.

With Interview Tactics!, you can create lots of different pitches so you can adequately decide which pitch you think is most appropriate to use, depending on who you're talking to and where you are. It's called knowing your end-user and being target-specific. Again, it's the right tool for the right time. The key to this is really asking a few questions of the person you're talking to so you can best chose the right one, so as to make what you're selling about *them.*

For example, when I'm networking with CEOs, one of my pitches is, "I celebrit-ize CEO's", which is a terrific attention grabber with head honchos, and they always want to know more. When I'm at Book Expo, I want to be just as specific with authors, so my pitch is "I celebrit-ize authors." And, when I'm at the Inventor's Expo, I'm pitch that "I celebrit-ize inventors." And I do all of the above. The funny thing is that it's the same job for all three, with a bit of tailoring.

You can and should be just as flexible with your pitching when your customer base is diversified. Think of the Hollywood Dry Cleaner. He cleans all the clothes in show business and they all need him, regardless of how diversified *their* businesses are. So he can brand himself as the Dry Cleaner to the Stars, the Studio Executive's Dry Cleaner, or George Clooney's Stylists Dry Cleaner! Guess what? His job is exactly the same regardless of whose dirt he shouts out.

Think about all the different markets your business serves and start expanding who you pitch to. Can you have a separate pitch for stay at home moms, seniors, astronauts, students, families, solopreneurs, reinvented entrepreneurs, scientists, insurance salesmen? You get the picture.

As for me, when I'm coaching or speaking about "Interview Tactics!" my job never changes, but my end-users do, so I stay keenly aware of all the businesses and markets that might need what I'm selling at any time, so I can pitch to them, too.

In my experience, the very best pitches are the ones that sell themselves. Meaning that they're easily repeatable, full of color and detail, visual, direct, concise and solidly to the point.

A "Killer Pitch" is so engrossing that people become compelled to move it forward for you, word for word, especially if it's clever.

You can create pitches that literally sell themselves by being target-specific. For example, everyone wants more time. How about instead of telling customers that they'll save time with your product, why not tell them exactly how much more time they'll have as a result of working with you? Do the math in advance and give them examples of extra time over the period of six weeks.

Or, who doesn't want to lose weight? By creating a Killer Pitch for your "Get Skinny Fast Diet," you can not only show people how to lose weight fast, but by following your directions they'll be 20 pounds lighter in 30 days. You're giving them a roadmap so they know what to expect and they can see the results of their hard work.

By being specific, you not only give your end-user a personalized message, you're also writing their script so they know how to comfortably pitch you to their friends, family, co-workers and the next person they meet. Or, even better, they can tell their boss exactly what you do and how terrific you really are, word for word.

Questions to self for creating "The Power Pitch"

- What problem does my business solve?

- Does it save my end-user time or money? If so, how?

- Will it make my end-user more money? How?

- Will it make them happier? Healthier? Younger? Sexier? Thinner? (You need to know how for all of these.)

- Will it buy them more time to play and be sociable? Spend more time with friends and family?

- Will they learn something of great benefit to their lives and the lives of their community or country? (Hint: This is important if your product is a charity, or on a medical, health/wellness or green topic.)

- Can your business, product or service jump-start their business?

It's important that you have at least two or three answers to each of these questions so you always have scenarios and examples about your business available to tell anyone at anytime.

One great way to stay on top of information about your area of expertise is by subscribing to Google Alerts. Google Alerts can be found on Google.com. When you subscribe, Google will send you an email every day, or weekly, listing all the internet chatter on your topic for that day or week.

Be sure to input your keywords and core message for maximum results. Your Google Alert will include the latest breaking news, the latest studies and the newest innovations in your field. This will keep you at the top of your game and ahead of the competition. You'll be such a know-it-all. Creating commonality with the person you're talking to is also a huge benefit, meaning taking what you do and relating it to everyday things that we all experience and think about. By breaking your business down in this way, you're actually expanding the base of your business and making your products available to a lot more people than you think. Remember, people have people.

Gayl Murphy is a Media Entrepreneur on a mission. Get the story; get it right and coach entrepreneurs to craft media messages that make millions! Gayl is a veteran Hollywood Correspondent, Media and Presentational Coach, Speaker and Author of *Interview Tactics! How to Survive the*

Media without Getting Clobbered! As a Media Expert Gayl celebritizes entrepreneurs in business and entertainment to successfully use media to celebritize themselves and their brands, so they can pitch it to promote it and tell it to sell it … anytime, any place. As a Showbiz correspondent, Gayl interviews the stars! She's interviewed over 15,000 of the biggest celebrities and newsmakers in the world on radio, TV and in print for ABC News, BBC News, SKY News, E! and HollywoodToday.net among others.

InterviewTactics.com
Gayl@InterviewTactics.com
01-323-417-5172

Print media

This area contains all printed materials via ink on paper—including newspapers, telephone books (The Yellow Pages), flyers, business cards, and brochures.

Advertising

Advertising attracts attention to the small or home-based business and creates the most favorable impression on the public. This in turn expands the growth and development of your business. It is a sales proposition in which you are getting the consumer's attention to mentally involve them with the product or service. Print pertains to flyers, coupons, door hangers, and anything not included in other advertising.

Direct mail advertising

Direct mail coupons and introductory letters are an effective advertising tool to get new business. A 1-5% return is considered good. There are two benefits of using direct mail:

its accountability and how quickly you know the results of your investment. Remember, even if you don't receive the response you expect from the first mailing, your business's name and service is still getting the most effective exposure available.

The way to achieve success in direct mail is to make the right offer, to the right prospect, at the right time, and in the right way. You must present your information in a visually attractive manner, and remember to make the offer irresistible. You must also create a consistent message and look.

Direct mail is highly effective because it creates a more intimate contact with the reader. With a direct mail campaign, you directly interact with potential customers in a personal way. Your letter or coupon goes directly into their home with their name and address on the envelope. Direct mail includes letters of introduction, newsletters, direct mail coupons and more.

Get a clear idea of a market that would find your products and services valuable. A demographic survey, which allows you to pinpoint who your potential customers are, will increase your chances of success.

"Testing" with direct mail is vital. Try several differently worded introductory letters, mail them to your target market and observe which letter creates the most responses. Start with your own customer mailing list: a) begin with your customer card files for current names, b) use names from previous contests or drawings, and c) ask current customers for names of friends and relatives (a referral list). Here's an idea: give a small gift in return for five or ten referrals. Now would be a good time to leave a customer mailing list form at your front desk.

Two crucial points in direct mail: a) it is better to send fewer letters to a well-targeted list of 300 than to send to a "random" list of 3,000 and b) to raise your response level to 17% (as noted by researchers who track this process) use up to four repeat mailings per prospective client.

Magazine and newspaper advertising

Recent years have seen the disappearance of numerous magazines and newspapers. Magazines are generally a poor choice for a small or home-based business advertisement. It's just too costly. A magazine's territory is too wide to benefit most small businesses. You will pay high exposure rates for consumers who live too far away.

However, if your business lends itself to magazine advertisements (a mail-order firm for example), the most effective number of placements is a minimum of five pages per year.

You may fare better with regional magazines or those that are directed toward specific industries: insurance, real estate, medical, or hospitality.

Yellow pages advertising

Classified ads in the yellow pages provide a certain amount of exposure. Yellow pages advertisements don't necessarily motivate people to buy from you or frequent your business. Once you have already motivated them with other media, the yellow pages pull them in.

The advantages of this media are that you have constant exposure, everyday, for 24 hours a day. Yellow Pages are most effective for businesses whose name begins with the letter A. Remember that every business and home has a phone book. However, recognize these two disadvantages to the yellow pages. You can't update your advertisement whenever you feel the need; restrictions require that you make changes at one particular time of the year when the telephone book is due for republishing. This may happen a year from when you need it, so you must plan accordingly. Secondly, a large ad can be quite expensive. You may or may not be able to recoup your costs.

Broadcast media—radio and television

Radio and television can help to supplement your advertising campaign by reaching a wider audience. Radio is less expensive and it also gives wide exposure. You will reach a broader range of consumers than through the newspaper or other media. Radio is everywhere: in our cars, our homes, in stores, on the streets, and on our headsets. There are many varieties of stations from which to choose: all-news, all-sports, top 40 music, classical, country, jazz, ethnic, and more.

There is a limitation of two minutes or less for radio spots, so you must make the sale in that time constraint. You must present a problem and demonstrate why your product or service can provide the solution. Make sure to state the price and possibly a money-back guarantee. Create a sense of urgency or a reason to act "now." It's helpful to use a phone number that is easy to remember. I recall that the authors of the *Chicken Soup for the Soul Series* used the phone number: 1-800-SOUP-BOOK.

The principles of radio advertising are:

1 Talk one-to-one with the listener (talk about benefits).

2. Focus on one idea, creatively expressed to get attention.

3. Stretch the listener's imagination by creating atmosphere.

4. Be topical by sending messages relative to the season (Christmas, Valentine's Day, Mother's Day).

5. Measure the response by asking new customers if they heard your radio announcement.

I used radio advertising a couple of times with only moderate success. I advertised in conjunction with a co-op agreement. The script was good and professional; however, consistent use is necessary to get a great response.

A program host at the station can read your radio advertisement or commercial. Listen at the time your announcement is getting airplay to hear how it sounds. Record it if possible. Remember that people are listening in their cars, not necessarily through a high-tech stereo system.

Having an announcer read your script live has drawbacks because he or she may have a bad day or read it too fast.

You can do pre-recorded messages yourself if you have a pleasing voice. Pre-recorded announcements in a voice that appeals to you will always sound the same and be delivered in a style that expresses your professionalism. Reading from a script will prevent errors, but practice enough to sound natural. Music evokes feelings and emotions without pictures.

Other than advertising, you can use talk and information shows as a vehicle to promote your business. Find a local station where the host interviews guest speakers. Talk about a specialty area where you are an expert.

Television requires a lot of money to buy advertising space. You must be strengthed at creating an attention-getting advertisement. You have only three seconds to grab the consumer's attention. Business owners find that hiring professional consultants or ad agencies may be necessary to gain the expertise needed.

Digital media

The Internet—online marketing

Your online presence is like having a marketing staff working for you 24/7. On your website, you can share your newsletters or offer customer education programs and sell your products in a catalog format. You can accept orders online, by fax or telephone. People are interested in websites that have up-to-date, interesting content. They also like interactive sites that are easy to navigate. Websites must be constantly updated and improved; otherwise, people will be bored and won't return. My co-author Tom Marcoux provides free material at his blog BeHeardandBeTrusted.com (with a new article every week) and his website TomSuperCoach.com. He gains subscribers to his free enewsletter "Success Secrets." Occasionally, he holds a special promotion around Valentine's Day and the Holiday Season that he promotes through his email list. Repeatedly, he gets immediate orders because he provides two details: (1) a deadline and (2) an enticing free offer (like an exclusive downloadable audio program).

Now, Danek S. Kaus introduces the online marketing process.

Get Started with Online Marketing

Danek S. Kaus

What to put on your website

Your website should be easy for people to navigate, that is, to find what they are looking for. One of the best ways to do this is to divide it into specific sections. Here are some of the pages you may want to consider:

The homepage: This is the first page people see when they visit your site. Its purpose is to introduce yourself to the world. You want to create a message that will draw people in so that they will want to visit the rest of your website.

Products/services: This section describes your offerings and may include pictures, if you have products.

Staff: Let people know something about who they will be dealing with, especially their experience and expertise.

About us/me: Depending on the nature of your site, this section might be unnecessary if you have already covered the staff. This is where you let people know about your company and its history.

Testimonials: Get other people to say good things about you and include them on this page.

Articles: In this section you can give people information related to the nature of your site. For example, if you're a CPA, you can write about various financial topics. If you don't like to write, hire someone to interview you and ghost write some articles for you. You can also get free articles from article directories. (More about them below.) Putting articles on your site and updating them gives people a reason to keep coming back to your site. If journalists have written articles about you, get permission to reprint them and place them here. This helps build more credibility.

Resources and links: On this page, you list places where people can find more information about the focus of your site. You might suggest books or put in links to other websites. Putting in links is easy. All you do is paste in the URL (website address). In some cases, you may need permission to do this, but few people will turn down the opportunity to get free publicity.

Press or press room: Make it easy for the media to get the facts they need by putting in your press releases and other information from your media kit. Journalists like this page because they can get what they need in a hurry, whether you are available or not.

FAQ: Stands for frequently asked questions. If there are some questions that people often ask, do them and yourself a favor by creating this page. All you have to do is state each of the common questions with their answers.

Forum: A forum is an interactive discussion. It can contain "threads" about various topics. People can write you questions as well as share information, ideas, and opinions with each other. Some of the companies that sell template packages offer this with the website designs or as a separate package. If they don't, you can buy separate software. If you start doing forums, you may need to consult a website geek to help you get started. Some software is user-friendly and some requires an experienced hand, initially. One of the biggest benefits of a forum is that it develops a sense of community and keeps people involved—and coming back.

Contact page: Make it easy for people to reach you. The contact page can include your phone number, fax number, and email address. You may also consider putting this information on each page of your website.

Blogs

Blog is short for web log. A blog lets you express yourself, offer tips, and easily add new information for your readers. A blog can be part of your website or a separate entity. In recent years, blogs have become powerful tools for reaching people with common interests.

Blogs work best when you do several short "posts" per week. Be sure your blog has a place for people to leave comments. Your posts can be your thoughts on a particular topic, the latest industry news—whatever you think is important to your readers (customers). At this writing, Google offers free blog templates and hosting.

Visit blogger.com to learn more. Of course you'll need to promote your blog. First, register it with the blog search engines. Also, send "pings" to ping services each time you post a new entry. Doing so will help get your articles listed in the search directories.

You may also want to syndicate your blog so that people can subscribe to it. Two popular providers are Atom and RSS (Real Simple Syndication).

Another way to promote your blog is to contact other bloggers who write about similar or complimentary topics to see if they will do a story about you or link to your website and blog. You'll need to interact differently with bloggers than you do with mainstream journalists. Few bloggers have journalism experience, though many consider themselves journalists. That discussion is outside the scope of this article.

Only a small percentage of bloggers who are not professional journalists either understand or adhere to journalistic standards. Instead, you must establish a relationship with them. One way to do this is to read their blogs and post comments. You can also email them a personalized request to help promote your blog.

Keep in mind, they may post anything you communicate with them, even if you indicate that it is in confidence. The blogosphere is vastly different from the world of mainstream journalism. So protect yourself.

When searching for appropriate blogs, look for those that have lots of links to other blogs and sites, as well as numerous comments, which indicate popularity and dedicated readership.

Podcasts

The term podcast is a combination of the words iPod and broadcast. A podcast is essentially an audio or video blog, also known as a Vlog. To create a podcast you will need special software to turn your audio or video source into a digital format. One of the most popular ones is Audacity. You can download it for free at audacity.sourceforge. net. The website has information that will help you get started in podcasting. Once you've created your podcast, you can host it on your site or on one of the many sites dedicated to hosting podcasts.

You can also upload them to YouTube and social networking sites such as My Space where they are exposed to potentially millions of people.

Another great advantage of podcasting is that people can download podcasts, put them on their computer and MP3 players, and enjoy them whenever they want, even on the go.

Article Directories

You can use article directories in two ways. An article directory is a website in which people who want to get free publicity submit articles on various topics, with their contact information, such as a website, at the bottom. They give them to the site for free. People who want material for their websites, blogs, and newsletters search the article directory for suitable articles, which they then copy and use on their sites, etc., for free. There are a couple of stipulations. They must use the article as is, with no changes, including author credit, and they must leave in the contact information. It's a win-win-win.

You get free publicity and the user gets a free article. The people who operate the article directory usually make their money from ads on the site.

There are hundreds of directories, and each has its own preferred submission procedure, so sending your articles to a number of them can be time-consuming. However, there are services and software that will do multiple submissions for you. Whichever approach you use, submitting to the directories can garner you a lot of exposure, if you can provide well-written articles that are interesting and/or informative.

An Internet search will lead you to the directories and to the submission services and products.

Forums

You name a topic and there's probably an Internet forum about it. Some topics have dozens of forums.

A forum is an interactive website (or part of a website) in which people interact by email. People write in about what they like or don't like about a subject. They exchange information. They ask for advice and offer it.

Forums usually have multiple "threads," each one about a different aspect of the forum. A small business forum may have threads on marketing, selling techniques, customer relations, and so on.

You can promote yourself by starting your own forum on your website or as a dedicated site.

Starting a forum is a great way to keep customers or organization members involved. It also offers you the opportunity to offer information and advice to keep people coming back.

If you want to promote yourself outside your group, you can participate in other forums that are related to what you do. You are usually not allowed to advertise or pitch a product or service, but you can create what is called a "signature" at the bottom of each post that includes the address for your website, blog, or newsletter signup page. People who read your posts may then decide to click on the links, especially if you are able to answer questions from other participants.

Adapted from the book, *You Can Be Famous! Insider Secrets to Getting Free Publicity*, by Danek S. Kaus.

Danek S. Kaus is a veteran journalist and publicist. He has published hundreds of articles in about 75 newspapers and magazines. His publicity clients have been featured in such media outlets as CNN, USA, the *New York Times*, and hundreds of newspapers, magazines, and TV and radio shows. He is also a produced screenwriter. To contact him, or get more publicity tips:

getfreepublicitynow.com
dkaus@sbcglobal.net

Another way to increase traffic on your website is to subscribe to a service such as Yahoo Directory. Such subscriptions improve your ranking in search results so potential customers get to your site sooner, and your company description will be written by a professional search director (that is, a person, not a machine). A number of website owners use Google Ads to bring potential customers to their websites.

Now Paul Gillin shares tips on how you can write your own blog.

The Power of Your Blog

Paul Gillin

The best way to sustain visibility, name recognition and search-engine love in our information-saturated world is to write a lot, particularly on a blog, which is a magnet for search engines.

But writing is hard for most people. Just coming up with a topic to write about and something new to say is often the biggest struggle. Write about things that inspire you and about which you have strong opinions. If the subject doesn't move you, it's hard to get motivated and create ideas.

I've learned a few tricks about how to overcome Web 2.0 blogger's block. We'll start at the beginning with how to find inspiration for a topic.

Use feeds: All blogs and most news sites support RSS feeds. In some cases, the feed delivers the entire content of the site. In other cases, they're organized by topic. You assemble feeds in an RSS reader.

RSS readers are basically mini newspapers you create out of information streams from online sources. I use Google Reader to set up topical feeds from bloggers and publishers I like who cover these topics. Another nice reader is NetVibes, which organizes feed content into kind of a personalized home page.

[On my website PaulGillin.com, I have] an example of a collection of RSS feeds I set up about journalism and news. It's usually a two-click process to add a feed to Google Reader, and another couple of steps to organize the feed into a folder. You can even republish the collection of feeds by generating a single RSS address for the whole group.

Topical feeds inspire great ideas. You can easily see if a topic is trending by the amount of attention it's getting. Feed collections also give you a quick idea of whether a topic is controversial, since you can easily see if a lot of people are writing about it.

Tweet and be tweeted. I'll admit to not being very good at jotting down ideas when I have them. My teachers always told me to carry around a notebook for this purpose, but I'd either forgot the notebook, the pen or both.

Twitter has helped me surmount this disability. Now when I see something interesting or have an idea, I tweet it. I can then go through my own tweet stream later and look for ideas that have since slipped my mind.

Twitter is also an endless source of ideas. If you carefully manage the list of people you follow, simply monitoring the topics they tweet will give you ideas. With the new Twitter Lists feature, I can now read tweets from people who share interests or affiliations. It's like the topical RSS feeds described above, only shorter and less predictable.

Bookmark: When you see an interesting article or video, bookmark it and write a comment. Services like Delicious, Reddit and Clipmarks make this easy. My personal favorite is Diigo, because it allows me to highlight and annotate the items I bookmark. [On my website PaulGillin.com, I have] my personal list of the most interesting articles I've bookmarked recently. Choose a tag you'll remember, like "ideas."

Listen to your audience: Conferences, meetings and consulting work are good sources of material because they tap into what's on people's minds right now. Read what people are commenting about. Find an article that interests you and look at how many comments it's drawing and how controversial it is.

Refresh old material: If you've been writing for more than a year, chances are there's some material in your archives that could use a fresh look. Revisit an old prediction and see if it came true. Or discuss new ideas on an old subject. Be sure to link to the original article to drive a little more traffic to it.

Writing it down: When it comes time to write, there are a few tricks you can use to get yourself in the mood and find a voice that works for you.

Defy conventional wisdom: This is an old newspaper columnist trick, but it works well. Think of a topic that most people agree upon and argue the exact opposite point of view. For example, try to build a case for why social networks are a passing fad or the New York Jets are the team to beat in the NFL this year. You have to think creatively to argue your point, and the result may be more satire than opinion, but just let the idea take you where it wants to go. Going against conventional wisdom is one of the best ways to fuel creativity.

Get angry: The best writing is driven by emotion. Think about something you've heard or seen recently that really made you mad. Are there lessons you can share? Or can you abstract the issue into more general commentary? Maybe you got cut off by a driver talking on a cell phone. That could lead to a bigger essay on distraction. Let your passion guide you, but be careful not to push the "publish" button till you've calmed down.

Aggregate other opinions: Go to a news/blog aggregation site like Alltop.com and browse a category that interests you. Find a topic that several people are commenting upon, summarize their comments and add your own. For an extra twist, try the tactic mentioned in the first item above and argue the opposite case.

Tell a story: It's the most powerful form of human communication. Reach back to an experience that was meaningful to you and start writing it down. What did you learn from that experience? How can those lessons help others?

Revisit: The simple act of scrolling through your past blog entries can yield ideas about new topics or new angles on old topics. If your predictions were wrong, tell why. If they were right, build on them.

Conduct a small research project. Two of my most well-received recent blog entries were quick experiments, each of which took less than an hour to conduct:

> I visited 15 corporate blogs shortly after the financial meltdown
> and looked at what they were saying about the economy. The

lack of attention to this hugely important story was stunning. It made me angry, and that's a good formula for writing.

I picked a stream of 100 tweets at random and analyzed them for content and value. The results surprised me and my essay generated quite a few tweets from others.

Make a list: This is the most popular organizational tool in the blogosphere. Pick a topic about which you have some expertise and offer quick hits of advice. For example: "10 Ways to Research a Company on the Web," or "Seven software utilities I couldn't live without." Or you can skip the numbers and just organize your thoughts in modules, like I'm doing here. I get tired of all the numbered lists after a while, but I have to admit, readers love 'em.

Predict: Predictions are hugely popular at the end of the year, but you can make them any time. To add variety, limit your time frame or endpoint. Neville Hobson and Shel Holtz did this effectively with the 500th edition of their "For Immediate Release" podcast by asking their listeners to predict what topics the two will be discussing during their next 500 shows. Pick a topic, make a prediction and argue your case. Then revisit later and write about how you did.

Recommend: Are there blogs, discussion forums, podcasts or how-to websites that you love? Write them down, tell what you like about each and share them with your readers.

Explore everyday things: This is an offbeat approach, but it's a great way to satisfy your curiosity while delving into little-known corners of the Web. Pick a topic about which you know very little and research it. For example, learn why golf balls have dimples or find the origin of the phrase "the whole 9 yards." This work may have limited relevance to your business, but it'll probably yield a fascinating tidbit of information and help you learn new ways to find things online.

Serialize: Take any of the ideas above and publish it as short thematic entries. Few people read long articles anymore, anyway, so break out those ideas and sprinkle them around. Just be sure to tag and categorize them appropriately so you can reassemble later.

There are dozens of other ways to generate ideas. If you find a blogger you like, write a note and ask what tricks work for him or her. Then blog them!

Paul Gillin is the author of *The New Influencers* and *Secrets of Social Media Marketing*.

Paul Gillin Communications Content Strategies for Social Media
    4 Thurber St., Framingham, MA 01702
    508-202-9807 office, 781-929-6754 mobile

email: paul@gillin.com
web: gillin.com
Twitter: pgillin, LinkedIn: paulgillin

Be careful about what you place on the Internet.

Consider submitting your blog entries to a team member or friend for comments before you publish your thoughts. Your associate could save you from needless embarrassment. My co-author Tom Marcoux says, "A blog and email are like cockroaches; they never go away. I am careful to have a team member look at the my broadcast messages to my e-subscribers because once the message is sent, I can't take it back."

Promotion Reminders

Plan each promotion from beginning to end, and review it periodically to implement improvements.

Make Final Decisions

1. Make the final decisions of events to promote.

2. Determine your budget allowance for each promotion.

3. Develop a theme and give it a tagline.

4. If needed, determine which products to order for the promotion, either pre-packaged items or additional stock.

5. Determine the suitable media or combination of media to use: Internet, billboard, radio, print, cable TV or other.

6. If using print media, decide which elements to use: coupons, direct mail, newspaper, flyers, postcards or other. Find out the cost of each.

7. Write your promotional pieces and target them to a specific audience.

8. When necessary, contact your graphic designer, advertising agency or printer to determine required lead time for printed pieces. Your local copy center is also a good source for short, uncomplicated photocopying.

9. Determine when to send out mailings, remembering that mail service is sometimes slow during the holiday seasons.

10. Remember to notify your employees of all promotions far enough in advance so they can verbally interact with clients. Train employees to use new services or product lines so they can speak from experience.

11. Increase your effectiveness by telephone follow-up calls.

12. Coordinate your social media marketing efforts with Twitter, Facebook, LinkedIn and your own blog.

List Exact Media Details for Each Promotion

1. Names and phone numbers of newspapers, radio stations, direct mail companies, cable TV, billboard sign companies and others.

2. Free publicity opportunities.

3. Costs of printed or photocopied materials.

4. Dates and sizes of ads.

5. Frequency of advertising.

Do a Product and Equipment Analysis

Begin with a description and cost for products: For each promotion, note which products to order and the expected costs.

Inside display: Acquire point-of-purchase displays for various promotions. Manufacturers provide displays that professionally showcase new products, novelty items or anything that applies to your retail business.

Equipment: Various promotions may require the purchase of additional equipment. New gimmicks and gadgets are available every year.

Include a Marketing Budget:

> Total marketing budget. . . . .$ _________
>
> Budget for each promotion. . . . .$ _________
>
> Budget for new products. . . . .$ _________
>
> Budget for new equipment. . . . .$ _________

Strategizing Summary

Take the following steps to access your hidden strength to strategize.

1. Market Strategies

    A. Determine your approach

    B. Create a sense of expectancy.

    C. Slice the Pie.

    E. Get ahead of your competition.

    F. Choose from Sixteen Strategies for Better Marketing

  2. Calendar Strategy

     A. Plan a calendar of events.

  3. Develop a Media Plan

     A. Promotion reminders.

When Do I Take These Steps?

In your Marketing Binder, answer the questions found in this chapter.Mark events into your calendars. Also look through strength 9—Activating for more ideas. It may take some time to determine which promotions will accomplish your primary objective. By all means, use frequency in advertising and keep it all in balance.

9

Energizing

Your Eighth Hidden Strength

Imagine you're at the computer and you type "The End" on your screenplay for a feature film you want to direct. With all your heart and soul, you feel it's going to be a hit. But without power this project won't take off. A perfect script is not enough for success; you need financial backing and excellent actors. Power also applies to your marketing campaign. If you want your audience to get excited about your business and strong marketer promotions, then it's going to need some power or energy behind it. You'll energize your marketing campaign with three powerful elements: a financial investment, your communication messages and your business identity system.

Strength 8—*Energizing* focuses on several effective ways to take your business from obscurity to popularity. You'll answer the one main question, "What will I do to energize my marketing, and get noticed by consumers?"

Complete the energizing *Action Steps* and your benefit is joyfully knowing that your business is empowered with a magical appeal.

Patricia Fripp, a top national speaker (and one of our contributing authors), says, "The answer is always 'no' unless you ask. The answer might still be no, but you still asked the question." Patricia uses networking, her website, demonstration audios, videos, press kits, and magazine articles to attract clients. She emphasizes that "the magic is in the mix."

Your Objective for the Energizing Strength

Your objective is to remember when you gave so much energy to something that it brought you to a place of joy, satisfaction, or even elation. Now, energize your campaign via your investment, communication messages and business identity system.

Energizing as a Natural Strength

We devote lots of energy to get, become or accomplish something meaningful. We always seem to be in pursuit of something: from an endless number of objects, to basic peace and quiet. We are born as energetic beings, and it's our natural state. Children constantly and energetically explore the world. As a teenager I loved to remodel my bedroom. I'd move the furniture around, change the pictures, and use different bedspreads. Over the years, my nephews used their energy to play video games—and even do homework.

As adults we use our natural energy any time we want to change or improve a situation. The energizing process takes on many forms: money, effort, support, or some particular action.

In 1980, I purchased my first home near Chicago. Apart from its charm, it needed extensive refurbishing. Over the next nine years, I replaced the roof, kitchen, floors, and so on. I invested plenty of time, money and energy into my home to make it comfortable and up-to-date. My abilities and resources energized it and gave it some real substance. I fulfilled my belief in the home's potential to become a spectacular residence.

Before you opened your small business, you invested some time in envisioning and creating a vision of your new business. To make that vision real, you invested time and energy into a business plan, an education, and some research. It took energy to get you where you are right now. It takes energy to get out of bed in the morning, fix breakfast, and begin the day. Let's face it, nothing happens unless you put your energy towards achieving what you want. Invest your time and energy into your business for it to become everything you desire.

Action Step

> List two examples from your past when you used your energizing strengths.

Sometimes, being strong about energizing is to make sure that you do something about things that drain your energy. Now my co-author Tom Marcoux will share helpful methods so that you can direct your attention and even jump start your energy.

How You Can Be a Marketer Who Goes to Sleep Happy

Tom Marcoux

Ever have too many thoughts racing around in your head? Have difficulty falling to sleep? How I could have used this next method when I was in college!

While in college, I would go to sleep disappointed. It seemed like my to-do list was never getting smaller. I felt on some level like a failure every night just before my head hit the pillow. And I wrote some of the most downhearted letters to my then-girlfriend. (Note to self: do not write an email or letter when feeling down. Second note to self: write the email in MS Word so I do not accidentally send an inappropriate email message.)

Here's the solution I have found:

Write for 2 minutes in a personal Daily Journal of Blessings and Victories. A blessing is something good that appears like a friend calls up out of the blue. A victory is something that you have accomplished like: "Came up with 3 possible designs for the logo."

So, as an effective marketer, be sure to write down your incremental accomplishments before you go to sleep. You can see and feel that you're making progress.

After my two-minute writing session in my Daily Journal, I grab a 3x5 card. For one minute, I write my next day's Top-Six-Targets. These are my most important tasks for the next day; and this plan serves as my "marching orders" for the next day.

Ahhhhh! Now I can go to sleep happy with my blessings and accomplishments. And my mind is cleared of worry about what I need to do the next day. This process protects my energy. Try this process, and you'll thank me.

Energizing Your Marketing Campaign

Soar higher and farther by energizing your campaign with two types of power: your financial investment and your communication system. Make sure that you devote sufficient attention to your communication system which includes your messages to your prospective customers and your business identity system (web site, brochure, business card, signage at your location and other related details).

Energizing With a Financial Investment

You'll energize your campaign by making an investment in its success.

Empower Your Dreams

Connect with your real purpose: the reasons you went into business and are following through with this marketing campaign. Now, you're connecting with the power that causes you to take action. Perhaps, you energized by imaging your expanding prosperity, happiness and fulfillment. Connecting with something that moves your heart and spirit will empower you to move forward with confidence.

Action Step

> What energizes you to focus on your marketing objectives?

Five principles to Energize your marketing campaign

These five principles will help you to focus your energy more effectively:

1. Believe in your strategies.

2. Trust that you have made effective decisions.

3. Make a financial commitment to your campaign's success.

4. Think of the money you spend on marketing as an investment.

5. Tell your readers what's in it for them.

Make a Financial Commitment

A marketing campaign needs a firm and enthusiastic financial commitment to assure a prosperous future. Don't be afraid to put money in this important area. Spend your money intelligently, and it will certainly return in business growth, boosted sales figures and rising profits.

Think of your financial commitment as an investment in your business. For example, when you invest in the stock market or in real estate, you invest your money for an eventual return in profits. When you buy a home, you are building equity in the home. The stock market or real estate investment is merely a vehicle which, when used adeptly, returns profits.

We all know that it takes investigating and identifying strengths to be able to choose the best vehicle. Envision your objectives and transform them by breathing life into them. Money is the required energy.

Energize your campaign with facts:

1. You are investing in the long-term success of your business.

2. Your advertisements and promotions are constantly making impressions on consumers.

3. The responses you receive will gain momentum.

4. It takes time and patience.

Use investment strategies to help you invest in your marketing campaign, and make that great first impression.

Always keep your primary objective in mind when you reserve financing for your campaign. Some objectives may not require a large budget, and others will demand a larger investment. If you have financial challenges, you may have to rethink your objective or find inexpensive, creative ways to promote your business.

Define Your Budget

Many business people ask how much energy is necessary? You'll first decide how far you want to go with this campaign: a little way, half way, or all the way to your destination. Make this choice first, then ask about necessity.

Business planners suggest that a new enterprise spend about 10% of their business's gross revenues on marketing during the first year in operation, implement a reduction of 5% the second year, then leveling off around 3% per year for the life of your business. Budgets vary depending on your industry. Get advice from your accountant. Be prepared to invest whatever is required to make an impression and to be valued. This amount may be more or less than the suggested costs.

Here is another formula for how much to spend on advertising. Higher rent + high visibility = less advertising. I used this concept for my salon business after moving it to a large mall. I marketed quite heavily in the beginning, since the mall location was brand new and partly vacant. I slowed down my marketing campaign after about five years, as the mall became more popular. I found it necessary to do some spot promotions around special events and again to introduce new products and employees. There was also a Mall Association that periodically promoted every store in the shopping center.

The potential for high foot traffic is good in most shopping centers. Once the community starts frequenting a mall or shopping area on a regular basis, you shouldn't have to spend quite as much money and effort on marketing. Always be aware when another competing business opens up nearby, or even in the same center. You may have to re-engineer your campaign.

Plan a Financial Strategy

You'll need a financial strategy that is not only aggressive, but also practical. Invest your money wisely on smart items that will increase awareness of your business, your image, your position and niche.

Your largest initial expense in the start-up phase will be to create your identity system (more about this a few paragraphs below). Decide on the pieces you need to begin your business: logo, business card, brochure, and stationary. The best way to find out what your identity system will cost you is to get at least three estimates. Estimates take between two and five days. Get time estimates too. Give the designer fairly accurate specifications in order to get realistic estimates. Be sure to get it all in writing: the work to be done, start and completion dates, the costs and anything else.

Then choose which promotions to use throughout the year, and which media to use. Estimate their costs, and budget money for each one. After your first three years in business, you should get a feel for the cost of various promotions and your budget for future years.

When you're marketing more than one business, the divided costs are much less per business. If you divide your marketing campaign budget by three or even twelve chain businesses or outlets, you are actually paying a very low cost per business and they all benefit from your marketing efforts.

I remember a small beauty shop in the town where I owned my business. It appeared to be a very quiet, nondescript, obscure business. No one ever talked about it, so it didn't have a good or bad reputation. One day I drove by it and thought to myself, "This business has never taken off." Not long after that, the owner started opening discount businesses in many nearby towns. This was when chain and franchise operations were starting to take hold in the United States. All advertisements and promotions served each of the eight to ten locations, and attracted consumers throughout that area of the state. The owner marketed her businesses very heavily, and she has done quite well.

Tip: You'll need to be creative to overcome these two obstacles.

1. The size of your company.

2. Your limited financial resources.

Don't be an ostrich with your head in the sand. Make a commitment to truly analyze and understand your numbers. Seek the services of an accountant and/or computer software that keeps track of financial data. Don't guess at how you're doing financially. It might be too late.

Action Steps

1. How much money can you realistically commit to a one-year marketing plan?

2. List 5 ways you can increase your marketing budget!

Your Communication System

Energize Your Messages

In Chapter 7—*Defining,* you defined your business image. You created a compelling image based on knowledge pertaining to your niche and its image requirements. Strength 8—*Energizing* will build further on that information by using your image to develop your communication messages.

The way to energize your message is to make quite deliberate decisions about how you're going to create a positive feeling in your customers. Use the physical characteristics (colors, style, tone) of your business image to enliven your media messages. For example, stay consistent. If your logo is purple, then purple would be appropriate for graphics in an Internet-based video. Ideally, you chose a color that creates the feeling that you want the person to experience while in your location (for example your restaurant or hair salon). Tom Marcoux's mentor Dottie Walters emphasized that warm colors (red, orange) can seize attention and get people to "warm up" to you and your business simultaneously.

Define benefits to customers

When we talk about "energizing", we need to realize that we're in the process of transferring energy to our customer. If you feel great about the warm colors of your logo (for example), you can transfer your good feelings to the customer. Benefits to customers include how they feel, not just that practical benefit like a haircut or a new website or a new set of dishes.

When you're thinking about benefits that you provide your customers, realize that offering multiple benefits can help you stand out in the competitive marketplace. Sometimes salespeople hesitate to up-sell or cross-sell, but they don't realize that they may be failing the customer in a way. The customer relies on you to give them the whole story and to help her solve her current—and perhaps, future problems. So up-selling and cross-selling can often be providing more and better service. Now Craig Harrison will elaborate on the process of up-selling and cross-selling.

Would You Like Fries with That?

Supersize your sales with up-selling and cross-selling

Craig Harrison

Congratulations! You've sold 'em. Now sell 'em more!

Recently while navigating an online bookstore I came across Napoleon Hill's classic book: *Think and Grow Rich.* As I read about this book I was informed that "readers who bought *Think and Grow Rich* also bought the Dale Carnegie's book *How to Win Friends and Influence People* and Dr. Stephen Covey's *The Seven Habits of Highly Successful People.*" Folks, I was being cross-sold, yet I wasn't cross about it.

The reality of business is that customers want to be sold. They love to buy for their own reasons. Not manipulatively bombarded with sales pitches or indiscriminately pressured with endless offerings, but intelligently informed, guided and suggested with related, logical and natural purchases that further their goals.

Up-selling and cross-selling are two sales techniques used by professional sales and service staffs to increase sales. Are you making the most of suggestive selling?

Up with selling

Up-selling refers to situations where your customer buys a product or service, and you encourage them to spend more for additional features or packages. They are upping the amount they are spending, albeit for more or better services or products.

Consider the customer seeking a point-of-sale solution for handling credit cards, yet opts to purchase a deluxe POS model for more money when learning of additional capabilities, security and flexibility.

You are shopping for a bare-bones SUV. The salesperson informs you that soccer moms tell him they love having the model with the DVD player in the backseat for the kids. Thus you buy that model with a fancy video system and then the extended warranty, too.

Sales crossing ahead

Cross-selling refers to situations where a customer buys a product or service, and is simultaneously sold related items that often complement their purchase.

For example: A customer buys a computer and is then sold training services or tutorial software to go with it at additional cost.

Ditto when a man buys a suit and is then offered a color coordinated silk tie and dress shirt to go with it. While we think of these as advanced sales techniques, they are actually rooted in the power of suggestion.

People, once they've decided to buy, are naturally swayed by more and better options, additional value and the excitement following their initial purchase. Many customers don't know about additional items or options, or how well they complement the initial item they bought. Up-selling enhances their initial purchase, making them more powerful, capable and effective. Cross-selling similarly enhances their purchase, often maximizing its impact on their business.

Suggestive selling salient in our lives

Quite frankly, we've been up-sold and cross-sold every day. And it's not necessarily a manipulative process. Consider the following examples:

"Would you like fries with that order?"

"For just 49 cents we can super-size that for you."

"When you buy 2 today you get 1 Free!"

"Would you like to purchase our extended warranty coverage on this? It's only … ."

I've worked with customer service staffs afraid to sell, others who felt it was manipulative and smarmy to sell. Yet here's a secret: It's really a form of service!

Service through sales

When you up-sell and cross-sell:

You are making informed suggestions as a knowledgeable rep.

You are apprising customers of options they may not be aware of.

You are often anticipating future needs.

It's a way to further help your customer ... to be more powerful, to enjoy more benefits, to maximize the usefulness of the products or services they're acquiring. Remember this, when you are the rep who is selling and serving:

You are in the business of solving problems, generating solutions and making customers happy, or even happier.

You are the subject matter expert when it comes to the products and services you are representing.

To the extent you listen and understand the situation of your clients, customers or constituents, you are ideally suited to provide solutions, recommendations and remedies.

To withhold this from others would be selfish, poor service.

Any time you can fulfill more needs, address more issues or solve more problems you are easing your client's/customer's life. After all, they already trust you, like you and are doing business with you.

So, how does one up---sell or cross-sell? It's easy.

Let's play Bridge

After you've completed the initial transaction or gotten the initial indication your customer wants to buy, you can then bridge to the Up- or Cross–sell:

Mr. Randle, while I have you on the line ... were you aware you can work in multiple advanced speech manuals at the same time?

Oh, by the way Ms. Kennison, did you know ... that the book you bought for new hires also has a companion CD for just $9 more?

Mr. Younger, I'd like to take a moment to ... inform you of a new nationwide program just for businesses such as yours ...

Incidentally ... were you aware that you are 2/3's of the way toward qualifying for a discount on shipping of your office supplies?

Using BRIDGE statements allows you to transition from your initial sale to up-sells and cross-sells.

Look anew at the offerings you're selling. For each, what is an up-sell? What can you cross-sell with it? Make sure your salespeople know the migration paths so they can suggestively up- and cross-sell with ease.

In closing, I'd like to thank you for your engagement with this material. Before concluding, could I interest any of you in a related article on up-selling and cross-selling? Perhaps you'd prefer a training course on suggestive selling? Shall I customize that for you? Consider yourself super-sized!

Craig Harrison founded Expressions of Excellence™ to help professionals express their excellence through stellar sales and service training.

ExpressionsofExcellence.com
Craig@ExpressionsofExcellence.com
(510) 547-0064

As we've learned from Craig's comments, you can provide better service when you look at what you're offering and discover more ways to help your customer. As my co-author Tom Marcoux says, "In a way, up-selling and cross-selling might even be a moral imperative. The customer has come to you for solutions, right?"

The general public feels that there are many great businesses, great products or services and great salespeople, so it becomes difficult to prove that one is "better" than another. To stand apart from other businesses, emphasize in your marketing materials what you do that is truly different or unique to the industry. The questions you answered in strength 6—*Defining your image* will help clarify what your small or home-based business has to offer.

Action Step

What benefits do you offer to your target market?

Define your message

To begin with, your marketing messages must persuade, inform and motivate. Second, they must offer something appealing that customers will buy. Third, learn how to stimulate feelings of perceived necessity. Make vivid suggestions about how your services/products will make the customer's life more comfortable, easy, luxurious, or meaningful. Choose your unique message and effectively deliver it to prospective customers in your advertisements and printed materials.

With strength 4—*Identifying*, you identified your target market, which enables you to "speak their language." When you do this well, the potential customer is more likely to mentally receive and accept your message. Something will "click" for them. Here's an example:

Upon opening my first salon business, I placed my first advertisement in a small local newspaper. I had no prior marketing experience, so I was essentially winging it. I read in a marketing book that effective advertisements used power words such as: discover, improve, free, guarantee, new, money, proven and save. So I decided to add a word I thought was powerful and appealing to my target market: "foxy"—to attract a younger clientele. "Foxy" was a popular expression for "trendy and beautiful." It may have come from a Jimi Hendrix song called Foxy Lady. Among other responses to the ad, one woman called right away and made an appointment. To my surprise, an elderly woman arrived for the appointment. When I asked how she wanted her hair styled, she answered, "Foxy, like you said in the ad." I did my best to help her look foxy. My mistake was assuming that only young people wanted to look foxy. I realized that people of all ages tune into powerful slang words such as foxy.

Define some compelling advantages for walking into your place of business. Be selective with whatever benefits/features are appropriate:

- **Talent:** the uniqueness of your employees

- **Comfort:** personal service

- **Full service:** one-stop shopping

- **Speed:** quick-service business

- **Convenience:** high visibility and easy accessibility

- **Atmosphere:** the ambiance and plushness of your interior

- **Extra amenities:** any product or service not normally expected (day spa, boutique, jewelry, child care)

- **Price:** cost for value received

- **Prestige:** acquired reputation

Action Steps

1. How much time are you willing to spend on your advertising and promotions?

2. What main message do you want your target market to believe from your advertising or promotions?

Educate the public

As a new business owner, you need to educate the public. How well you do this may determine your response rate. Consumers have less time to spend on educating themselves, so your educational messages must be brief and to the point. Simplicity is the key.

Educate consumers through a) verbal interaction while they are visiting your business and b) the media to develop their awareness of your products and services. Educate the public on how what you can do for them is different from the others, and the advantages of utilizing your services or products. You help them make an informed decision. They'll remember you and your small business as the one who created that awareness for them. People want to know the facts, which is why so many people watch television news and explore the Internet.

Action Step

What is involved in your efforts to educate the public about your product or service (brochures, newspapers, direct mail, others)?

Two major reasons for marketing a service business is to make your image known and to stimulate interest.

Add impact to your messages

The first thing customers want to know before giving you their attention is what's in it for them? Before you even consider communicating with consumers in the media, you need to clarify how you will benefit them with your products and services.

With so many businesses bombarding the public with information, your media messages must stand out in a simple and profound way. To reach your target market, your messages must be simple and eye-catching in a creative way. Write your message out on paper and repeat it back to yourself. Does it sound right?—comfortable?—true? Ask your friends if your message stands out in their minds. Is it different from your competition? Will it appeal to your target market? Is it a slogan that is easily remembered? It's important to increase communication effectiveness. Take some time to think this step through and test your messages.

Action Steps

1. What do you hope to accomplish with these media messages (primary objective)?

2. List some strategies for accomplishing these results.

Build a strong foundation for success by doing a thorough job of presenting your business to the public. To create a long-term successful business make a long-term financial commitment.

Energize with a Graphic Identity System

Three things are essential for profitability: a) a detailed business plan, b) an organized marketing campaign, and c) a well-designed identity system and meaningful printed pieces. You previously focused on your business's image and defined your benefits. Now it's time to energize your marketing campaign by developing a congruent communication system.

Produce a Graphic Identity System so the public can pick you out of the crowd. Your basic identity system will consist mainly of a logo, which you will display in a prominent place on your business cards, brochures, letterheads and envelopes (and website). Four elements will contribute to your graphic image: logo, color, typefaces, and paper.

Take the time to think—and feel—your pieces through, step-by-step, to get a sense of clarity. I stress clarity because communication systems can be rather expensive to develop, and mistakes can be even more expensive to correct.

Analyze your competitors' graphic identity system

Analyze the identity system and print media of each of your competitors. You did this in an *Action Step* in strength 3—*Investigating* your competitors. After comparing images, be certain to use a logo, a design, and colors that are unique to you. Using identical messages and designs will confuse the public. Make it a point to look different.

Seek examples from noncompetitive or product/service-oriented businesses. Implement innovative ideas into your designs.

Action Steps

1. Analyze at least three of your competitors' I. D. systems. What image, style, colors, typefaces, and paper do they use?

2. How is each one appropriate and effective?

Logo design

A logo is a symbol for communicating identity. Logos often project an image of reliability. They should be distinctive, project a positive image, express your personality, be something that you can protect legally, have lasting appeal, and be reproducible in a variety of sizes. A logo must also differentiate your business, product, and services from similar ones.

Design an eye-catching logo

Logos are a powerful media and marketing tool that define your uniqueness. In order to choose or design the best logo, have a clear understanding of your products and services, your niche, company image, goals, and your target market. Define what you need the logo to do and how it will be used. This process determines the logo characteristics that will best communicate the essence of your business. It will also attract your target market. Review your answers to the *Action Steps* to find the best solutions for your small or home-based business logo. Logos can be difficult to design, so look through logo and trademark books at bookstores to get some creative ideas.

Some businesses prefer to use abstract symbols; others like a stylized rendition of their names or a combination of both. Sketch out ten good first drafts, using different typefaces and symbols. Note if a particular shape or type of line communicates your identity. Try various sizes, placement, boldness, and degrees of balance. See how each solution works on a business card and stationery. Your logo, if typographic, must be readable at any size. Use Tom Marcoux's *Choice Market Testing* process: Show two options to many people and ask "Which do you prefer?" . . . "What about your selection works for you?"

Whichever style you choose to make that first good impression, choose a design that is simple, eye-catching, and easy to remember. It must also be inexpensive to reproduce. Develop a simple black-and-white version of your logo for various media.

Use your logo on everything from stationery (*i.e.*, letterhead, envelopes, and business cards) to websites, shopping bags, receipts, signs, flyers, labels, brochures, your business menu, all retail merchandise, and every bit of promotional and advertising print materials. When people see it they will identify it with you and your business.

Buy a professionally designed logo

Your logo is your most important graphic element, so if your time or creativity is lacking, hire a graphic designer or advertising agency. Interview several graphic designers before choosing one and ask to see their portfolios. Some probable questions to ask are:

- What are your best portfolio pieces and why?
- What services do you provide?
- Do you prepare camera-ready art?
- Do you oversee production?
- Does my piece interest you?
- How are you with deadlines?
- How much will you charge?
- When would you be available for my work?
- May I have references and call them?

My co-author, Tom Marcoux, suggests asking references: "Were there any problems, and how did it go?" Also, have the designers check to be sure the logo they create is not already being used or that yours is not uncomfortably close to a corporate identity. There are trademark restrictions, so be careful about what you choose.

You will pay more for a logo from a first-rate design firm. To bypass budget limitations, use the services of a design school student or seek a freelancer with reasonable fees. This is a tricky decision because sometimes new business owners must seek a better professional to "undo a mess" by someone who is not suitably experienced.

Your answers to the *Action Steps* are valuable insights into your business and will assist a graphic designer in understanding your business and image, so remember to take this book and your notes with you.

Contact an Art School and Engage a Student

Some entrepreneurs have found success by engaging a student from an appropriate art school. My co-author Tom Marcoux teaches graduate students at Academy of Art University. He has a number of interns, some of whom he has engaged to illustate book covers and even design websites. You might consider holding a contest and offering a cash prize to a student who submits a winning logo.

Action Step

Sketch your first ideas for a logo.

Choose Coordinating Colors and Typefaces

Unique typefaces and interesting color combinations can make your printed pieces look incredible (especially on glossy paper stock). Choose colors and typefaces for your printed materials that coordinate with your business's image. Typefaces are unique and tend to have a certain personality. Try to match up a typeface or two with the personality of your business. Look at corporate logos and printed materials to see examples of how that works.

Keep in mind that identity systems with two or more colors are more expensive to reproduce. For new ideas on what design styles are currently popular, seek the services of a graphic designer or look through design books located at your library, bookstore or online.

Action Step

1. What colors would compliment your business or company image?

2. What typefaces would be complementary to your company image, and match your business's personality?

Choose Paper Stock

The paper you choose for your identity system will have as much impact on your image as the other elements: logo, color and typeface. Before you choose the paper, decide if you are going to do it yourself on your home computer. If so, purchase a specific paper for your laser printer. An office supply store or a mail-order paper company will have many styles, designs and colors from which to choose. Purchase business cards, stationery, brochures, and message cards specifically to be used in your laser printer. Mail order catalogs offer software templates that will help you to easily format your designs.

Choose light-colored paper and dark ink if the piece is to be photocopied or laser printed. White paper projects a contemporary or business-like appeal, and cream projects an elegant, classic, or antique look.

Check with the post office to make sure it can be mailed (there are regulations affecting weight, size, location of information and type of fold).

Papers come in a large variety of colors, textures, grades, weights, and finishes. The printer will need to know what it will be used for, and how it will be distributed. You must be aware of cost, availability, and opacity. The most important factor is the look of the paper. Paper conveys a subtle message to the reader. It sets a mood through its feel, texture, and quality. Sometimes it is better to go with a more prestigious grade of paper to make an impression.

Printers often have a large quantity of paper available that they call 'house stock' that may be available at a better price than a special order. Call several and ask for more information.

Ask about paper 'weight'; and the weight you choose will depend upon the purpose of the piece and whether it will be mailed or handed out. Common bond paper is usually 20 lb., 24 lb., and 28 lb. Bond is used for stationery and flyers. Cover stocks, which come in coated and uncoated, usually weigh 60 lb., 65 lb., and 80 lb. Cover stock is used for business cards, folders, invitations, menus, booklets and anything requiring a heavier paper stock. Text paper, which comes in 70 lb., 80 lb., and 100 lb. weights, are used for self-mailers, booklets, and brochures, and often come in a variety of finishes.

Ask the printers questions. They'll help you save money, time, and headaches.

Business Card Guidelines

Business cards are the most easily transported advertisements for your business. Never underestimate the importance and recognition of a beautifully designed business card.

Design a professional-looking business card with your name, address, email, website, fax number, and phone number on it. Try to capture the essence of your business image. Create something that will appeal to your target market.

Add your logo or slogan and any pertinent information about your business. You may choose to use both sides of the card. On the reverse side of the card you could reserve space for the date and time of the client's next appointment or your business hours. List services that customers may not know about.

Folded business cards are also available, and serve as mini-presentation pieces. There is plenty of space for slogans, detailed business descriptions and other motivators to get customers to call you.

Print enough cards and distribute a sufficient number to your employees. Don't spend too much money in the beginning, in case you want to change your design or information. Once you are comfortable with your business card design, print each employee's or team member's name on their own supply of cards.

For a convenient temporary design system, purchase blank business cards from a stationery or office supply store and print them on your laser printer. You'll find a large variety of preprinted papers which come in professional-looking four-color designs. You can also get matching envelopes, letterheads, tri-fold brochures and postcards. Printing establishments have generically designed business cards. When appropriate, switch to your own unique materials.

Have plenty of your business cards and literature available at your front desk. Make it convenient for customers to access necessary information about your business. Ask customers to pass your promotional material around to friends and family.

Emphasize to your employees the importance of being generous with your business cards. They stimulate interest and make your image known.

Action Step

Sketch your first ideas for your business card.

Design Your Brochure

Brochures are a vital part of your identity system. They're a great promotional tool which highlights your business. Your brochure informs, motivates, sells, educates and persuades. Brochures or pamphlets are effective marketing pieces, usually getting a 10% return as reported by researchers who track this process.

Write to persuade

Write paragraphs (the "body copy") to express how you will benefit the reader, proof that your offer is credible, what action you want the reader to take, and how and when the reader needs to respond. For more information, read the Five Secrets To Better Brochures (a few paragraphs below).

Be crystal clear in your communication. Focus on price, advantages, features, benefits, convenience, quality or a time-limited offer. Support your ideas with text, charts, illustrations or testimonials. You want a brochure that is interesting, accurate, and specific. Make certain that the words flow. Plan graphics based on content.

Experts maintain that readers actually understand bar charts better than pie charts since bar charts require only a line-length judgment. But if one measurement is 90% or more use a pie chart.

Proofread your copy carefully and avoid costly errors.

Illustrations and photos

Excellent illustrations and photos already exist and often can be found for a nominal price on the Internet. They help set the mood or tone of the brochure. If you have original images available to you, you can easily place them on a page by scanning them into your computer first. Remember that photographs motivate more powerfully than drawings.

Find a good printer

When it comes to printing, your local printer can make suggestions that are within your budget. Take your ideas to them in the early stages of development.

Don't waste time, money and effort designing a brochure that is too expensive to print. It is also possible to photocopy your materials for short runs. For longer runs over 1,000, it's more economical to have it printed. In either case, make sure that copy is laid out so the brochure will fold properly with the cover on the outside.

Calculate delivery costs into your budget. The heavier paper weight will add to the cost of mailing a large amount of brochures.

If you choose to have your graphic pieces printed at a quick print shop, ask for their help in choosing an appropriate paper.

They'll have a sample swatch book to look at, and will give you estimates on your job.

Will cutting costs to save money hurt the finished product? Only you can decide if a more professional look is worth spending more money. If you are not happy with and proud of a cheaply made product, then you may hesitate in giving them out. Such hesitation impairs your quick progress and success.

Five Secrets to Better Brochures

Secret 1: Appeal to the needs of your target market. A direct approach is often superior because it motivates your customer to make the next move by taking advantage of your offer, coupon, postcard, etc. To be effective, your brochure must be attractive and believable, and provide a call for action. Include your name, address, phone number and business hours. Add your email address and website. If you feel a need to list your prices, do so on a separate insert. Updating information is easier, and you won't have to pay for a full printing.

Secret 2: Describe how the customer will benefit from your products and services, what problems you will solve and what the results will be. Establish credibility by using testimonials.

Secret 3: Provide credentials such as contests you or employees have won, customer endorsements, success stories and any guarantees you might offer.

Secret 4: Show things happening by using action photos, but not too many. Too many are distracting and take attention away from the copy. Use a single visual on the cover.

Secret 5: Use proven power words: improve, discover, you, free, health, guarantee, new, proven, safety, save and money.

Action Step

1. What is the primary purpose of your brochure?

2. What else can your brochure do for your business?

3. What image do you want to project in your brochure?

4. What will make your brochure more appealing to your target market?

5. What benefits do you want to emphasize in your brochure?

6. What photos would be useful and appealing?

7. Who is your message for?

8. How long will your brochure be in use?

9. What do you want people to do regarding your brochure?

10. How will you know if your brochure has achieved its objective?

11. Have you set a deadline? (My co-author Tom Marcoux says, "Avoid delaying too long to begin your actual selling efforts by trying to make a 'perfect' brochure. Remember, customers need to *talk* with you to begin to *trust* you."

Small and home-based business menu

Small business menus are a bit different from brochures in that they include a detailed description of your services and prices.

The secret here is to save money by using a separate insert for your price list. Update it whenever necessary, without having to reprint the whole menu.

How to Develop a Timeline

Develop a scheduled plan to receive your brochure or identity system by a certain time. You can do either a week-by-week schedule or a backward schedule. A timeline will vary as to whether you do it yourself or delegate it to a designer. The designer's schedule varies, depending on how busy he or she is. These timelines are also useful for your promotions.

The week-by-week schedule

The week-by-week schedule begins with the date you generate ideas or hire a designer, and continues until your pieces are in the customer's hands.

The sample week-by-week schedule flows as follows:

Example Schedule

Objective:

Target dates

Generate ideas or hire designer. . . . . June 1

Talk over concepts, costs and schedule . . . . June 10

Talk to copywriter and get costs and schedule . . . . June 15

Choose photography and illustrations . . . . June 20

Deliver writing to designer . . . . June 30

Review printed pieces. . . . . .July 6

Final edit and copy approval . . . . July 12

Printer. . . . . July 15

Delivery. . . . . July 18

Have in customers' hands. . . . . July 21

Step 15-2. The backward schedule

The backward schedule will begin with the date that you want your printed pieces to be in the customers' hands, and you work backward from that date.

The sample backward schedule functions as follows:

Example Backward Schedule

Objective:

Time required, target dates

Have in customers' hands. . . . . July 21

Delivery. . . . . .3 days, July 18

Printer . . . . .3 days, July 15

Final edit and copy approval . . . . .3 days, July 12

Review printed pieces. . . . . 6 days, July 6

Deliver writing to designer . . . . one week, June 30

Choose photography and illustrations . . . . 10 days, June 20

Talk to copywriter and get costs & schedule . . . . 5 days, June 15

Talk over concepts, costs and schedule . . . . 5 days, June 10

Generate ideas or hire designer. . . . . 10 days, June 1

Hire Outside Professionals

If you decide to hire a professional graphic designer for a brochure, be sure to get at least three bids for your design work. Ask the designer to assist you in choosing a paper stock that will print well with the type, illustrations or photography you have chosen. Order your paper early enough so that it is available by the time your job is ready for the printer.

Plan ahead for printed materials, and you'll get a better production and controlled costs. Allow ample time for each phase of the process: designing, copywriting, photography, retouching, typesetting, proofreading, printing and bindery work. Constantly check on how your job is progressing, and include time for corrections. My co-author Tom Marcoux advises his clients: "It helps to discuss a 'cap' (or limit) for the project budget. If you do not have a 'cap', you might get a bad surprise in that the professional has devoted too much time and incurred costs that are too high. Protect yourself. You can say something like: 'This project cannot exceed $1500. Let's keep me posted. If this project seems to start to go over budget, I require that you and I talk about this. I may need to cut something out.'"

Elicit the services of a professional business copywriter if you aren't certain what to say, or how to say it in a comprehensive manner.

Another important point: spending lots of money on a lavish printed piece does not guarantee its success as an effective communicator. Ensure your brochure is clearly readable with effective use of white space to make the main ideas stand out.

Action Step

Look in the yellow pages or call friends for referrals. Choose at least three graphic design firms to contact for estimates. Call for an appointment to review each designer's portfolio, then answer these questions:

1. Do you like the sample pieces in the designer's portfolio?

2. Would you like your brochure to look like these?

3. Does the designer charge a rate you can afford?

4. Does the designer appear reliable and conscientious?

5. Would you enjoy working with this person? (Have you talked with three references?)

6. In seeking a student graphic artist, what art schools are in your area?

Five Methods to Attract New Customers

Every business, large and small, is competing for the consumer's attention. Penetrating consumers' minds is no easy task, but it is possible. That's why it is essential that you do your marketing right the first time and make a lasting impression. Your communications need to be effective. Here are some important guidelines:

Method 1: Do your demographic research. In order to receive the best response from targeted mailings, they need to be sent to your target market.

Method 2: Make your communications personally relevant to the client. When using direct mail, place the client's correct name on the envelope. "Free offer inside" also helps entice people to open the envelope. Another consideration is to customize your messages for different groups of people.

Method 3: Engage the reader by educating them with useful information. Offer valuable tips, facts or how-to information. Make a handy chart: a bulleted list of secrets, principles, short cuts, rules, procedures or some useful information regarding your field or industry. Consider using a map if your business is particularly difficult to find. If you use charts, keep them simple. Consumers are more likely to respond to products or services they know something about.

Method 4: Make your brochures, newsletters, advertisements and flyers easy to read. Use appropriate larger-size print when directing campaigns towards our aging population. Create shortcuts by breaking up text into smaller sections, organize information into bulleted lists, use bold headlines and plenty of white space. Be certain that your message is clear. Ask someone to read your materials first, before they go to the printer.

Method 5: Keep visual similarity on all media pieces. A consistent look and feel assists consumers in identifying your communications as uniquely yours. For effective name recognition, use the same symbols or images, the same typefaces and colors. Keep a consistent attitude for the highest success rate.

A consistent look and feel among all your graphic identity pieces will provide a sense of congruency and professionalism.

Energizing Summary

Take the following steps to access your hidden strength to energize.

1. **Energize with a financial investment**

   A. Enable your dreams

   B. Make a financial commitment

   C. Define your budget

   D. Plan a financial strategy

2. **Energize with a communication system**

2A. *Energize your messages*

   A. Define benefits to customers

   B. Define your message

   C. Add impact to your messages

2B. *Energize with a graphic identity system*

   A. Analyze your competitors graphic identity

   B. Logo design

   C. Choose coordinating colors and typefaces

   D. Choose paper stock

   E. Business card guidelines

   F. Design your brochure

   G. How to develop a timeline

   H. Hire outside professionals.

I.   Five methods to attract new customers.

When Do I Take These Steps?

Before you can do any active marketing, you need to figure out how much money you have to invest. How much money you appropriate determines the extent of promotions and advertising you can do for the year. It also determines the quality of your marketing campaign. Your financial commitment to increased awareness of your business brings profitability.

Take this step of energizing and developing your message after completion of all previous strengths, especially the imagine strength. Base your identity system on your image, and your messages on the needs of your target market.

10

Activating

Your Ninth Hidden Strength

While gathering information for your next vacation, you consider the options: the type of vacation, a destination and time of year. Will you fly, sail or drive? Will you go alone or with a friend? Will you visit family or go to a new place? We all know that successful vacations are the result of making the best choices and decisions. Act in accordance with what you want by taking consistent steps and following through to completion. You may want to visit a foreign country, explore museums, meet exotic people, and eat different food. Go to a deeper level with your desires and you may discover that what you really want is adventure. So adventure empowers you to make decisions, and it is the connection between where you are now and where you want to be. You call the travel agent and say definitively, "I'm looking for adventure, what destinations do you suggest that I consider?" You've just shortened the process by getting right to the point. Take a few moments to reconnect with your hidden strengths before you read on. Activate your marketing campaign by eliminating the extra work and frustration, and get right to the point.

Strength 9—*Activating* focuses on the actions you'll take to reach your objective. You'll answer the one main question, "What actions will I take to make my marketing successful?"

Upon completing the *Action Steps*, you will benefit by raising customer awareness and escalating your public image. It helps to plan ahead and prepare for a number of situations. For example, Gale Anne Hurd, movie producer (*Terminator 2, The Incredible Hulk*) takes consistent action with confidence. She activates excellent plans. She says, "I tend to operate on a worst-case scenario basis. I imagine the next day's [filming] and what could possibly go wrong, and come up with A, B, and C plans."

To act with determination and strength you need to empower yourself. Now Dr. JoAnn Dahlkoetter shows you how.

Your Self-Esteem Can Boost Your Marketing

Dr. JoAnn Dahlkoetter

Motivation is energy, and a sense of self-directedness is one of the most powerful sources of energy available to an athlete or business person. The good news is that building and maintaining a high level of self-motivation is a learned strength that anyone can acquire. From internal motivation you gain the willingness to persevere with your training, to endure discomfort and stress, and to make sacrifices with your time and energy as you move closer toward realizing your goal. From working with many clients from CEOs to Olympic Gold medalists to small business owners, I have observed that people do better when they feel better. You can have the energy to do your marketing efforts when you take good care of yourself physically. Excercise is a must. And exercise boosts feelings of self-esteem!

The 3 P's for Your Performing Edge

Here are three tools for improving your ability to consistently exercise.

Positive images: Use your mental training and images throughout your workout to create feelings of speed and power (e.g., if you're walking or running and you come to an unexpected hill, visualize a magnet pulling you effortlessly to the top). Use visualization before, during and after your training to build confidence and new motivation.

Power words: Make positive mental training self-statements continually. Negative thinking is common; everyone has an inner critic. Become aware of these thoughts early on. Don't fight with them; simply acknowledge their presence, and then substitute positive power words. (e.g., When you're thinking: "This hurts too much, I want to lie down and die"; say to yourself: "This feeling is connected with getting healthier and doing my absolute best").

Present focus: Practice your mental training by being in the present moment. Remind yourself to stay in the here and now. Let past and future events fade into the background. Remember, Exercise improves your self-esteem, and good self-esteem gives you the energy to fulfill your marketing goals.

Dr. JoAnn Dahlkoetter, peak performance expert, sports psychology coach, best-selling author of *Your Performing Edge*, is a Stanford Performance Consultant, sports psychologist to Olympic Gold Medalists and CEOs, winner of the San Francisco Marathon and 2nd in the World. Championship Hawaii Ironman Triathlon. She is an internationally recognized Keynote Speaker, columnist, and frequent TV expert commentator on NBC, ABC, and BBC networks. Dr. JoAnn provides corporate training and personal coaching programs for sports, business, wellness, and reaching your potential in life. DrJoAnn.com Phone: 650-654-5500 Email: info@ sports-psych.com And to learn so much more about how to perform and feel your best, Dr. JoAnn invites you to download her free Online Mini e-Course for Personal Excellence with private coaching, video training tips, and valuable articles at drjoann.com/2009/12/tips/.

Your Objective for the Activating Strength

Your objective is to remember those times when you acted with determination and strength to attain something you really wanted. As a result you gained a sense of power, and it made you enthusiastic enough to do it again and again. You'll activate those memories now to strengthen your presence in the marketplace and get control of the ball.

Activating as a Natural Strength

Children demonstrate their activating strengths at a very young age. I remember when my youngest brother Tony took his first steps as a one-year-old. I had been holding him up, helping him to develop strength in his legs, and showing him how one foot went before the other. At first he held onto the chairs and sofa, until one day he finally let go of the furniture and darted happily across the room. My family and I made a big deal over his ability to activate his walking strengths. Children activate friendships by quickly talking to and playing with other children. They activate their televisions, video games and computers by pressing or pulling on buttons and knobs. Teenagers activate their driving strengths by taking a driver training class.

Because you've acted on something, made a decision and followed through to completion, you are an activator. We take action to accomplish objectives, and to become a successful person. We take action every day in one form or another, from the time we turn off the alarm and get out of bed, go to work and to the time we go to bed.

Our activating strengths take various forms. When I wanted to enroll in college, I sent in my application form and a check. I took tests, spoke with a counselor, and chose the classes I wanted to attend. All of those actions activated my college education. You can probably think of many ways that you have used your activation strength to affect your experiences in life.

Action Step

List two examples from your past when you used your activation strength.

A Celebration of Your Life Transformed—Really?

Tom Marcoux

Have you done some of the *Action Steps* in this book? Okay. Take a deep breath. Some readers will just read a book like this. Instead, I invite you to do something.

Take just 20 seconds and write something down in response to a question. You have just tripled the value of this book to your life. How do you enjoy a life transformed? You take one step forward at a time.

Recently, I was offered a new class to teach at the university where I currently teach eight classes. How did that happen? Some months earlier, I heard that a new department was forming. I went directly to the leader of that new department and expressed my experience and qualifications for the job. That is marketing. She can trust that I will do an excellent job of teaching the students skills that they'll use for a life-long career.

So now, your chance to transform you life begins with one step forward:

What do you want?

What do you want to feel?

What will your new life look like [after you effectively market your product or service]? How will your new life feel?

What will make all of your marketing efforts feel worth it?

That's it—answer the questions. Your transformation beings now:

Become a Catalyst for Change

Think of yourself as the activator or catalyst for change. You are in a position powerful enough to bring value through your products and services into the lives of other people. Most products and services bring a level of comfort, well-being, education, joy, or some degree of mental, physical and emotional pleasure or peace. Whatever your role is, if it contributes to your community in some positive way, then you are a catalyst who can make a difference.

Action Step

How does it make you feel to know that your products and services make a difference in a customer's life?

Develop Ethics in Advertising

It is valuable to keep your advertising copy reputable. Now, my co-author Tom Marcoux will share some guidelines:

Being Good Means "Good for Your Business"

Tom Marcoux

Have you heard about the topic "ethics in advertising"? Long-lasting companies build their business on long-term relationships with customers. Ethical advertising opens the door maintaining the relationships throughout the years.

"Genuine gifts, given with the right intent and a respectful posture meet our sniff test," wrote Seth Godin, known as the most influential business blogger in the world. Seth consistently holds the place as one of the twenty-five most widely read bloggers in the English language. About gifts, Seth also wrote: "If I create an idea, the Internet makes it possible for that gift to spread everywhere, quite quickly, at no cost to me. Digital gifts, ideas that spread--these allow the artist to be far more generous than he could ever be in an analog world."

What kind of gifts? A song, an e-book, a recording of a speech, a photo, a poem, a free chapter—it's up to you. YouTube.com is a compelling and influential outlet that allows people to post their song, video or recording of a speech. A number of people surf YouTube.com and discover new offerings everyday, and YouTube.com has reportedly over one billion views per day.

Here's an example of how an offering on YouTube.com took off. First, the song may have been a clever way to complain. But the humor and musicality of the work became a form of gift. A singer/songwriter Dave Carroll posted a song "United Breaks Guitars" detailing how his Taylor guitar was broken by United Airlines personnel and no one stepped forward to help the situation. As I write these words, the song/video has been viewed 10,255,305 times. My colleagues have said, "That song and video placed Dave Carroll on the map. I bet it helped his career."

Let's continue this conversation along the lines of advertising. How do we express good ethical behavior in advertising?

First, realize every consumer uses the "sniff test" on every bit of advertising. It's a self-defense reflex. Consumers seek to protect themselves from poor products that waste their money.

Second, begin your process with the right intent with your advertising: Sell something that will help the buyer!

Third, have your advertising include a respectful posture. How? Don't lie, exaggerate, or "bait and switch." Consumers hate being promised one product (the bait) and being told that another product (the switch) will suit them just as well—since the "bait-product" is somehow no longer available.

Do tell the truth. Substantiate your claims with proof. Disclose your guarantee or warranty. Have real people give true testimonials.

Use that respectful posture in advertising and you can begin long-term relationships with customers.

Another way to do good with advertising and public relations efforts is to connect your product with doing something benevolent. For example, authors Jay Conrad Levinson and Shel Horowitz announced "a portion of the authors' net profits from the book *Guerrilla Marketing Goes Green* launch will be donated to Green America (greenamericatoday.org), a not-for-profit organization founded in 1982 (as Co-op America) with a mission to harness economic power—the strength of consumers, investors, businesses, and the marketplace—to create a socially just and environmentally sustainable society."

A personal example: My family counts on Walt Disney Resorts to provide top notch service and friendly, courteous interactions. My sweetheart said, "Let's go to Alaska." I replied, "Okay. Let's take the Disney Cruise."

Customers appreciate businesses who are ethical in advertising and customer service. My vacation example shows how consumers will buy again and again from businesses who are trustworthy. Be reliable. Be consistent. It is simply good business.

Tip

Remember that advertising is not a cure-all for a business that is not doing well. There may be other factors that need to be looked at, such as management and cash flow.

Now Tom will talk about another aspect of marketing—since we opened with discussing ethics.

Can Marketing Be Spiritual?

Tom Marcoux

One of my friends appears to have frequent good luck. People call him with new opportunities. New clients arrive by referral. There's something in particular that I notice: he is always helping someone. During a recent conversation, I learned that he was looking at a stranger's resume at 1:43 AM. He did some work for this stranger by using Google.com to look up a couple of resources. My friend replied via email to the stranger with the links he found.

What's going on here? My friend is always seeking to serve. For some things he gets paid. For other things, it's just his way of flowing with each day.

Can marketing be spiritual? Yes! My friend is an example of seeking to make a contribution. Similarly, I have focused on my personal mission as "I help people experience enthusiasm, love and wisdom to fulfill big dreams."

My company also has a mission:

We create encouraging, energizing entertainment and edutainment in joy of contribution because our work enlivens us and outlives us to serve humankind's rise.

TOM MARCOUX MEDIA, LLC
Mission Caption

Every effort that my team members and I do for marketing is dedicated to a higher cause—"to serve humankind's rise."

So yes!—marketing can be spiritual.

And now I ask you: What good are you doing with your marketing efforts? How will your clients benefit from your product or service? This is where you start.

We can get a sense of personal mission and fulfillment when we take an extra moment to align our marketing efforts with a wholesome purpose. For example, one of my colleagues told me of a tire salesman who expressed philosophical nuggets in his television ads; he became both a legend and millionaire—in Tucson, Arizona.

Choose Your Distribution Methods

When I was a salon owner/stylist I worked with various chemicals that dramatically changed my client's hair color. In order to bleach or lighten hair, I mixed a bottle or tube of color with a developer. But to get more strength from the mixture, I needed to add an activator or booster. It made all the difference in the finished product. In marketing, you have your identity system and your money, which work like a bottle of color. But it's nothing without a developer, which are your mailers (brochures, newsletters, business cards, flyers). The real activating agent that makes your marketing campaign powerful is the media or distribution method. Put the three together, and you have a powerful mixture for success.

A strong marketer uses distribution methods to send his/her messages to their target market—in the form of flyers, direct mail coupons, newsletters, web pages and others. Your answers to the *Action Steps* are the signposts that will direct you to make the best decisions. Review your strategies for more ideas.

Your regular customers will find out about your promotions when they interact with you and your employees, so you don't necessarily have to mail them announcements, unless you prefer to do a mailing. You can hand them brochures, coupons, flyers, newsletters or other promotional materials before they leave your business. Make a media connection with rarely seen customers and prospective clients.

You've come a long way in your journey towards success and profitability, and now it's time to put your strategies into action. This Activating strength empowers you to use many methods of distribution to stimulate awareness.

Action Step

> List names and phone numbers of website designers, newspapers, radio stations, direct mail companies, cable TV, billboard sign companies, blogs and others.

Launch Your "Rocket Ship"

Think of your marketing vehicle as a rocket ship, and activating the rocket is like pressing the button that launches the ship into space. Pressing the button says to everyone, "This is it; this is what my business is all about." Activating your campaign means to set your plans in motion. It's a positive, direct action to achieve your primary objective.

Actualize

Take another look at your primary objective and realize how much it means to you, your employees, your business, and your community to have it become a reality. Review your transforming strength and anchor your success. Growing a business means nurturing that which you care about, while still remaining practical.

Plan

Plan for all possibilities by staying aware of what is going on in the marketplace and in your community. Activate the most logical promotions. Remember that your marketing campaign is not written in stone. It's basically a road map to your destination. Detours are inevitable, and sometimes they can become a welcome blessing.

Repetition

Use frequent and repetitive messages to guarantee that your campaign gets noticed by your target market. Activate your marketing campaign to consistently make impressions that 'wow' consumers and get control of the ball.

Action steps

1. Plan for increased education of employees. Reinforce your campaign through verbal support from your employees. For higher sales, offer employees a commission on retail sales.

2. Choose the most effective media to reach your target market.

3. Maintain consistent media coverage.

4. Prepare your business: You'll need business displays, samples to give away, product information handouts and plenty of products to sell.

Activate your marketing campaign

1. Public relations,

2. Advertising, and

3. Promotions.

Activate public relations

Additional information can be found in the Chapter 7, *Develop Your Media Plan.*

Press Releases

Begin your public relations campaign with press releases which inform the public that you're making important changes. Design press releases to 'release' information about your business. Use it for newsworthy events like the opening of your new business, new location, new employee, or an award you or an employee has won.

Attract the attention of the editor with a 'unique angle' or a strong purpose. Your press release must contain information about something new, interesting, and of benefit to the public. A well-written presentation is important.

Limit your release (often called a "media release") to one page, use your letterhead stationery and make your presentation well-written, simple and easy to read. Double-spaced paragraphs are standard format. List a contact person in the top right corner of the page.

Use "who, what, when, where, why and how" to convey your message of your major event. Write the first paragraph in an inverted pyramid style, with the most important information first, then less important information, and finally the least important information. It is likely the last paragraphs will be cut in newspapers or other media.

The press release format:

1. The release date

2. Headline

3. Body

4. Source information

5. Conclusion

Guidelines for more effective press releases:

1. Use adjectives to make your copy dynamic.

2. Make sure the information is grammatically correct.

3. Be brief.

4. Be concise.

Where to send your press release:

1. City editor at the newspaper office

2. Contact people at appropriate Blogs and websites

2. News director at the radio station

3. The assignment desk people for television news shows

You'll have a better chance of getting exposure with a small newspaper. Also, read the newspaper to find an appropriate editor or reporter to call. When you call to find out whom to send the press release (the "media release") to and how much lead time is necessary before newspaper deadlines. Remember to send a thank you note to the person in charge. Often, you'll be using email to seen your press release. Also, remember to contact appropriate bloggers because they can be quite influential.

Action Step

1. Why do people need the information in your potential press release.

2. Note your first ideas for a press release.

Press Kit

Send a press kit to professional associations, trade magazines, radio stations and local newspapers. This will most likely get you an interview. Included in this 9 x 12 inch packet of information is the press release, photographs, articles about you and your expertise, your brochure, a business card, video or audio clip, and any other pertinent information. Include an energetic cover letter to capture the editor's attention.

Be sure to mail it on time, or deliver it to the editor yourself. Several days before the event, call the editor to be certain he or she received your packet. Ask if the editor has questions or comments concerning the press kit. It is always appropriate and recommended to send a thank you note to acknowledge the reporter who covered your story.

If you don't get noticed the first time, don't give up. Continue to send releases until you receive the exposure you want. Also, many business owners have a link on their homepage labelled "Media" which leads to a webpage that includes downloadable material (from the press kit).

Strategic publicity power

The following strategies will activate your public relations efforts:

1. Be certain that your public relations efforts support your objective.

2. Place your business first in the public mind by spotlighting particular events.

3. Choose the media that will best reach your target market.

4. Send out related materials and follow up with phone calls.

Most importantly, don't give up. It takes time to gain exposure for your business.

Activate direct mail marketing

Direct mail marketing is the most popular way to impress your business's image into the minds of potential customers.

Be certain your messages are clear and concise, and present your image appropriately. Keep your mailers cost effective by using lightweight paper, one color of ink and bulk rate mail. Ask several people to look at your ideas before you spend money to send out direct mailings or advertising. It's also good to test it a couple of times before committing to a large mailing. A poor response rate will make it obvious that your idea isn't attractive.

Additional information can be found in Strategizing— *Develop Your Media Plan.*

Nine secrets for planning a direct mail campaign

Secret 1: Get to the point quickly. State your offer in the headline and make it clear.

Secret 2: Make sure the offer is right. Avoid your mail going in the trash; the right offer encourages the prospective client to study the potential purchase. Carefully craft your offer to be genuine, valuable, and believable. Don't give so much away that no profit exists for you. Determine whether you will be able to make a profit with a .5% response, a 1% response or a 2% response.

Secret 3: Use the envelope to grab the reader's attention and motivate them to buy. Use something to evoke their curiosity: a cartoon, a quote, an interesting graphic or the promise of valuable information. Get them to open the envelope by offering something "FREE inside."

Secret 4: A visually interesting letter is often better than a brochure. Longer letters typically get higher responses. Ask for the sale. Emphasize that the offer has a time limitation. Remember to use a P.S. — research shows that people read P.S. messages. Repeat your call to action in the P.S.

Secret 5: Remember to match the tone of your letter to the target audience and the subject. This involves knowing your target market very well. Review your demographic research in strength 4, and identify the characteristics of your target market.

Secret 6: Treat the potential customer as a friend. A more personal letter creates a sense of camaraderie rather than a cold, impersonal message.

Secret 7: Offer a free consultation. Experts agree that an introductory service stimulates responses. Offer trial size products to first-time customers.

Secret 8: Put together some *before and after visuals.* They are effective and show potential customers how you can successfully create change.

Secret 9: Keep your mailers cost-effective. Use lightweight paper to keep your mailing costs down, and one color of ink on white or colored paper to lower printing costs. Try cost efficient postcards before letters. Buying the right mailing list will also keep your costs down. Remember that a "tightly" selected mailing list of 300 people, to whom you mail separate pieces four times, can help you get a 17% response rate. This multiple mailings process is more effective than sending one piece to 3,000 "widely" selected prospective clients.

Send your mailers to people who have a need for your product or service, and you will certainly reap the rewards of smart planning.

Apply the same rules for introductory letters and direct mail coupons.

Introductory letters

The purpose of the introductory letter is to introduce your business and your benefits. Use a professional-looking letterhead from your identity system. In writing a letter, introduce yourself and what you do, then focus on how your services can benefit them. Remember that the most visible areas of your sales letters are the first sentence and notes handwritten in the margin.

In writing the letter use the words: "you, your benefits, your advantage" instead of "we offer, we provide."

Send introductory letters to local professionals such as health clubs, clothing stores, etc., who might like to share mailing lists and/or exchange services. Contact them within a week to discuss how to continue.

Test your direct marketing by varying the elements: a letter rather than a card, reflecting certain seasons, price differentials, diverse colors, unique layouts or special offers. Know what has worked for you in the past. Look at the effective direct mail you receive. Notice which elements continue to arrive in the package; they are the successful ones.

Action Steps

1. Draft your first ideas to make the envelope grab the reader's attention.

2. Note your first ideas for a P.S. part of the introductory letter.

Direct mail coupons

Direct mail coupons give the first-time buyer an added incentive to invest in your products and services.

Four mailings a year, one each quarter, are a consistent way to promote your business and determine if direct mail is the right marketing approach for you. Consciously direct your mailings to people who can benefit from your products and services. Another approach is to do four mailings within forty days: you send out a mailing and then another mailing to those who did not respond to the first one. Experts, including Dan Kennedy, say that this approach increases the usual 1.5% response to 17%.

Properly done, direct mail can build trust. Consumers welcome value-oriented information. Establish rapport and help the consumer trust you, your products and services, to lift your message out of the "junk mail" category. Notice what appeals to you when you receive a direct mail packet. Use successful ideas as a model for your own coupons.

Restate your offer on the coupon. List payment, delivery options, and a phone number. Include the expiration date and any other rules. Repeat your address in case the coupon gets separated from the rest of the mailing. If you are sponsoring an event, enclose free tickets that are activated when the prospective client calls you. For the tickets, use warm colors like red and include the location, phone number and other necessary information.

If you plan to include a coupon on a flyer or sales letter, place it in the lower right hand corner for easy removal.

Visit your local library for books on direct mail. Apply all the great advice, forms and ideas to your own campaign. Some list brokers offer free guides with pages of advice on direct mail. Ask your broker if they have one. Market to people outside your existing customer base by renting a mailing list; rental fees vary according to the nature of the list, the number of names ordered and the number of uses paid for.

Request a copy of the Consumer's Directory of Postal Services and Products from the U.S. Post Office. It's free and filled with facts on minimum size requirements, bulk mailings, class mailings, postage meter rentals, address protocol and more.

Your objective is not to save money, but to rent the right list. You don't want to mail your expensive direct mail piece to the wrong audience. You'll find list brokers featured in the yellow pages under "Advertising/Direct Mail." Ask for references.

Direct mail catalogue

Create your own direct-mail catalogue. Customers who are unable to come to your small business could order products from you by telephone or email. List available mail order products on your order sheet. Add the price of each item, tax, shipping and handling. Customers pay by check or credit card.

E-newsletters

E-newsletters are a wonderful way to stay in touch with customers, establish credibility and build rapport. Writing your own newsletter establishes you as an expert in your field when you inform your customers of trends and future events.

E-newsletters are long-term, ongoing marketing tools that constantly keep your business's name in the customer's mind. Give your newsletter a name and a tagline that includes the subject of your e-newsletter. It doesn't have to be long; two pages can be enough.

When designing your e-newsletter, make sure it's easy to read, conversational in tone and focuses on providing useful information. To make your e-newsletter more helpful and well read, pack more information into a short publication.

Add unique information that appeals to your customers. Add anything that pertains to the development of your professional business image. Your charity work, dates of public speaking engagements, and television or radio broadcasts are especially important. Refrain from writing only about your business. You will lose credibility if your e-newsletter sounds like a long advertisement. Instead, always provide value, including some tips that your reader can use.

Send your e-newsletters to existing customers as well as potential customers. [Make sure that a visitor to your website can easily sign up for your e-newsletter.] Send e-newsletters to past customers, especially if they are familiar with other members of your customer base. E-newsletters keep them informed of current events. You never know when they might become dissatisfied with their current services and be motivated to return. Continuing to keep them on your mailing list says you are looking forward to seeing them soon.

Send your newsletter to customers at least on a quarterly basis. My co-author Tom Marcoux has prewritten more than two years of e-newsletters (24 monthly e-newsletters), and anyone who signs up for his free e-newsletter "Success Secrets" receives the first one no matter what time of year the person signs up.

The quarterly distribution of your e-newsletter gives you enough time to collect pertinent information and write the copy. Create the newsletter on your home/business computer or with a graphic designer.

Increase your distribution by giving extra copies to walk-in customers. You can also give them to other businesses which you cross-promote.

Helpful hints for e-newsletters

1. Include sections on trends, quick tips, sales, new product information, and announcements about your business.

2. Include interesting brief news from magazines and reputable online sources. Be careful not to plagiarize. Quote sources and give credit where credit is due. Add your own personal ideas or ideas from your employees, customers or networking partners.

3. Add information on products and services, updates on the small or home-based business industry or specifically your business.

4. Create how-to articles in your area of expertise.

5. Add birthday acknowledgments of both customers and employees. Perhaps, formally recognize graduations, marriages, anniversaries, births and deaths.

6. Add cartoons, illustrations and photographs to give a new dimension to your newsletter.

7. Include coupons as well as specially designed inserts (for the printed version), such as flyers or testimonials.

Action Step

Note your first ideas for an e-newsletter.

Now, Ed Gandia will share ideas about including an e-newsletter in your marketing mix and how to follow-up with prospective clients.

Don't "Throw Away" Your Prospects

Ed Gandia

Did you know that only 10% of the energy used by an incandescent lightbulb produces light? The rest is given off as heat.

Seems like a lot of wasted energy, doesn't it?

It's no different when you're a freelancer, consultant or other solo professional and you're prospecting for clients. Most of the energy that goes into a self-promotional effort is wasted in the search for those few golden nuggets. That's life.

But the difference between just getting by and always having a steady stream of work lies in what you do with prospects who aren't ready to hire you.

Take, for instance, a direct mail campaign. Or maybe a cold-calling effort. If you're lucky (and with the right list, call to action, copy or script), you might get five leads out of 100 pieces mailed. From that select group, maybe a single lead will become a client.

It's not that the other four who responded don't need or want you. Assuming there's a good fit, they might just not have a current need. Or maybe they don't have the budget to hire you today.

That's why I call these prospects the "not today" group.

But here's where many solo professionals drop the ball. Instead of trying to nurture these prospects (the four who expressed interest but couldn't hire you at the time), the tendency is to forget about them.

Sure, they might attempt a follow-up call here and there. But many such calls take the wrong approach. Often, they go something like

"Hi, Susan. Kevin Smith here. Calling to see if you have any projects I can help you with."

That comes across as desperation more than anything else.

What few folks ever try to do—and what you should attempt in order to become a truly successful solo professional—is to start a meaningful dialogue with this "interested but not now" group. Regardless of their timing to hire you.

In other words, you should work diligently to nurture this group of prospects over the long haul. Not with calls to see "if they have a project." But with carefully timed value-added information.

Think about it. These people have expressed interest. They've responded to your call to action. Most of them are qualified to do business with you. You've had some honest dialogue. In other words, you've already done most of the heavy lifting. Now you just need to stay top of mind. That way, the next time they need help in your area of expertise, you're the first person they think of!

Not staying in touch in a meaningful way would be wasteful. And crazy.

How can you strategically nurture this "not today" group? Here are some practical ideas:

1. Ask permission to add them to your newsletter distribution list. A highly targeted newsletter with valuable, insightful and practical content gets read. It builds credibility. It positions you as an expert in your field and as someone with great ideas. Better yet, it helps keep you top of mind with hundreds of potential prospects. But don't just stop there …

2. Send an occasional email with relevant news. Have a new service offering? A new capability? Have an impressive case study of how you helped a similar company solve a key problem? Thought of another

way you can help the prospect? Send him or her a quick email every couple of months. Be brief, but be personal. And if you really want to set yourself apart …

3. Also stay in touch by sending relevant articles. Personally, this is my favorite way to become memorable. While I use the other two strategies above, I love to send my clients and prospects articles I think they'll find interesting and useful, based on what I know about them and their businesses.

Want to really make an impact? Send the actual cutout (or printout) of the article via postal mail with a handwritten Post-it note. Either way, be genuine and relevant. And again, always be personable without coming across as a stalker. And don't send everyone the same article—make sure what you send is relevant to each prospect.

Make it a point to institute a prospect-nurturing program. Make this part of your marketing process. And watch your marketing efforts skyrocket.

No reason to let all that valuable prospecting time, money and energy go to waste.

Ed Gandia is the co-author of *The Wealthy Freelancer: 12 Secrets to a Great Income and an Enviable Lifestyle* (Penguin/Alpha) and co-founder of TheWealthyFreelancer.com, a popular blog with strategies and insights for getting the clients, income and lifestyle you want as a solo professional. An expert on the topic of successfully transitioning from employee to self-employed, Ed took his part-time freelance business from zero to a six-figure income in only 27 months—without sacrificing his day job or putting his family's financial future at risk. Ed has written marketing copy and consulted for more than two-dozen clients in the high-tech industry. His advice and insights have been featured in publications such as *DM News, AirTran Airways' Go magazine, The Writer* and *WhitePaperSource,* among others. A self-proclaimed wine geek, he lives with his wife, son and hyperactive dog in Marietta, Georgia.

Activate Advertising

Advertising attracts attention to your business and creates a favorable impression on the public. The objective of advertising is to provide information consumers want, present a problem to which you have the solution, and present a situation with which they can identify. An effective advertisement will arouse their curiosity, lure them into your world and invite them to participate. Provide appealing images and words that answer consumers' question: "What's in it for me?" Your answer must demonstrate how your services are quicker, more quiet and relaxing, a better price value, more convenient, full service or other benefits.

Advertising approaches

Use any or all of these seven approaches to more effective advertising:

> **Humor:** Use a humorous story or quote that puts your business in a positive light.

> **Human interest story:** Use a true example of how your own experiences contributed to your success.

> **Comic strip:** People enjoy a new and refreshing style of advertising. Create your own characters.

Testimony: Use quotes from satisfied customers; high-profile customer quotes work best.

Problem solving: Show how you solved a common problem.

Emotional appeal: Tell how your product or service made a difference in someone's life.

Projective approach: Paint a picture (in words) of a customer using your product or service with good results.

Advertising decisions

When you create an ad, answer these questions:

1. Are you going to do a single advertisement or a series?

2. What size is the advertisement going to be?

3. What is the shape of the advertisement?

4. Is it going to be in black and white or color?

5. How long will the advertisement be in length?

Include no more than 1-3 selling points, with the most important on top. Look at other advertisements to see new trends.

Closing an advertisement

There are three ways to close an advertisement: a direct close, a soft suggestion, and an implied suggestion.

1. A direct close uses the last sentence to tell the reader what you want them to do: call for an appointment, write a letter, come into the store, send a fax or e-mail, ask for a catalog or talk to a salesperson.

2. A soft suggestion says to the reader to 'think of me' before you go elsewhere.

3. An implied suggestion suggests what is lost if the service or product is not purchased from you.

Create another sign in your small business which states "satisfaction guaranteed" and mean it. My co-author Tom Marcoux says, "Don't be shy. Close with 'Call (phone number) and get your free (offering) today.'"

Free Advertising

Word-of-mouth: Of course your best advertising is by word of mouth and a satisfied client. It's always appropriate to ask for referrals. Give your customers business cards and brochures to hand out, and please send them a thank you note for their effort and good intentions.

How do you recognize customer satisfaction? You know when they call for another appointment or return to purchase more products and services. Customers can express pleasure and be supportive of your business by telling their friends, family and co-workers. Reassure business customers that you will also refer your customers to them for products and services. Get their business cards, and do it.

To encourage repeat business, use some combination of these methods: thank you notes, discount coupons, brochures, business cards, referral coupons, new customer packet, and appreciation certificates.

Action Step

How are you going to create excellent word-of-mouth?

Advertising media

Magazines: Magazine advertising is generally too expensive and tend to cover too wide a territory to be effective for a small business with a local store. You may benefit from magazine advertising if you belong to a regional or a nationwide chain store or a franchise, or if you sell by mail or email.

By advertising in a trade magazine, you can be selective as to the type of person reading your advertisement.

Newspapers

Additional information can be found in the Chapter 7, *Develop Your Media Plan*. In recent years, many newspapers have gone under. Still a local newspaper may be an appropriate venue for your advertising. Here are six advantages to newspaper advertising:

1. Flexible.

2. Fairly reasonable in cost.

3. Changeable with one or two days' notice.

4. Adaptable to geographic targeting. You can choose a specific area in which to advertise.

5. Set up for good timing to reach a certain audience. Many newspapers have morning, afternoon and evening editions.

6. Good for seasonal promotions.

Ethnic newspapers

Many communities have a large ethnic population. Small ethnic newspapers are a good place to attract clients from a multicultural neighborhood. Analyze the benefits of targeting an ethnic area. You or your employees need to fluently speak the language.

Action Step

Which ethnic newspaper could you target?

College/university newspapers

Consider advertising in local college newspapers. Perhaps, pay a student to hand out flyers, or tack them up in the student union and on school billboards. Offer special discounts to students with an I.D. Make the offer during slow times of the day, on slower business days, or just when you need more business.

Action Steps

1. Which area college newspapers could you target for advertisements?

2. What type of student discount can you offer?

High school newspapers

Don't neglect your local high school newspapers. Their rates are often very reasonable and it's a low-cost way to reach local teenagers. They do care about maintaining their image, and many have good-paying jobs and a disposable income. A satisfied teenager is a great advertisement. They'll tell their friends about you and generate excitement about your business.

Action Step

Which area high school newspapers could you target for advertisements?

Local newspapers

As mentioned, in recent years, a number of newspapers have shut down. If you decide to use your local newspapers to reach customers, focus on what makes you unique or a provider of special benefits to people in your immediate vicinity. Impress the public with your image, grab their attention and motivate them to call you.

Call the newspaper to discover their prices and column specifications before you design an ad. The column inch is the accepted system of measure. You'll get a better rate by signing a long-term contract.

Offer a benefit in the headline. Appeal to the reader's self-interest or state some news. When writing your copy, make it easy to read. Use capitals and lower case letters in the text.

Avoid text in all capital letters, which is difficult to read. 'Sans serif" type, like Helvetica, is best for headlines and display type, while 'serif' type, like Times Roman, provides easy readability for the text.

Remember to use simple layouts. Avoid a cluttered ad with too many photos and multiple typefaces. A dramatic or outstanding photo or illustration with a brand name can deliver a clear message. Many experts feel that the headline is crucial to spark the reader's interest.

Experts agree that photos work better than artwork and offer compelling visual evidence. A caption under the photo gets twice as much readership as body copy. A picture with a caption can be an advertisement within itself.

An advertising agency or your newspaper's sales representative can direct you in your advertising campaign. Due to the rising costs of advertising, it's often a smart decision to consult with a qualified professional.

Action Steps

1. Identify local newspapers that could be an advertising vehicle for you.

2. Sketch your first ideas for a display ad. Include ideas for a photograph.

3. Schedule the date when you will develop your advertising and set a deadline for presenting it to area newspapers.

Yellow pages advertisement

The yellow pages tend to be rather expensive, and a large advertisement is not always better. You can purchase space in the yellow pages in varying sizes. Choose from one-line listings to quarter-page or full-page spreads. Still, many frugal business owners choose to avoid an elaborate yellow page advertisement.

Update your advertisements yearly. In order to be more competitive, add new information as trends change.

Action Step

Sketch your first ideas for a yellow pages ad.

Activate Outdoor Advertising

Outdoor advertising will extend and balance your marketing campaign, reminding consumers of brand names, brand images and brand positioning.

Here are some outdoor advertising tools:

Balloons

Balloons attract the attention of passersby. I know of a small restaurant whose owners consistently hang colorful balloons outside their door. This business is on a side street, so balloons draw the attention of people who might not realize the business exists. The balloons give the business a cheery, party look.

Billboard advertising

Here are the advantages to using billboard advertising:

1. It is observed by many people.

2. It can be local.

3. It may have an enormous impact.

The billboard retailer does research to learn how many cars travel past the sign and the number of viewers likely to see it. The standard size of most billboards is 12 feet by 24 feet.

Design your advertising message to grab the readers' attention quickly and deliver the communication instantly. The rules for successful billboard advertising are to keep it simple and easy to understand. You need only one picture and no more than seven words of copy. Make it memorable. Humor works well and will appeal to bored travelers. Avoid offending people.

Use creative work that is distinctive and perhaps enhances the environment. Sign makers use computers to give us more options. Use high-impact graphics and bold lettering. The use of primary colors will grab the reader's attention. Black on yellow is the most visible combination. Location is of prime importance. You will pay more for the most visible location and a reduced amount for a less conspicuous site (which may not be worth the investment). Consider the idea of a billboard on your business's roof or sign on your company car's roof.

Action Step

Sketch your first ideas for billboard advertising.

Bus stop: Use bus stop advertising to gain additional outside exposure. Be brief, colorful, and compelling.

Call your local transit authority for details and cost quotes.

Front door: Use your business's front door for advertising or decorative purposes, especially during a holiday. It is always useful to have an "open" and "closed" sign on the door and to state your hours of business.

Message board: Present a simple and attractive message (sandwich) board outside your door to advertise your business. This is especially effective if your small business is on the second floor or out of view.

State your name, phone number, hours of operation, etc. Attach a Plexiglas holder for brochures or flyers to inform passersby and entice potential customers to try your services. You may prefer to secure your message board to a pole or a concrete block. Check with local ordinances before you go to the expense and effort of creating a board. Some cities prohibit the use of message boards.

Action Step

Sketch your first ideas for a message board.

Where in your neighborhood are message boards located (grocery stores, cafes, laundromats)?

Outdoor sign: Another form of free advertising is your outdoor sign. Light it at night to attract the people who pass by.

Sidewalk art: Use colored chalk on the sidewalk in front of your store. Develop a unique design to create interest in your newest promotion. Consider having an artist illustrate an appropriate image for your business. Get news coverage on it.

Plane pulling a sign: This is a unique way of getting your message across to the general public. You'll reach the widest audience during special community events.

Window: Create a startling display that will attract attention to your business. Your window will act as a salesperson to every passing individual. Be colorful and daring. Use unusual props. Consider an interactive display—perhaps, an electric eye that activates a toy train. Set up product displays with banners or plastic lettering to develop your own unique promotions. Notice what other businesses use to attract attention. Department and clothing stores generally have interesting and eye-catching displays.

Decorate your window for special events and during the holiday seasons. Include new products, stocking stuffers and any pertinent information. I once had an artist come into my business and paint Christmas scenes on my windows. My customers enjoyed this customized decoration. It was a fun departure from the usual displays.

Action Step

Sketch your first ideas for window advertising.

Activate Broadcast Media

More information can be found in the strategizing strength, Chapter 7, —*Develop Your Media Plan.*

Cable television: Consider local cable television as a good source for reaching local consumers. Call your local cable company to get quotes on advertising.

Action Step

Identify the name and phone number of your local cable television network and prepare copy for cable television advertising.

Radio and television: The strategizing strength, Chapter 7—*Develop Your Media Plan,* has information regarding radio and television advertisements. Review, then complete the following *Action Step.*

Action Step

Note your first ideas for a radio or television ad.

Activate Digital Media

Online marketing costs a fraction of the amount of direct mail and results are available much more quickly. Find the most effective ads by testing a variety. Then count the number of downloads each one receives. Your local bookstore will have many in-depth books about online marketing, online etiquette, and creating a website.

More information can be found in the Chapter 7, *Develop Your Media Plan.*

Now, Allison Bliss will guide us to make our website do some profitable activity.

Converting Web Traffic Into Sales

Allison Bliss

So, you've done some great SEO (search engine optimization) to build traffic to your website. (If you haven't, take a look at the end of this article*).

But are you making the sales or growing your clientele? That's what 'conversion' is all about. Converting visitors to take action, to learn more, and to make purchases of your products or services.(for marketing coaching or services from our marketing agency, email us exactly what you need). But for converting visitors to buyers, here are a few tips we use and some we've learned from a few experts this week:

1. Be certain to add Google Analytics to your site so you can measure where your visitors come from, which pages are most popular, which percentage of visitors actually purchase items from

....

* Still haven't done the SEO to build traffic on your website? Allison suggests: "Visit me at AllisonBliss.com for useful options."

you and other critical factors that can be analyzed to convert traffic to sales. Sign up for free at: google.com/analytics/sign_up.html. If you need our programmer to add this code to your website, just email us a request.

2. Build your Social Network outreach (Twitter, Facebook, LinkedIn, etc.). It's free, but you should devote a half hour daily to learn to maximize its potency for your business. We've a tool to save you dozens of hours by showing you exactly how to set up your social media to make it work for you: allisonbliss.com/services. htm#socialmedia. Is it worth 50 hours of your time to learn top techniques in social media? If not, you can get this action tool for only $17.

3. Create a blog, free report, ezine, downloadable pdf with instructional info, or free ecourses to test which work best to get your web visitors converting to purchasers.

Why? If you add up the long term value of a typical client, you may find for small professional service businesses that they're worth $4,000 over the course of a year.

If you're only getting 1 out of every 100 web visitors to convert into a client, you're not making your "conversion tools" work hard enough. Let's say you test different tools (*i.e.*; a webinar instead of a free report, or ecourse instead of an ezine, for example) and increase your sales to a 3% conversion. You've just turned $4,000 into $12,000 a year. (Thanks to internet expert & trainer Tom Antion for this lesson!)

4. Build your Affiliate income. Let's say you're a writer and I've got a great service that benefits your clients or web visitors so they stand out from the crowd (that's called "positioning" in marketing parlance). Perhaps you'd want to offer them this "Knowledge is Bliss

Positioning Package" of ours for sale on your website—you'd help your clients so that your writing would be even more effective—without guessing at the positioning, too!

For each package sold through your site, you might receive a $200 commission. And best of all you helped your clients at the same time. Win-win, right? And you didn't even spend 2 minutes doing any work. Ahhh, now you get the picture!

Free Tip: The top affiliate sales experts recommend that the best affiliates sell ongoing 'residual or continuous' sales products—like classes or subscriptions for which people pay large monthly fees. That way, you get continual monthly commission payments. And over time, this adds up! But I suggest you start with products or services you personally recommend and know will help your clients.

So, who could you partner with that has these products on their site that you could be selling? Maybe you work with a transcriptionist who could help your legal clients. Or maybe you sell a series of CDs that train people on dog behavior tips and know a vet who would love to sell your CD's on their website. Put some brainstorming into it and watch your income grow. Need help with that? Of course you can call us!

Free tip: If you need a super inexpensive, easy-to-operate shopping cart to make this work, contact me and I'll recommend one.

Go forth and prosper: Follow Your Bliss …

Allison Bliss is founder of Allison Bliss Consulting, a Bay Area marketing and communications agency that helps service professionals earn more income by creating marketing action plans that actually bring success. She brings 20 years working on Hollywood feature films and TV shows, running dozens of businesses and leads her teams of writers, designers, internet marketing, and social media specialists to activate marketing plans into reality to help independent professionals earn more income.

As a 2009 winner of The Woman-Owned Business Award, Allison brings her successful resources, ideas, tools & resources to her Marketing Coaching service, which is geared for small business owners to increase clientele. The agency also creates promotional materials, web development, television commercials, the "Knowledge is Bliss" business evaluation, podcast production, search engine optimization, marketing services, branding, and marketing plans. The company can be reached at 510-864-8500. abliss@allisonbliss.com

---

Allison has encouraged us to take action to gain more profits from our website. Another approach to online marketing is to make the most of free social media processes. Now, Danek S. Kaus guides us to increase our following on Twitter.

Want a Huge Twitter Following?

Here's how to get more twitter followers

Danek S. Kaus

If you're on Twitter you know what a powerful marketing tool it can be. But the key to success is finding and keeping followers. Here are 11 steps you can take to get more Twitter followers.

1. Create a great Twitter bio. One of the key factors in whether or not people decide to follow you is the quality of the information in your bio. If you have a relevant website, be sure to include the URL.

You only have 160 chracters, as opposed to the 140 allowed in tweets, so use them well.

2. If you're new to Twitter, create about 10 or so interesting tweets before looking for followers. You have to give people a reason to want to follow you.

3. If you find an interesting article on the web, tweet about it with a link. Because most links will be too long, you can shorten them by going to tinyurl.com. Simply paste in the old link and it will give you a new "tiny" link to use for free.

4. Tweet inspiring or humorous quotes. You can find a lot of great quotes that your Twitter followers will enjoy at BrainyQuotes.com

5. Tweet links to interesting videos from YouTube and other such sites.

6. Help others by re-tweeting their tweets. Many will return the favor, which will expose you to other people who may then decide to follow you.

7. Join the conversation. Reply to other people's tweets, give them a compliment or thank them for sharing. These people may also decide to send you @ messages, which will also make their followers aware of you.

8. Thank people who re-tweet you. Just hit the reply button and send a thank-you note. If you don't thank them, at least some of the time, they will probably stop re-tweeting you and stop following you.

9. Become active on Follow Friday. Each Friday, recommend some of your favorite tweeters to your followers by typing in "#FollowFriday or #FF" and then their Twitter handle, such as "@JaneSmith." Others will do the same for you. This is a great way to get more Twitter Followers.

10. Follow all of Twitter's rules about following and un-following. Don't become too aggressive or your account will be suspended.

11. If you are marketing something, try to keep a ratio of about one marketing message for every 10 or so tweets. If all you do is try to sell people something, they will stop following you. Doing nothing but marketing tweets could get you labeled as a spammer, which could result in being banned. Remember Twitter is about being social first and marketing, if you do any marketing, second.

> Danek S. Kaus is the author of *You Can Be Famous! Insider Secrets to Getting Free Publicity*. He has helped people to get featured in *USA Today*, CNN, the *New York Times*, and hundreds of other newspapers, radio and TV shows, and magazines. His website is getfreepublicitynow.com Write him at dkaus@sbcglobal.net.

Danek has introduced us to Twitter-related strategies. A number of effective marketers choose to take action 30 minutes (or more) a day related to Twitter, Facebook and LinkedIn.com. And, now some marketers are developing groups at Ning.com. This website (and service) describes itself in this way: "Ning is the social platform for the world's interests and passions online. Millions of people every day are coming together across Ning to explore and express their interests, discover new passions, and meet new people around shared pursuits."

At the time of this writing some noteworthy details were released about Twitter:

- Twitter has 105,779,710 registered users.

- 300,000 new users sign up each day.

- The site brings in 180 million unique visitors each month.

- 75% of Twitter traffic comes from outside the site (*i.e.* third-party apps)

Now, Beth Barany gives us more hints about Twitter.

Promotions on $0 Budget: Use Twitter for a Purpose

Beth Barany

Twitter is a lot of fun! I'd be the first to admit it. And it's a time suck. In researching this article I spent WAY too much time playing on Twitter, doing good things—which I'll get to later—but it's distracting nonetheless. Lesson: set a time to write the article [done!] and a time limit on Twitter. [I'm going to have to work on that one!]

You may think that using Twitter is a complete waste of time (see above), but actually it's a gold mine of promotional opportunities for authors. If you use Twitter to grow your fan base, you can build your book buzz, and ultimately sell your books. And Twitter will be worth all your time away from your current work in progress. Yah!

Before we begin—Twitter basics

To get started on Twitter, create a free account and fill out your profile information.

Choose a picture, background and bio that is aligned with your author brand.

Import your contacts from your email account. Start searching for your favorite authors, media folks, and interesting people to follow. In Twitter, who you follow won't necessarily be who follow you back, though they may. You also don't have to follow those who follow you. I do recommend you follow your fans, once you've identified them. Which leads us to our first main opportunity: grow your fan base.

Grow your fan base

Whether you're a newly published author or have a few books under your belt, Twitter is a great way to have direct and timely contact with your readers. By direct, I mean you can send them a message via Twitter called a direct message or DM for short. Handy, huh?! By timely, I mean right away! Okay, when it's your social networking time.

Regarding DM's, individuals can only send you a direct message if you're following them. So, follow back if you want to use this feature.

You can also write a Twitter post (often called a tweet) directly back to someone and mention them. Everyone likes some Twitter love.

Actual Twitter Example: "@ann_aguirre We'll miss you while you're gone. Enjoy *Dragon Age*".

For as yet unpublished authors, you can use Twitter too! Connect with your potential fan base by chatting (DM'ing in twitter parlance) with fans of your favorite authors. Share about your favorite authors in the genre in which you write. When it comes time for you to chat about your first book, your fellow fans can get excited about your book and become your fan.

Continue the conversation by occasionally inviting followers to visit your site or blog and sign up for your newsletter, if you have one, or sign up for your RSS feed for your blog.

Build your book buzz

You can build buzz around your book by getting other people to buzz for you. One way to do this is to talk about other people's books a lot, as does Ann Aguirre, paranormal romance author, twitter.com/ann_aguirre, and romance author, Bella Andre, twitter.com/bellaandre, among many others.

Another way to build buzz is to interact with the buzz builders: book reviewers.

By following romance author, Carolyn Jewel's twitter (@carolynjewel), I found LimeCello (twitter.com/limecello), an avid book reviewer who interacts with the authors she reviews and raves over. It was fun to follow her send up of various authors and see them answer back.

Find book reviewers by using Lists, a fairly new Twitter feature that allows you to collect groups of Twitter folks under one, well, list. Anyone can create a list. I'm sure I was not the only one to create one for book reviewers: twitter.com/BethBookCoach/book-reviewers. Check out the reviewers' sites to be sure they cover your genre, then engage the right ones in a Twitter conversation.

Book sales

While it may be difficult to track book sales because of Twitter, you can increase your author platform—the size of your audience—by using Twitter to point out how great and awesome you are! I mean, how your books rock the house. Or, how absolutely smart and snarky you are. Whatever fits your book, your style, your author brand.

Above all, have fun with Twitter! Interact with new fans, build buzz, and shine a light on your books!

Related links:

List of Book reviewers on Twitter:
twitter.com/BethBookCoach/book-reviewers

LimeCello:
twitter.com/limecello

Bella Andre, romance author:
twitter.com/bellaandre

Carolyn Jewel:
twitter.com/carolynjewel

Ann Aguirre, paranormal romance author:
twitter.com/ann_aguirre

This article was first published in *The Heart of the Bay*, in the column "Promotion Posse"—a monthly column spotlighting promotional strategies for authors, written by members of SFA-RWA with a knack for PR.

Author, speaker and columnist, Beth Barany, can be found raving about books, authors, and the ever-changing publishing and book marketing world at twitter.com/bethbookcoach. Beth speaks to writing groups all over the San Francisco Bay Area and across the United States. Beth Barany works with aspiring authors. She helps them actually get their books completed and out into the world. Beth Barany is the author of *The Writer's Adventure Guide: 12 Stages to Writing Your Book* and *Overcome Writer's Block*. She is also a columnist and editor at *The National Networker*, and a contributing author to several anthologies, including *Writing Romance* (managing editor), and *Creativity Coaching Success Stories*. She edited an anthology of stories by UC Berkeley alumni called *When I Was There*. Beth works with clients in the US, Canada, and Europe, and gives talks nationally and internationally. She also writes young adult fantasy novels.

Beth Barany: Let's have a conversation!
Site: bethbarany.com
Blog: writersfunzone.com/blog
Twitter: @bethbookcoach
Facebook: facebook.com/pages/Beth-Barany/102635213105386
Linkedin: linkedin.com/in/bethbarany

The important thing to remember is that you must be subtle and gentle with the various forms of social media. Why? Because people expect a conversation—not marketing. Look upon social media to be like an online party. People seek to have fun. So take it easy.

Activate Transportation Advertising

The advantage of transportation advertising is that you'll reach a broad base of the population. The copy on bus and taxi advertising should be similar to a headline—brief and to the point. Buses and taxi cabs offer advertising that is a bit expensive for most small businesses. However, many small towns don't have buses, and the few taxis wouldn't give you much exposure.

Research indicates that advertising in subway stations is well-read by commuters. Bright, cheerful ads are most effective as subway stations tend to be dark.

Activating Summary

The following steps will access your hidden strength to activate.

1. Become a catalyst for change.

2. Develop ethics in advertising.

3. Choose your distribution methods.

4. Launch your rocket ship.

    A. Activate public relations

    B. Activate direct mail marketing

    C. Activate advertising

    D. Activate outdoor advertising

    E. Activate Broadcast Media

    F. Activate Digital Media

    G. Activate Transportation Advertising

When Do I Take These Steps?

The activation strength is a monumental movement toward getting your messages to your target market and reaching your primary objective. Start choosing your distribution methods, write them into your Events Calendar and call the appropriate media. You are now ready to distribute your messages.

11

Evaluating

Your Tenth Hidden Strength

Imagine that you lived your life on earth, and it's now time to enter the Pearly Gates. Reviewing your life, St. Peter asks, "Why you did you stop short? What held you back when everything was provided? You were given incredible resources: imagination, intuition, strengths, and many helpers. It could have been different. All you had to contribute was a little willingness."

Now, imagine that St. Peter gives you a different review, one of amazing fulfillment, prosperity and success. You accomplished all your visions and objectives, and you did so with confidence. Now you get a chance to evaluate your life, its high points and low points, before you take a rest.

The review and evaluation process is a big part of our daily lives. We use it to make an improvement for personal growth and expansion. As you similarly evaluate your marketing campaign, you'll review performances: your choice of media, promotions, mailings, press releases, and all the high and low points of this experience. There are two critical areas that call for evaluation: the results of your campaign and your strengths.

The focus of the evaluating strength is on evaluating each part of your campaign, as well as the overall results. You'll answer the important question "How close did my marketing campaign come to reaching my primary objective?"

On completing the *Action Steps*, you benefit from an increase in confidence and a better understanding of what is needed to put together a successful campaign.

Evaluating can help you in another way. You can learn from another person's experience. Then you can avoid certain mistakes. When my co-author Tom Marcoux interviewed Susan RoAne, best-selling author of *How to Work A Room*, he asked this powerful question: "Knowing what you know now, what would you have done differently?" Susan replied that knowing what she knows now about the publishing industry, she would have tripled her fees when her book was profiled in *USA Today* and *The Wall Street Journal*.

Your Objective for the Evaluating Strength

Your objective is to remember those times when you evaluated your actions. You reflected on the value or effectiveness of an experience. You realized the intensity of your efforts and successes. As you reminisce through those phases or life experiences, bring back with you the remembrance of the lessons you learned. You'll apply that value and evaluate your marketing results. This is the most interesting time when you'll reflect upon previous promotions, and the entire campaign.

How Can You Evaluate a Marketing Campaign— and Keep Up Your Morale?

Tom Marcoux

Why do business owners shy away from evaluating a marketing campaign's results? Pain. That is, hoping to avoid pain.

Unfortunately, not facing the truth creates great pain on the subconscious level—sometimes referred to by researchers as "free-floating anxiety."

So the better plan is to use a three-step process to face the truth and take care of yourself simultaneously.

Step One: Identify your goals on three levels

Many marketers only measure their effectiveness based on a dollar amount. That's too limiting. You can include these levels: a) dollar amount earned, b) how we served people, c) how we positioned ourselves for more and better results.

Step Two: Find some way to praise yourself

What did you do right? What worked? What did you learn?

We need to remember that it took courage to try something. An old phrase is: Success goes to the activist. Praise yourself for trying something, learning and positioning yourself to do better next time.

Step Three: Find the Lesson and Place It into Your "Next Time Plan"

Every marketing campaign yields lessons. Find them. Write them down. Place them into your plan for next time.

I remember a powerful comment bestselling author Marianne Williamson's father said. Marianne had devoted $10,000 to a particular event that turned out in a disappointing fashion. Did her father say "Oh no, what a mess you made"? No! Instead, her father put his arm around her shoulders and said, "You can absorb this." In essence, he expressed his faith that Marianne was more than this temporary setback.

My mentor, Dottie Walters, said: "Failure? I never encountered it. All I ever met were temporary setbacks."

As an entrepreneur, I have produced many products and marketing campaigns. And I've learned from each one!

As I wrote in my book *Be Heard and Be Trusted, 3rd Edition:*

> *Harvest the wisdom from an error and you are twice blessed: you won't repeat the error and you know what to compensate for.*

Evaluating as a Natural Strength

Babies only a few hours old are able to recognize their own mother's picture over that of a stranger. In order to recognize Mom's face, the baby evaluated facial features. When I was a little girl, I practiced learning how to skip like other children. It took some self-evaluation before I was able to skip properly. Children evaluate themselves as they participate in school activities, and interact with brothers and sisters. Many times, children exclaim "I did that better than you!" They evaluate television programs, toys, food, clothes, and teachers.

As adults, many of us devote significant time to looking back at our past experiences, reviewing and evaluating what we did or didn't do, how it worked or didn't work, and its overall effects on our lives. Our evaluation strengths help us to gain new perspectives.

We often gain valuable knowledge by evaluating with hindsight our experiences related to marriages, careers, child rearing and many other aspects of life.

Obviously we can't change what we did in the past, but we can bring the lessons we learned with us into the next experience to make it better.

> *We're all doing the best we can in any given situation.*
> *When we learn how to do something better, we do.*

We can empower ourselves by starting with the above principle. However, some of us may find ourselves hesitating to do the actions of evaluating. Why? As Dr. Elayne Savage discusses below, we may fear disappointment.

Get Out Of Your Own Way—Overcoming Ambivalence and the Fears That Hold You Back

Elayne Savage, Ph.D.

By its nature, marketing yourself invites Rejection. Big time.

Fear of Rejection is huge, yet it's just a part of the Fear Team: Fear of Failure (evil twin of Rejection). Joined by Fear of Judgments and Criticism, Fear of Success and Fear of Being Visible. Here's a sneaky one which causes so much trouble—the Fear of Disappointment. When you look closely at Disappointment, you'll see it is often Rejection in disguise.

Still, Fear of Rejection is the team leader, the foundation for all the other fears.

For many years I struggled with these fears. There are other voices as well. They become a shouting match in my head:

"I can make a difference!" "No you can't!"

"I can!" "No, you can't!"

"I can!" "No, you can't!"

Opposing voices swirl around. "You can't do it! You can't do it!" answered by "Yes, I can! Yes, I can!"

In this haze of confusion, I can't see clearly. Sometimes it feels like I don't have choices. That's when I used to get immobilized.

And What About You? Have you ever felt this stuck? Unable to make choices? Paralyzed?

Let's sort it out. We can start by looking at that exhausting tug-of-war between those "voices." The clash between the voice of confidence and the voice of doubt is ambivalence. Ambivalent thoughts and feelings have so many variations, and some are so subtle it's easy to miss them. And missing your distinctive signs of ambivalence can be a barrier to attaining your marketing goals.

Ambivalence is natural to all of us. It's the presence of simultaneously conflicting feelings, ideas or wishes competing with each other. It's a tip off that you're ambivalent when you experience uncomfortable inner conflict and can't make a decision.

You feel stuck, like you're straddling a fence. Ambivalence drains your energy, and it can prevent you from taking action with your marketing.

Where does ambivalence come from?

Ambivalence is usually influenced by messages we heard in our early years.

"You're such a dreamer."

"What makes you think you can do that?"

"Who do you think you are?"

Many of us receive admonitions from parents, teachers, or peers. We hear these warnings as rejecting messages. They discount, dismiss and diminish. Over time we come to interpret these warnings as "Be careful." Cautions like these surely aren't conducive to putting yourself out there, which is the essence of marketing.

Putting ourselves out there can bring up all kinds of fears: Fear of Rejection or Failure or Success; Fear of Visibility or Disappointment.

Uncertainty, confusion, anxiety

You have probably faced confusion or fear about taking on new marketing challenges. When two internal voices start skirmishing with one another, this conflict leads to uncertainty and confusion.

The confusion creates anxiety, that can cause you to freeze up and become immobilized. This degree of ambivalence surely isn't productive. It takes a lot of energy to deal with these conflicting voices. Wouldn't you rather put your energy into some other activity?

Tips for taming ambivalence

By moving past the ambivalence, it's possible to make space for making marketing choices and taking action. Here's how:

1. Give both voices a chance to be heard. When you're only listening to one voice you are, in effect, rejecting the other. You might even encourage the voices to talk to each other. Out loud. Writing to each other works, too. In other words, you'll be giving voice to both sides of the ambivalence. You'll be honoring both voices. One way to do this is to make two lists: a "What I Have to Gain" list and a "What I Have to Lose" list.

2. It's a good guess that it's some type of Fear that is immobilizing you. You can begin to move forward by naming the Fear. Is it Fear of Rejection? Of Failure? Of Success? Of being Visible? Of Disappointment? Of Judgment? Try naming the Fear to yourself. Next, write it down. Then say it out loud. Hearing yourself say it allows you to see it differently and recognize possible options. Or hear yourself by talking out loud to someone else. A marketing coach can be a terrific help here. These steps can lead to a "Wow! I never saw it like this before," experience. (By the way, these fears are not only attached to your early experiences but also to family messages which are passed down from generation to generation. You can be the first one to break free.)

3. Next, approach the Fear with some detachment. I call it "walking alongside yourself." This means stepping back enough to recognize when you may be starting down that old path of doubt and fear. It

means providing enough distance from your emotional tug-of-war to create choices.

4. Then, ask yourself, "Do I really want to continue down this path?" Say, "I could retrace my steps and make the choice to return to the fork in the road. I can go down a different road."

5. You can learn more about your own early messages by asking yourself these questions:

If I put myself "out there," it would mean . . .

If I fail, it would mean . . .

If I succeed, it would mean . . .

Might I feel disloyal to someone? To whom?

If I feel too visible, what might happen?

When conflicting ideas lead to uncertainty and confusion, call a "time-out" with yourself. Step away from the confusion and sort things out. Putting your confusion into words gives it a container and definition. This allows enough room for choices to emerge.

By understanding your barriers, fears and ambivalence you'll be able to see your options more clearly.

This allows you the space to move forward with Full Strength!

Dr. Elayne Savage, The Queen of Rejection,® is a communication coach and expert on ambivalence, taking things personally and the fear of rejection. A professional member of the National Speakers Association, she is a workshop leader, trainer, and consultant. Her relationship books, *Breathing*

Room—Creating Space to Be a Couple and *Don't Take It Personally! The Art of Dealing with Rejection* have been published in 9 languages.

Website: http://www.QueenofRejection.com
Blog: http://TipsFromTheQueenOfRejection.com

When we appropriately confront our feelings of ambivalence, as Dr. Elayne Savage advises, we free up our personal energy. With more energy, you can take in the lessons you uncover during the evaluating phase of your marketing campaign. You can profit from your experience.

While having a particular experience does not necessarily make us an expert, it does give us a certain amount of credibility. It puts us in a position to further express our evaluating strength. We can then transfer that strength to other areas of learning, such as the evaluation of a yearly marketing campaign.

Action Step

List two examples from your past when you used your evaluation strength. How did that help you?

Evaluate Critical Areas

You'll get better results from your evaluation process when you address these critical areas pertaining to your primary objective:

Value received: Use accurately tracked results of every promotion to analyze your value received. Every new customer gained is a value to your firm. Clients refer their friends, family, co-workers and even strangers. I've seen it happen where one satisfied customer with lots of contacts can create a snowball effect, resulting in many valuable new customers. It feels great to be on the receiving end of a positive snowball situation.

Quality and worth: Take some time to evaluate the quality of your campaign. Use the *Action Step* questions to determine the quality and worth of your marketing campaign.

Effectiveness: Determine the effectiveness of your campaign by how much it contributed to your primary objective. If your objective was more image-oriented, then surveys and verbal feedback will give you the necessary data.

Action Steps

1. How would you rate your graphic identity system on a scale of 1-10 with one the lowest and 10 the highest?

2. Is your identity system appealing and does it contribute to the image you want to project?

3. Were your promotions balanced throughout the year?

4. Did you invest enough money to make your promotions effective?

5. Were your communication messages clear and to the point?

6. Were your advertisements attractive and inspiring?

7. Are you happy with how your products and services were showcased?

8. Are you happy with the quality of the information you used?

9. Are you happy with how your business was represented?

10. The main question is "did you execute a quality campaign?"

Measure Short & Long Term Results

Short term results are often difficult to measure, unless you receive a massive amount of immediate responses. Advertising and promotional efforts are generally measured by long term results. Long term efforts for the year often yield specific results because your efforts gain momentum at some point. As you effectively develop your marketing strengths, you will see at least a gradual upswing in business. A steady climb of increased profits is quite desirable. It means you're not overwhelmed and growth appears secure.

Measure results by using your data sheet. Write in your objective for each event. After each event, jot down pertinent details about the event and the effectiveness of each advertisement or promotion. State specifically how many coupons were returned, how many customers said they saw your advertisement and the particular media that was used. Keep track of sales and profits. The *Action Step* below covers critical questions that need to be answered before you judge the overall value of your promotions and advertising efforts.

Action Steps

1. How many repeat customers and referrals did you get?

2. Did you contribute to your mailing, telemarketing, or e-mail lists?

3. Were you able to sell more products or services?

4. Was your image or reputation improved?

5. Were you able to get control of the marketplace, or is the ball bouncing around between competitors?

6. What will you do next year that could help you get control of the ball?

7. Did anything happen which brought joy into your life, or that of customers and employees?

Review Your Vision

Always review the initial vision you created for your business, and your primary objective for the year. Use both as a gauge to measure your accomplishments. If you met your objective too quickly during the year, maybe it wasn't challenging enough. If you had too much trouble meeting it, perhaps you were unrealistic in your projections.

Action Steps

1. Did you surpass your objective or barely meet it?

2. Was your campaign unfocused and did it go off in another direction?

3. Did something unexpected happen in the marketplace to cause your campaign to make a detour? Detours can be blessings in disguise.

Keep a Marketing Ledger

Be aware of different strategies that would contribute to the future success of a similar promotion. Write it down in your marketing ledger. Log all promotions from year to year and refer to your ledger whenever you begin a new campaign. Use your ledger when planning your next year's campaign.

For example, last year you used only flyers to promote your Back-to-School promotion and increased your student clientele by 30%. Now, you plan a combination of flyers, newspaper advertising, and an online campaign, that you project will bring twice or three times as much business. Using newspapers that reach your target audience, and creating a timely and enticing offer can help you reach your new goal. But then again, the cost of extensive newspaper advertising could eat up your profits and not bring in enough new business to cover costs. If your message wasn't clear or was insignificant, it would be ignored. So what do you do? Education and preparation will put you in a better position for devising strategies and receiving profits.

Include Your Team Members

Remember that meeting objectives is a team effort. Include your employees/team members in your evaluating process. Their feedback is valuable, and when they realize you value their opinions, they'll be motivated to act on behalf of your business and the security of their jobs.

Action Step

> When will you meet with your employees to discuss and evaluate your marketing campaign?

Learn Strength Enhancement

Your evaluating strength, and thus all strengths, become more polished as you practice them in day to day situations. You'll use your strengths with ease and comfort once you have a successful experience. Their value increases and expands your self-confidence. I have discovered three keys that open the door to improving your expression of your strengths:

1. Ask the right questions.

2. Seek promising solutions.

3. Be able to make necessary changes.

Here are the benefits of exercising your hidden strengths in marketing or any other area of your life:

1. You gain value from your first-hand experience.

2. You become a more clever problem-solver.

3. You are able to make improved decisions based on past performances.

Action Step

What will you do next to enhance expressing your strengths?

Data Sheet

Create a data sheet to track marketing results. Each marketing campaign is different and every industry has unique elements. It is best for you to write down your own vital data points. Use the following questions to help you decide what is most important for you to track:

1. What were your results? (both good and disappointing)

2. How much time did you devote? How does it break down—that is, how many hours per each new prospect contacted, each new customer, and each sale?

3. What did you learn so that you you can do better next time?

4. Was your offer, its timing and the media selection right?

5. Were the results what you expected?

6. What would make this promotion more profitable?

7. Was this promotion worthwhile?

8. Who participated in this promotion to make it successful?

As people, products and markets change, you will eventually need to find a fresh approach to promoting your services and products. Also, remember that you need to continually supplement your marketing campaigns with networking efforts. Now, Jill Lublin reminds us that networking can be an energizing process.

Networking Encouragement

Jill Lublin

Networking can be a magical, joyful experience. First, prepare by clearly identifying your purpose—what you want and need. Clarity of purpose opens the door to possibility. People know who you are and what you want with absolute certainty. See nothing but possibility in everyone you meet. Every encounter you have with someone new or someone in your network is an opportunity to create magic. Then, magic spills out from your generosity in these encounters, and from your gratitude for every connection you make and every person you meet.

Aim high in your networking strategies. You always risk getting less than you want if you stop short of your ultimate dreams. Make your request known by getting out there and playing big. Take immediate and decisive action with every chance meeting or planned encounter.

Once you are in action, playing big, giving and receiving on a regular basis, the true magic of networking will happen in the form of new friends, higher quality associates, and more opportunities than you've ever had. Think big, play big, and fall in love with giving to those in your network. No matter what happens with your business, you'll always have this tight network of friends at your side.

Jill Lublin authored the bestselling book *Get Noticed ... Get Referrals: Build Your Client Base and Your Business by Making a Name for Yourself* (McGraw-Hill, 2008). She is also the coauthor of two other national bestselling books, *Networking Magic* which rose to No. 1 on the Barnes and Noble charts, and *Guerrilla Publicity*, the PR bible. Jill teaches *Crash Courses in Publicity* in cities throughout the United States and Canada. Jill hosts the TV program, *Messages of Hope*, and the nationally syndicated radio show, *Do the Dream*. Jill is a popular international speaker who teaches powerful publicity, networking, and how to be influential techniques. As the CEO of the strategic consulting firm, Promising Promotion, Jill has trained companies in innovative techniques to improve bottom line results. In the past twenty years, she has worked with ABC, NBC, CBS, and other national media, and knows what the media wants. She can be reached at (415) 883-5455, info@JillLublin.com, or through her website, www. JillLublin.com.

Jill Lublin reminded us that networking is more than just making business connections; it's an uplifting part of life. If you have a storefront, it helps to have employees support your marketing efforts by asking new customers how they heard about your business.

Evaluating Summary

Take the following steps to access your hidden strength to evaluate.

1. Evaluating critical areas.

2. Measure short term results.

3. Review your vision.

4. Keep a marketing ledger.

5. Include your team members.

6. Learn strength enhancement.

7. Data sheet.

When Do I Take These Steps?

After each promotion or advertising effort, write the results onto your data sheet. Refer to this information throughout the year to repeat a successful promotion. At the end of the year, review the results of your entire marketing campaign and note how close it came to accomplishing your primary objective.

A Final Note from Linda

Many important discoveries were made throughout my own marketing campaigns and during the writing of this book; one of which is "thinking small doesn't benefit anyone." Tom Marcoux encouraged me to write this book. After investigating the market, I was concerned about trying to surpass competitive books. Tom encouraged me to proceed anyway, and I did so with some reservations. This book is a niche product and the result of the *ten hidden strengths*, my own marketing experience, and creative guidance. It's proof that there is room for innovation, and one can overcome doubt and fear.

I've come to believe that the Earth is a school and we are constantly learning to make better decisions. The best we can do in any situation is to use these strengths to get information and then utilize our good sense and intuition to carry out our plans.

As small business owners and managers, we are not infallible. Similarly, people who operate multi-million dollar corporate empires make mistakes and lose money for their company. Or they don't act at all and lose money for their company, because while they are sitting on their decisions, someone else is forging ahead, ready for change, ready to take the risk. Those entrepreneurs who are forging ahead are not allowing fear to stop them from beneficial change or appropriate risk. They welcome the opportunity to respond to the growing needs of a complex society.

It is often said that knowledge is power. Tom Marcoux says, "Knowledge is potential. Consistent action is power."

Learn new management, leadership, communication, and marketing strengths, and your business will expand and become prosperous. My wish for you is that your small or home-based business grows into whatever your vision happens to be. Believe in yourself and it can happen.

Please send your comments and/or testimonials (with permission to use your testimonials) to:

Linda

Linda L. Chappo
HeartToHeartLiving.com

A Final Note from Tom

As we come to the end of this book, I would like to take this final opportunity to discuss a few more details with you. I'm inspired to share material that I expressed on my blog: www. BeHeardandBeTrusted.com.

Have you ever flinched about having to sell something? Was it your product or your car or something else?

Some of us find selling to be such a problem that we proclaim, "I don't like to sell."

I can feel the pain of well-meaning, dedicated professionals when they cringe about marketing (and selling). These people often fail to get out the word about their product and service. The pressure they endure hurts them and their families.

If you own your business, you're not just a product or content creator. To succeed, you need to realize that you're the chief advocate and voice of your product or service.

Here I'll provide powerful methods that my clients have found valuable. I call them the Five Forward Steps:

1. Coach to Action

2. Set Effort Goals and Result Goals

3. Make it a game you can win

4. Keep Score and Achieve More

5. Use your "for the team" tendency

Coach to Action

Some people hesitate about marketing. They see it as pushing people. No! That's not it. The process is for you to be a "coach to action." What does a coach for an Olympic athlete do? He or she guides the athlete to do what's necessary to win gold.

Think of marketing your product in this way: "always be helpful." You're in the business of finding the right fit. You find the customer that can truly benefit from your product or service. You help that customer see the value of what you're offering. And you coach that customer to get involved with your product or service. Finally, if what you offer can't help the customer, you see if he or she will refer you to someone who is a good match for your product or service.

Set Effort Goals and Result Goals

Some people get stuck and their morale hits bottom. Why? Often it's because they have not separated Effort Goals from Result Goals. Let's say you decide to make ten prospecting calls a day. That's an Effort Goal. Then, from those calls, your aim is to set four appointments. That's a Result Goal.

We don't control results. We influence them. For example, you could call ten people and only get voicemail. No appointments have been set. Perhaps you didn't know about the industry conference that pulled all ten people out of the office. You can be proud of your success when you set and meet your Effort Goals.

Make It a Game You Can Win

Do you need to make marketing calls? Then avoid starting with a goal of 200 calls in a day. Build up to it. Start with five calls and then reward yourself when you succeed. This is a process of "make it a game you can win." Particularly when you begin a new discipline, think it through. Avoid unnecessary frustration caused by a goal that's too high for your current level of experience. Start small and build up from there.

Keep Score and Achieve More

I find it self-motivating to keep score when I write a book. I record how many pages I write each day. Often we discover that many projects require us to maintain discipline, day in and day out. Without discipline, we won't hit the big peak of achievement.

The same process applies to making calls or contacting new people. When I began on Facebook, I made an Effort Goal of contacting 20 people a day. I set up a form and noted my daily progress.

Use Your "For the Team" Tendency

Have you met a mother who won't take five minutes out of her day to quietly have coffee but will spend three hours helping her son with his homework? She is what I call a "for-the-team" person. She will do more for her family (or team) than for herself. (As a sidenote, I would advise that mother to also take care of herself. Taking breaks is a valuable habit to form.)

If you notice that you have a "for-the-team" tendency, then you can turn it to your advantage in your marketing efforts. For example, one of my clients, Mary, discovered that she was more likely to devote efforts to marketing if the process somehow benefited someone she cared about.

Mary wanted to help her friend Tara, who had been laid off from her job. So Mary hired Tara to promote her speeches to women's associations. The initial plan was for Mary to pay Tara an hourly wage to make the marketing calls for her.

But then Mary had a new idea. She would motivate herself to do the necessary follow-up calls by adding in a benefit for Tara. Tara would receive a bonus for each sale Mary closed (setting a speaking engagement). With this, Mary had her "for-the-team" tendency kick in, which was an important motivating factor for her. And, in so doing, Mary felt accountable for something good happening to Tara.

Implement the Five Forward Steps:

1. Coach to Action

2. Set Effort Goals and Result Goals

3. Make it a game you can win

4. Keep Score and Achieve More

5. Use your "for-the-team" tendency

Take these steps and you'll feel great each day. You will begin see good results blossom.

Finally, I encourage you to go back to the chapters in this book and benefit from working with the Questions and Action Steps. When you use this book like a workbook, your benefits double.

It has been a joy to share my ideas with you throughout this book. I hope to work with you again; please go to FullStrengthMarketing.com to gain free material and enroll in a Full Strength Marketing Teleseminar or an event like the Full Strength Marketing Boot Camp—or subscribe to special training with Full Strength Marketing Inner Circle—or gain one-to-one coaching.

The best to you,

Tom

Tom Marcoux
(415) 572-6609
TomSuperCoach@gmail.com
www.TomSuperCoach.com
Blog at www.BeHeardAndBeTrusted.com

Special Offer for Our Readers

Bring Tom to your company, conference, or church and get a 10% discount on his fee. TomSuperCoach@gmail.com.

Tom's popular topics include:

- Be Heard and Be Trusted
- 10 Seconds to Wealth
- Nothing Can Stop You This Year!
- Full Strength Marketing
- Double Your Sales in Half the Time™
- 10 Best Kept Secrets of Persuasion Masters
- Truth No One Will Tell You
- Say Yes to Yourself: Reduce Stress and Increase Ease
- Empower Your Personal Brand

To view a downloadable page of these topics, go to:

bureau.espeakers.com/simp/viewspeaker5261&multimedia

Don't miss a special offer for readers of
***Full Strength Marketing* at:**

TomSuperCoach.com/ReaderOffer.htm

Get FREE reports and e-newsletter subscription, *Success Secrets* (a $195 value!). Order books and audios — list at front of book.

Glossary

Glossary

For easy reference, here are listed all the specially defined terms used in this book.

Activating (Strength Nine)—This is the process in which you take action and become a catalyst for change. You choose your distribution methods: digital media (social media, your web site and more), public relations, direct mail marketing, traditional advertising, outdoor advertising and/or Broadcast Media.

Brand, Personal—This is what makes you unique and trustworthy to your listener. Your personal brand is the answer to the question, "What are you best known for?" The clearly expressed personal brand establishes credibility. It is also part of the process of rising to the QuickBreakthrough Level, on which you have rapport with people and can even get access to their intuition! Here are the four elements of your personal brand:

1. The answer to "What am I best known for?"

2. A story that moves emotions

3. A sound bite

4. A moniker (label)

Catchphrase ⇒ "Hook"

Charisma—A charismatic person expresses compelling messages—messages which have a powerful and irresistible influence. These messages overpower inertia, low moods, and procrastination.

Courage—Ambrose Redmoon stated, "Courage is not the absence of fear, but rather the judgment that something else is more important than fear." I (Tom) emphasize to my audiences—*Courage is easier when you're prepared.*

Decision, Good —Here are some hallmarks of a good decision:

1. It's timely

2. It's proportional (devoting too much time to trivial details can keep you from your real priorities)

3. It may be informed by the expertise of others

4. It feels "intuitively right" (For example, Walt Disney felt his vision of Disneyland was worth overcoming the objections of his wife, brother/business partner

Roy and the board of directors. Walt had to cash in his life insurance policy to fund the initial stages of Disneyland.)

Defining (Strength Six)—This is the process of making your business image into something specific. Then you will:

1. Differentiate your business from other businesses.

2. Attract customers who are seeking what you have to offer.

3. Assimilate all the features of your small business into one integrated image.

4. Create a more professional marketing presentation.

Elevator Pitch—An elevator pitch is your expression of your personal brand in a mere 30 seconds. Many times, it is a way to tell people how you can help them or someone they know.

Energizing (Strength Eight)—To energize your marketing campaign, use these five principles:

1. Believe in your strategies.

2. Trust that you have made effective decisions.

3. Make a financial commitment to your campaign's success.

4. Think of the money you spend on marketing as an investment.

5. Tell your prospective customers what's in it for them.

Envisioning (Strength One)—Remember how you have used imagination to bring forth an image or idea of something you wanted with all your heart and soul, and apply that remembrance to creating a vision and primary objective for your marketing campaign.

Evaluating (Strength Ten)—The review and evaluation process is a big part of our daily lives. We use it to make an improvement for personal growth and expansion. As you similarly evaluate your marketing campaign, you'll review performances: your choice of media, promotions, mailings, press releases, and all the high and low points of this experience. There are two critical areas that call for evaluation: the results of your campaign and your strengths.

Expert—An empowering definition of an expert is someone who has devised a system that people like and use.

Higher Power—This is a non-denominational designation for the theist presence in the universe, with no reference to any particular faith. Higher Power as referred to herein has the following characteristics: (1) compassion for the human condition, and (2) concern for the well being of individuals.

Hook or Catchphrase—Make your hook short, simple and articulate. Make sure it encapsulates the heart and soul of your goal. When you repeat it to yourself, make sure it brings up powerful emotions and gives you a strong sense of direction.

Identifying (Strength Four)—You will need to let go of biases in your personal approach. To accurately assess who your potential clients are, you need to be realistic and use good judgment. Discover your target market by making observations and then reflecting on what you have found.

Investigating (Strength Three)—For your business, you observe and search into how your competitors have a competitive edge and why. This information will save you from making unnecessary mistakes. Your thorough search helps you create an effective, new identity system or new marketing materials.

Journal of Victories and Blessings, Daily—To counteract feelings of underachievement and depression, keep a Daily Journal of Victories and Blessings. In it note down each day's joys and accomplishments, regardless of scale. This will promote feelings of gratitude and blessedness.

Journal, Personal—A vital record of your journey through this book. To get the most from this book, be sure to write down the answer to each *Action Step* in your personal journal as you proceed.

Manipulation—Manipulation is a dark practice where someone selfishly focuses solely on their own benefit to

the exclusion of concerns for the listener's welfare. *Also* →
"Persuasion vs. Manipulation."

Mentor—Your mentor knows the shortcuts, the time-savers and the little tricks.

Mission Caption—Some authors emphasize the need to write a mission statement. How many people have memorized their mission statement? Often a mission statement is several pages long.

Instead, the Mission Caption can appear like a caption below a photograph. It will help you gain access to your intuition.

Network—Identify the key contacts, the people who control huge networks of people.

Personal Brand → "Brand, Personal"

Personal Journal → "Journal, Personal"

Persuasion vs. Manipulation—It is critical to distinguish persuasion from manipulation. For this book, let us make the following distinction:

> **"Persuasion"** is helpful because we start with benefits for your listener in mind.

"Manipulation" is a dark practice where someone selfishly focuses solely on his or her own benefit to the exclusion of concerns for the listener's welfare.

Positioning (Strength Five)—This is the process of placing what's uniquely different about your small business into the minds of consumers. You must get them to think that your business and its employees do something special or unique that no one else can do as well.

Power Time Management—Tom Marcoux's unique method of coaching so that clients and audiences use their natural brilliance to get more done with less stress. Innovations including Time-Leverage™ and the Easethrough™ to help the individual let go of resistance, procrastination, and inappropriate behavior-patterns. Clients learn to rise to the QuickBreakthrough Level so that they create more fulfillment and attract more opportunities and success. *Also* ➠ "Time-Leverage" and "QuickBreakthrough Level."

QuickBreakthrough Level—The empowered state of the QuickBreakthrough Level is one of heightened awareness and flexibility. When you are functioning on the QuickBreakthrough Level, you have the flow of:

- Intuition
- Cooperation
- Connection

- Creativity

- Integrity (wholeness)

- Excellent communication

- Effective action

At the QuickBreakthrough Level, you are free from distraction, pain, worry, limited thinking, judgments, and emotional baggage. You do not procrastinate. On the QuickBreakthrough Level, you have the full use of your resources and strengths to gain the cooperation of other people.

Sound Bite—A sound bite is the expression of your message boiled down to a simple, clear, hard-hitting point.

Story, Good—Stories reach us on our subconscious and emotional levels, going around our natural resistance. For your story to be compelling, you need to provide:

- An attention-grabber

- Suspense and tension

- A release

Strategizing (Strength Seven)—This process helps us save time, get things done quickly and easily, and gives direction to our lives. Strategies help us to influence each other and the mass population. It's done everyday on the Internet, television and radio—and in books, magazines, newspapers. An effective marketer looks at the basic human motivators and builds his or her marketing campaign to reach the hearts and minds of consumers.

Support, Three Levels of—Facing your fears often involves gaining the insight and support of others. Sometimes we cannot get support from others at the time we need it. So, a good plan has three levels:

> *Level I*—Support that takes little or no energy. (Example: devoting time with a pet.)
>
> *Level II*—Support you can provide for yourself. (Example: taking a walk.)
>
> *Level III*—Support that arrives when you ask for help. (Example: phoning a kind friend.)

Team—Team members fill in the gaps in your strengths set.

Time-Leverage™—The process of reducing resistance and going into action quickly with the least energy required. In this way, Time-Leverage provides an Easethrough.™ With Time-Leverage, you neutralize your own resistance, a source of procrastination.

Time-Leverage is better than standard time management. This process uses your emotions as a fulcrum. That's how Time-Leverage gets you into action. Standard time management, using only a written list, does not give a person the energy to get into action.

Transforming (Strength Two)—Remember how, in the past, you changed a situation in your life and as a result gained valuable experience, knowledge, and fulfillment. For your business, you learn to discover your needs and move beyond fear so you act to fulfill your vision.

Victories ⟹ "Journal of Victories and Blessings, Daily"

Bibliography

Further Reading

The following list of books and audio programs provides the reader with select landmarks in the rich literary landscape which has informed this book. Valuable tips and methods are in these books Enjoy!

Chappo, Linda L., *Marry Your Self First: Your Key to Manifesting Loving Relationships: Affirmations, Ceremonies, Discovery Tools, Prayers and Visualizations - A 40-Day Program to Awaken the Love Within*, 2010, Heart Publishing, 978-0-9823279-1-3

Hayden, C.J., *Get Clients Now!: A 28-Day Marketing Program for Professionals, Consultants, and Coaches*, 2nd Ed., 2007, AMACOM

Godin, Seth, *Linchpin: Are You Indispensable?*, 2010, Portfolio

Joyner, Mark, *The Great Formula: for Creating Maximum Profit with Minimal Effort*, 2006, Wiley

Kawasaki, Guy, *Reality Check: The Irreverent Guide to Outsmarting, Outmanaging, and Outmarketing Your Competition*, 2008, Portfolio

Levinson, Jay Conrad, *Guerrilla Marketing: Easy and Inexpensive Strategies for Making Big Profits from Your Small Business*, 4th Ed., 2007, 384p, Mariner Books , 978-0618785919

________; Rick Frishman; Michael Larsen; et al., *Guerrilla Marketing for Writers: 100 No-Cost, Low-Cost Weapons for Selling Your Work*, 2010, Morgan James Publishing

Marcoux, Tom, *10 Seconds to Wealth: Master the Moment by Using Your Divine Gifts*, 2nd Ed., 2011, Tom Marcoux Media, 978-0-9800511-7-9

________, *Be Heard and Be Trusted: How You Can Use Secrets of the Greatest Communicators to Get What You Want*, 3rd Ed., 2009, Tom Marcoux Media, 978-0-9800511-4-8

________, *Nothing Can Stop You This Year!: How to Unleash Your Hidden Power to Persuade Well, Get More Done, Gain Sudden Profits, Command Intuition, and Feel Great*, 2nd Ed., 2010, Tom Marcoux Media, 978-0-9800511-5-5

________, *Truth No One Will One Tell You: How to Feed Your Soul, Save a Business, or Get a Job in a Crisis*, 2010, Tom Marcoux Media, 978-0-9800511-6-2

Vitale, Joe, *Hypnotic Writing: How to Seduce and Persuade Customers with Only Your Words*, 2006, Wiley

Index

Index

A

Academy of Art University
– XXXIV
accomplishments – 32, 41, 69, 92, 95, 97, VII
accountability – 281
action – X, XI
Action Steps – 10, 16, 21, 25, 27-28, 30-32, 38-40, 42-44, 46-48, 51, 58, 61, 72, 74-75, 77-78, 80, 82, 87, 93-100, 102-103, 105-106, 111-112, 115, 118, 122, 124, 127-128, 137, 140-141, 144, 146, 150, 152, 164, 169-170, 174, 178, 187, 189, 192-193, 195, 203, 205, 210, 212, 214, 216, 218, 227, 229, 232, 235-237, 248, 250-255, 257-263, 267, 274, 304-305, 308, 312, 319, 321-324, 326-328, 331, 334, 339, 344-345, 347, 349, 354, 358, 363, 367, 374-380, 382, 396, 404-407, 409-410, 421, VII

activating – 5, 301, 343, 344, 346, 354, 355, 394, III
advertising – 35, 47, 50, 57, 59, 67-68, 76, 78, 89-91, 103, 105, 108, 110, 129, 137-140, 153, 165, 168, 193-196, 216, 219-220, 250, 254-255, 261-262, 266-267, 273-274, 280, 282-285, 298-299, 301, 310, 319, 321, 325, 342, 349, 350-351, 356, 360, 364, 366, 371-374, 376-382, 393-394, 406, 408, 413, III
affirmations – 22-23, 28, 83, 96-98, 239-240
America's Communication Coach – v, XXXIII
Ash, Mary Kay – 149
associates – 54, 110, 152, 211, 297, 411
attitude – 39, 56, 63, 78, 83, 115, 157, 174, 177, 192, 202-203, 206, 212, 215, 217-218, 340

B

Bambo, G. – XXXVII

bankers – 52, 54

banks – 54-55, 97

benefits – 17, 26, 30, 40, 41, 47, 55-56,
66, 72, 77, 101, 105-106, 114,
117, 122, 136, 140-142, 147, 150,
155, 157, 165-166, 168, 187,
189, 192, 196, 205, 210, 226,
229, 237, 241, 248-249, 258,
261-262, 265, 279-280, 282,
284, 287, 304, 311, 313-314,
317, 319-320, 322-323, 331,
333-334, 341, 344, 353, 357,
362-363, 371, 374-376, 384,
396, 409, 415, 418, 420-421,
VII-IX, XXXIII

Big Picture Forgiveness Process
– III

Birkenstock – 150

Blessings, Log of Victories and
➠ victories & blessings,
journal of

book – i, vi-vii, ix, 423, III, VII-VIII,
XV, XXXIV

brain – 155-157, 162-163

brand – iv, 423, III-V, VIII, XXXIV

Branding Instructor, Personal
– XXXIII

Branding, Personaltainment – VIII

brand, personal – iv, 423, III-V, VIII

Bring Calm Steps – IV

brochures – 34-37, 55, 59, 76, 133,
136, 154, 168, 219, 260, 265-
266, 280, 307, 311, 321, 323,
325, 328-335, 338-341, 354,
359, 361, 373-374, 380

Buddha – 149

budget – 55, 92, 102, 153, 168, 246,
271-273, 275, 298, 300, 309,
311-312, 326, 332, 338, 341,
368

business – 3-5, 9-10, 16-26, 28-32,
34-37, 39-40, 43-59, 61, 65-69,
71-72, 74-78, 80-81, 84, 88-90,
92-93, 95-96, 98, 101-116, 118,
121, 123-128, 130, 134-141,
143-145, 149-154, 158, 164-166,
168-169, 171, 173-174, 176-179,
181-183, 185-189, 191-197, 199,
202-207, 209-219, 221-224,
226-231, 233-237, 241, 243,
246-249, 251-253, 255-261,
263, 265-284, 291, 297, 300,
303-305, 307-314, 316-317, 319-
331, 333-334, 338-340, 342,
344-346, 349, 351, 354-357,
359-360, 362-363, 365-367,
369-371, 373-376, 378-381,
384, 386, 397, 406-409, 412,
415-418, IV-V, VII, IX, XII

business cards – 59, 136, 145, 219,
231, 280, 307, 311, 323, 325,
328-331, 354, 359, 373-374

C

California Employment Dev. Dept.
– XXXIV

California State University – XXXIV

campaign – 4-5, 12, 31, 33, 39, 48-50, 66-67, 92, 97, 101, 103-105, 109-111, 115, 123-124, 138-139, 147, 182, 193-194, 235, 237, 247, 249, 251-253, 255-256, 259, 263, 268, 270, 274, 281, 283, 303-304, 307-311, 323, 342, 344, 354-357, 364, 368, 377-378, 396-398, 404-410, 413, V-VI, XI

Cannes Film Festival – XXXIV

career – 35, 73, 95, 97, 113, 187, 218, 237, 264, 348, 350

caring – 175, 189, 218

Carnegie, Dale – 149, 175

Catchphrase ➠ hook

change – 72, 75, 77, 98-100, 117, 264, 348

charisma – IV

clients – i, ix, 4, 6, 14, 26, 34-37, 44-46, 51, 66, 79, 89, 91, 104-105, 125-126, 142, 152-153, 158, 161, 167, 174, 176, 186-187, 189, 193, 198, 200, 217-219, 225-226, 228, 236, 243-244, 248, 255-256, 258-260, 265-266, 270, 282, 291, 299, 304, 317, 330, 338, 340, 345, 352-354, 361-362, 364, 367-368, 370, 373, 375, 384-385, 393, 417, 420, VII, IX, XXXIII

coach – i, XXXIV-XXXV

Cogswell Polytechnical College – XXXIII

communication – 54, 132, 159, 232, 252, 322, 324, X, XXXIII-XXXV

company – 423

compassion – VI

competition – 5, 11, 45, 55-57, 108, 122, 124, 128, 135, 137, 140-144, 146-148, 177, 198, 203-205, 207, 212-213, 215, 233, 241, 246, 248, 251, 267, 279, 300, 322

confidence – XXXV

connection – IX

con's ➠ pro's & con's

consumers – 28-29, 45-47, 49, 66-68, 104-106, 108, 127, 129-130, 134, 146, 153, 168-169, 177, 189, 191, 193, 198, 204, 210, 212, 216, 219-220, 228, 242, 246, 249, 252-253, 261-263, 265-266, 268, 280, 282-283, 285, 303, 309, 312, 321-322, 339, 340, 350-351, 356, 364, 371, 378, 382, IX, XI

cooperation – IX-X

Copperfield, David – 211

corporation – 54

courage – IV

creativity – X

credibility – III

credit lines – 55

customers – 7, 21, 23, 28, 34, 43-44, 46-48, 50, 55, 59, 67, 77, 83, 88-90, 96, 101, 106, 108-110, 113, 116, 121-122, 125-126, 128, 130-133, 135-138, 140-144, 150, 152-153, 165, 167-171, 174-180, 182, 190, 192, 199, 201, 203-206, 209, 212-214, 221, 223, 225, 227-230, 240, 250, 252-257, 262-263, 265-267, 269, 277-278, 281, 284-285,

288, 291-292, 307, 313-319, 322, 330, 333, 335-337, 341-342, 344, 349, 351, 354, 360-362, 364-367, 372-374, 376, 380-381, 404-407, 410, 412, 418, V

D

Dahlkoetter, JoAnn – i
DeAnza College – XXXIV
decisions – 19, 34, 56, 90, 97, 100, 116, 118-119, 123, 128, 151-152, 154-159, 162-164, 174, 177, 181, 219, 248, 253, 257, 273, 298, 308, 313, 321, 326, 343, 347, 354, 377, 401, 409, 415, IV-V
defining – 5, 62, 76, 209-210, 212, 214, 233, 246, 313, V
direct mail – 280-281, 360, 363-365
discernment – IV
Disneyland – IV-V
Disney, Walt – 10, 145, 149, 351, IV-V
distinction – VIII
dog – IV
dreams – i, iii, XXXIII

E

easethrough – IV-V, XI
Edison, Thomas – 149
education – 101, 104, 119, 321, 331
effective – XXXIV
effective listener ⟹ listener, effective

emotions – IV, VII, XI
employees – 4, 29, 39, 40-42, 44-46, 50, 54-56, 76, 81, 85, 107-108, 110, 115, 127, 138, 168, 170, 173, 177, 179, 188-189, 194, 199, 202, 204, 206, 210, 214, 217-218, 229-230, 256-258, 260, 265, 267, 269, 270-271, 299, 310, 320, 330-331, 333, 354-357, 367, 370, 375, 407-409, 412, IX
empowered state – IX
empowerment – iv, 97-98, 308, 344, 399, 423, VI
energizing – 5, 219, 303-304, 307, 313, 341, V
energy – XI
envisioning – 4, 9-10, 12-13, 16, 21, 39, 52, 68, 74, 95, 145, 152, 246, 305, VI
Ephron, Nora – 73
evaluating – 5, 395-396, 398, 412, VI
exercise – VII
Experience Unlimited – XXXIV
experts – VI, XXXIV
expression – V, X

F

faith – VI
fear – IV, XI
feelings – VII, XXXIII
flexibility – IX
Fraser, Margot – 150

friend – 57, 73, 77, 82, 84, 111, 113,
136, 158, 161, 186, 196-197, 231,
244, 297, 306, 343, 352, 361,
420, XI

funds – 55, V

G

Gandhi – 149

goals – 13-14, 18, 26, 31-32, 39-48, 54,
56, 59, 63-65, 68, 71, 77-79, 81,
85, 93, 95, 118, 153, 157, 188,
243, 247, 251, 315, 324, 345,
397, 400, 408, 419, VI

good story – X

gratitude – VII

G.R.E.A.T. process – X

growth – 25, 40-41, 49-51, 55, 61,
71-72, 74, 115, 117, 146, 196,
227, 247, 261, 280, 308, 395,
406, VI

H

health – vi, 13-14, 41, 109, 199, 273,
279, 333, 362

heart – VI

hidden – 9, 71, 121, 149, 185, 209, 235,
303, 343, 395

Higher Power – VI

hire – 37, 41, 54, 217, 269, 287, 325,
335, 336-338, 368-369

hook – IV, VI

hypnotherapy – 77-78, 139, 260

I

IBM – XXXIV

identifying – 4, 17, 69, 149-153, 165-
166, 174, 180, 182, 192, 212,
246, 309, 319, 340, 411, VII

identity – 45, 49, 76, 124, 303-304,
307, 311, 323-328, 331, 335,
340-342, 353, 362, 405, VII

image – 4, 5, 12, 21, 28-29, 45, 50,
76-77, 79, 104, 110-111, 128,
137-138, 140, 142, 152-154,
165, 173, 209-220, 227-229,
232-233, 241, 245, 247-248,
261-262, 265, 272, 311, 313,
319, 322-324, 326-329, 331,
334, 342, 344, 360, 365, 376,
381, 405, 407, V-VI

image, personal – 218

image, public – 218

impressions – 27, 99-101, 127, 210-
211, 215, 218-219, 232-233, 247,
259, 280, 309-310, 325, 329,
339, 356, 371

influence – IV, XXXIII

innovation – 51, 77, 104, 137, 140-141,
190, 201, 215, 228-229, 255,
258, 323, 412

insurance – 55, 277, 282, V

integrity – 25, 90, 109, 144, 212, 218,
231, 259, X

intuition – 26, 156-160, 162-163,
218, 240, 248, 395, 415, IV,
VIII, IX

investigating – 4, 121-124, 147, 152,
165, 192, 212-213, 246, 309,
323, 415, VII

J

Jefferson, Thomas – 149

Jesus – 24, 149

jobs – XXXIV

journal, [personal] – VII-VIII

judgment – IV, X

K

Kawasaki, Guy – XXXIII

Kennedy, John F. – 149

Kunst+Aventur – vi, XXXVII

L

leader – XXXIV

leadership – XXXIV

learn – IX

letterhead – 59, 219, 325, 357, 362

leverage – v, XI

Levinson, Jay Conrad – XXXIII

L.I.K.E.–M.E.–N.O.W. process – VII

Lion – VII

listener, effective – VII

listening – III, VIII, IX

loan – 55-57

log of victories & blessings
        ⇒ victories & blessings,
        journal of

love – iii

Luskin, Fred – XXXIII

M

Mac Leod, Johanna – vii

magazines – 55, 68, 77, 91, 117, 126,
        139, 152, 191, 204, 215, 220-
        221, 237, 253, 264, 282, 291,
        304, 359, 367, 370, 374, 388,
        X, XXXIV

management – XI

manipulation – VII-IX

Marcoux Media, LLC – vi

Marcoux, Tom – i, iii-vi, 5-7, 10-11,
        41, 60, 78, 107, 109, 126,
        137, 180, 186, 231, 240, 242,
        244, 268, 285, 297, 306, 313,
        318, 327, 338, 347, 349, 352,
        353, 366, 396-397, 415-416,
        421, 423, IX, XVI, XXXIII,
        XXXVIII

marketing – i, 3-7, 9-13, 15-16, 21-25,
        31-39, 42-45, 47-52, 56-57, 62,
        65-67, 74, 78, 83, 88, 90-91,
        96-97, 101-111, 113, 115-116, 119,
        122-130, 135, 137, 138-141, 147,
        152-154, 169, 177, 179-182, 186-
        187, 189-190, 193-195, 197-198,
        200, 202-203, 207, 212-214,
        216-217, 219-222, 225-227, 231,
        233, 235, 237-238, 241-243,
        245-252, 254-256, 259, 261-
        263, 265-266, 268, 270, 272,
        274, 285-286, 291, 299, 300,
        303, 307-312, 318-319, 322-
        324, 331, 339, 342, 344-345,
        348, 352-356, 360, 363, 365,
        367, 370, 378, 382-386, 388,
        392-402, 404-406, 408-409,
        410-413, 415-420, III, V-VII,
        X-XI

marketplace – 4-5, 26, 49, 50, 90,
        104-105, 121-123, 125-127, 141,
        143, 147, 185, 190, 195-196,
        198-199, 201-202, 207, 230,
        238, 245, 247, 252, 254, 264,
        314, 346, 351, 355, 407-408,
        XXXIV
market research – 55, 169, 191, 229,
        237
mastermind group – VIII
media – i, 45, 50, 66-67, 87, 104-105,
        111-112, 143, 170, 179, 196-197,
        216, 219-220, 222, 226-227,
        231, 239, 248, 250-255,
        270, 273-274-275, 279-280,
        282-283, 287, 291, 298-299,
        311, 313, 321-325, 340, 354,
        356-358, 360, 384, 386, 390,
        393-394, 396, 406, 410, 412,
        III, VI, XXXV
meditating – 149
memorable phrase – IV
merchandise – 151, 213, 256, 325
mission caption – iii, 353, VIII
Mohammed – 149
moniker – VIII

N

National Assoc. of Broadcasters
        Conf. – XXXIV
National Speakers Association
        – XXXIV
natural – 12, 73, 123, 151, 188, 210,
        236, 304, 346, 398
news media ➠ media

newspaper – 50, 55, 60, 138, 153, 194,
        222, 260, 275, 283, 294, 298,
        319, 358, 374-377, 408
nonattachment – VIII

O

objectives – 4, 10, 12, 27-33, 38-48,
        52-53, 59, 65, 67-69, 73-77,
        80-81, 92-95, 97-98, 105,
        109, 113-115, 118-119, 123, 151,
        153, 187, 193, 195, 203, 210,
        235-236, 246-247, 250-251,
        253, 270, 272-273, 275, 301,
        304, 308, 309, 322, 334, 344,
        346-347, 355, 360, 364, 371,
        394-396, 404-408, 413, VI
Obst, Lynda – 72-73
opportunities – 24, 41, 58, 80,
        106-107, 148, 195, 197, 204,
        223, 242, 253, 256, 299, 352,
        389, 411, IX

P

pain – X
peacock – VIII
performance – 10, 41, 53, 254, 345
persistence – VIII
personal brand ➠ brand, personal
Personal Branding Instructor
        ➠ Branding Instructor,
        Personal
personality styles – VIII

personaltainment branding
➠ Branding,
Personaltainment

persuasion – iv, 423, VIII

persuasion vs. manipulation – VIII

plan, business – 5, 52-58, 61, 69, 84,
92, 109, 114, 123, 205, 214, 251,
305, 323

planning – 15, 111, 218, 235-237, 362,
408

positioning – 5, 185, 187-190, 195,
207, 385, IX

power time management – 423, IX

practice – VII, IX

praise – i

prestige – 43, 62, 99, 121, 167, 199,
210

priorities – IV

procrastination – IV, X-XI

products – 12-13, 15, 17, 23, 25, 28-29,
30, 44-48, 56-58, 66-67,
107-109, 125, 127, 130, 134, 137,
142-143, 145-146, 150, 152-154,
166-179, 190-195, 197-198, 200,
204, 205-206, 213-215, 217,
221, 223, 225, 228-230, 243,
247-252, 256-257, 260-261,
264-271, 273, 278-281, 283,
285-286, 290-291, 298-300,
310, 315, 317-324, 333, 340,
348-351, 353, 356, 361-367,
372-373, 381, 383, 385, 398,
405, 407, 410-411, 415, 417-418

professionalism – 101, 218, 227, 284,
340

professionals – vi, XXXIV

profit – 30, 41, 54, 57, 106-107, 114,
256-257, 262, 267, 272, 351,
361, 404

profit and loss statement – 54

profits, sudden – XVI

project – 41, 63, 210, 216-218, 272,
295, 303, 324, 334, 338, 369,
405, 408

project binder – IX

projection – 55

ProMatch – XXXIV

prosperity – 28, 38, 41, 67, 81, 92, 99,
107, 146, 150, 238-240, 248,
307, 395

P's, four – 107-108

psychology – 139, 151, 242

publicity releases – 55

publisher – vi

Q

quality – 25, 29, 46-48, 51, 71, 80-81,
101, 104-105, 108, 110, 141-142,
146, 151, 153-154, 157, 176, 194,
198, 204, 211, 219, 227, 259,
263, 265, 274, 329, 331, 342,
386, 405-406, 411

questions – III

QuickBreakthrough – i, v-vi, III,
IX-X, XXXVIII

QuickBreakthrough Publishing – vi

R

rapport – III

real estate – 55, 106, 282, 309

Redmoon, Ambrose – IV

relationships – vi, 14, 25, 55, 66-67,
73, 88, 96, 109-110, 112, 126,
133, 146, 158, 160, 175-177, 215,
221-223, 249-250, 289, 349,
351, 403

religion, comparative – XXXIV

representative – 110, 377

reputation – 56, 76, 90, 101, 141-144,
218, 259-260, 265, 269, 312,
320, 407

resistance – 41, 265, 267, IX-XI

resources – 144, 213-214, 223, X,
XXXVIII

restaurant – 46, 105, 154, 215, 217,
266, 313, 378

Roddick, Anita – 149

S

Safeway – 108

sales – XXXIII

schedules – 41, 114, 237, 270, 335-337

secrets – i, XXXIII

security – 41, 84, 315, 409

Seek, Shannon – i

Silicon Valley Bank – XXXIV

skills – X, XI

solution – 11, 27, 49, 133, 149, 157,
162-163, 221, 233, 245, 266,
275, 283, 306, 315, 325, 371

sound bite – X

spirituality – vi

Stanford University – XXXIV

stories – IV, XXXV

strengths – 3-7, 10, 13, 21, 32, 34,
39-40, 51, 54, 61, 74, 76,
80, 90, 95-96, 101-102, 108,
110-111, 115-117, 122, 124-126,
139, 143, 150-152, 177, 188-189,
195, 207, 212, 214, 217, 229,
235, 237, 246, 269, 305, 309,
342, 346-348, 355, 395-396,
399, 406, 409-410, 415-416,
VI, X-XI

strengths, hidden – 7, 21, 40

stress – 423, IX

success – 10, 16, 32, 34, 38, 44, 46,
48, 51, 53, 57, 63, 65, 72, 74,
81, 83, 85-86, 91-93, 96-97,
102, 104, 110, 114, 118, 139, 156,
164, 180, 188, 190, 193, 199,
218, 228, 238, 252, 258, 274,
281, 284, 303, 307-309, 322,
327, 333, 338, 340, 354-355,
371, 385-386, 395, 397, 408,
419, 423, V, IX

Sun Microsystems – XXXIV

survey – 126, 167-168, 171, 174, 178,
182-183, 257, 281

T

target – 4, 41, 60, 92, 94, 105,
112, 127, 129, 135, 137-138,
150-154, 164-166, 168-170,
179-180, 182-183, 194, 198,
206-207, 210, 215-216, 220,
228, 233, 235, 241, 245, 248,
250-252, 254-256, 261, 265,
266, 272-273, 275-276, 278,
281, 298, 319, 321-322, 324,

329, 333-334, 337, 339, 342,
354-356, 360-361, 375-376,
394, 408, VII

teaching – XI

teaching moment – XI

team – ix, 12, 40-42, 90, 115, 143, 217,
230, 235, 240, 246, 257-258,
295, 297, 330, 353, 400, 408,
413, 418-420

thoughts, negative – 96

time – IV, VIII, XI

time-leverage – v, IX, XI

Time-Leverage Detective – v

time management – IX

time management, power ➠ power
time management

TomSuperCoach – vi, 421, 423,
XXXV, XXXVIII

trademarks – 55, 324, 326

transformation – 4, 38, 68, 71-76,
80-81, 95, 99, 103, 114, 117-119,
152, 186, 246, 309, 348, 355,
XII, XXXV

trust – III

truth – i, iv, 423, XII

Truth No One Will Tell You – i,
423, XII

U

universe – VI

V

venture capitalists – 54

victories & blessings, journal of –
VII, XII

W

Wells Fargo – XXXIV

"what are you best known for?" –
III, IV

Wieder, Marcia – i

wisdom – iii

word-of-mouth – 103, 219, 266, 374

About the Authors

Linda L. Chappo

Linda L. Chappo became a marketing specialist to enhance her first business which did so well that she sold it and traveled the world. She then earned degrees in graphic arts and culinary arts. Her current businesses relate to those fields, to spirituality, and to coaching small business owners. Linda helps small business owners overcome fears that may keep them from reaching their full potential. Her focus is on how small business owners already have everything they need within them, for successful marketing and for a successful life. Linda is also the author of *Marry Your Self First: Your Key to Manifesting Loving Relationships* and is the founder of both HearttoHeartLiving. com and WeighLessExpress.com. She authored *How to Organize Your Marketing Campaign* and *How to Make it Big in the Hair Salon Business.*

Reach Linda through HeartToHeartLiving.com

Tom Marcoux
America's Communication Coach

Tom Marcoux helps people like *you* accomplish big dreams. As Tom says, "I help people like you *command the Wow!* in your audience. When presenting, branding, or communicating one-on-one, my coaching helps you make people feel good and *want* to follow your lead." Further, Tom helps people get more done and feel good doing it.

Tom is also a prolific author, including *10 Seconds to Wealth*, he has published 11 books and 21 audio programs, with sales in 15 countries. These have included both fiction and nonfiction. Prominent among his publications is *Be Heard & Be Trusted*, 3rd Ed., which, in a prior edition, was a required textbook at Cogswell Polytechnical College. The Third edition features contributions by Jay Conrad Levinson, Guy Kawasaki, and Dr. Fred Luskin, among others.

When you want *to influence others*, join Tom's many clients who benefit from his secrets on branding. Tom is described as "the Personal Branding Instructor" by the *San*

Francisco Examiner. Helping people become more effective job candidates, he has presented to ProMatch, Project Management Institute and chapters of Experience Unlimited (affiliated with the California Employment Development Department).

Holding a degree in psychology, Tom is also a personal and professional coach and guest expert on TV and radio In addition to being featured in technology and communication magazines, he earned a special award at the Emmy Awards. For six years, he addressed the National Association of Broadcasters Conference in Las Vegas on topics like, "Online Secrets to Build Your Brand."

Tom is an award-winning speaker and corporate workshop leader (to professionals from IBM, Wells Fargo, Sun Micro-systems, and Silicon Valley Bank). He is a member of the National Speakers Association.

Tom is also a faculty lecturer in public speaking, science fiction and fantasy literature and cinema, and comparative religion at Academy of Art University. He has been a guest lecturer at Stanford University, DeAnza College, and California State University at Los Angeles, among others. In addition to traditional classroom forums, he teaches online and has authored several online courses. He also presents workshops to fellow faculty at the Academy of Art University's Teacher Conferences.

In a more artistic vein, Tom has written, directed, and produced feature films, including one that went to the Cannes Film Festival market, where it gained international distribution. He performed as an actor in feature films and commercials. Presently, he is leading teams working on book-film projects titled *Crystal Pegasus* (children's fantasy) and *TimePulse* (science fiction). In addition, his audio programs and audio novels often feature orginal soundtracks composed by Tom.

When you need to enthrall audiences or effectively communicate your message to the media, engage Tom as your media coach. Tom will clarify your message, build your confidence in speaking, and craft compelling sound bites and stories for the press. Tom will help you excel!

(415) 572-6609
TomSuperCoach@gmail.com
www.TomSuperCoach.com
Blog at www.BeHeardAndBeTrusted.com
www.TenSecondstoWealth.com

Visit **www.FullStrengthMarketing.com** for free material and opportunities to learn via teleseminars, special training through Full Strength Marketing Inner Circle (by subscription), events like Full Strength Marketing Boot Camp—or through one-to-one coaching.

Designed

and set by gBambo of the graphic
and cartographic atelier:

kunst**+**aventur

Named for the slim booklet *Kunst
und Aventur* (Art & Enterprise),
published in Strasbourg, France in
1440, in which Johannes Gutenberg
(*c.* 1398–1468), a German goldsmith,
unveiled his epochal mechanization
of printing, vastly accelerating the
pace of learning and human progress.

The text was set principally in Minion
Pro, Zapf Humanist, Poor Richard,
Fontin, and Gill Sans families. The
body font, Minion Pro, was designed
by Robert Slimbach based on classical
old style types of the late Renaissance.

The design was executed in Adobe's
excellent Creative Suite 5, including
Photoshop, Illustrator, and InDesign.

Write kunst.aventur@gmail.com
about design inquiries large or small
or feedback.
Enjoy!

Collophon

Get what you really want ...

use the methods found in Tom Marcoux's books!

For special discounts, order at:
www.TomSuperCoach.com/SpecialOffer.htm

For more QuickBreakthrough resources, see

www.TomSuperCoach.com
blog at BeHeardAndBeTrusted.com